Praise for *Monastery and High Cross*

"Early Christian Ireland is a riddle wrapped in a mystery inside an enigma. All the more mysterious are its connections with monks in remotest Egypt. This book will transport you to a fascinating place you never knew existed. You will love every blessed page."

— Mike Aquilina, author of St. Patrick and His World

"This work does us a great service. Connie Marshner's work is built upon the first discovery of archaeological evidence of a direct relationship between early Christian Ireland and Egypt in the discovery of the Faddan More Psalter in 2006. Inspired by this discovery, Marshner, a Melkite Catholic of Irish descent, marshals a wide variety of earlier texts that underline the connections between early Christian Ireland and the Christian East in general and Egypt in particular."

— Fr. Neil Xavier O'Donoghue, Ph.D., Director of Liturgical Programmes, St. Patrick's Pontifical University, Maynooth

"In *Monastery and High Cross*, Marshner gives us a zesty and intriguing portrait of Irish Christianity as it was before the Romans came. It was a Faith that traveled over well-established trade routes, reaching Egypt, Constantinople, and points further east and returning over land and sea to the far-west land of Ireland. In the last fifty years, the archaeological evidence for this has blossomed, making this a fascinating story."

— Frederica Mathewes-Green, author of *Facing East: A Pilgrim's Journey into the Mysteries of Orthodoxy* and *Welcome to the Orthodox Church*

"A thoroughly Catholic work. Marshner reminds us of the truly universal nature of our Faith and replenishes our forgotten roots. Her book should serve as a bridge from East to West and across the ages. I can think of no nation more in need of this reminder than Ireland. Our story is even richer than many of us know, but in Mrs. Marshner, we have a reliable storyteller and an honest historian. She unveils the universal through the particular, as a good Christian scholar should. It's a peculiar irony that a daughter of the Irish diaspora is the one who can bring us home again."

– Marcas Ó Conghaile Muirthemne,
founder and host of *More Christ*

"This is the best book on the history of true 'Celtic Christianity' I have ever read. No other work so clearly explains the previously missing links that connect early Christian Ireland with the Levantine birthplace of the Faith. In addition to its reverent use of older sources, it is filled with information on the latest scholarship and discoveries that illuminate the Gaelic world's Eastern patrimony. With an Ireland that today is so secularized and anglicized, I believe Connie Marshner's *Monastery and High Cross* holds the key to an authentically Catholic revitalization of the Church in Ireland, Scotland, and anywhere on earth the descendants of the Gaelic people live today."

– Séamus Ó Fianghusa (Fennessy), historian,
Donegal Association of New York Inc.,
author of *Heaven Help Us, Now!*

"Half a century ago, I recall a discussion in our Christian Archaeology class concerning a particular ancient fresco. Was it a depiction of the Last Supper? Was it a Refrigerium Mercy Meal? Was it a Philosopher's Symposium? The professor, the late Rev. Johannes

Quasten, finally cautioned the class: "Gentlemen, do not impose twentieth-century questions on third-century Christians." The statement was an eye-opener. How often we underestimate the expansive cross-fertilization of the early Christian world. Connie's book will help us open our eyes and our minds."

— Rt. Rev. Mark Melone, pastor, Holy Transfiguration Melkite Greek-Catholic Church, McLean, Virginia

"Having my personal ethnic roots almost exclusively from Ireland and having had two appointments at the Norbertine Abbey of the Holy Trinity (no longer in existence) outside the town of Ballyjamesduff in County Cavan, I found Connie Marshner's work an engaging read. I am genuinely pleased to recommend it to anyone interested in Irish ecclesiastical history, in the connection of the Christian East with Ireland or in the beauty of the Irish literary mind, imagination and soul.

"I found the work to be thoroughly researched, with an extensive and most informative bibliography. The conclusions reached are based on facts emerging from thorough research. Certainly, one is left with no doubt at all about the central thesis of the work, the irrefutable fact of the Eastern roots of Irish Christianity.

"While Connie Marshner indicates which direction further research might profitably take, she has made a major contribution to bringing the question to a juncture from which further research may go forward. Her style of writing is engaging for the reader. I found it hard to put her work aside as I returned to monastic observance and pastoral apostolate.

"This short work deserves a wide readership!"

— Rev. Fr. William Fitzgerald, O.Praem., B. Theol. (Melbourne College of Divinity), S.T.L., Pontifical University of St. Thomas Aquinas (Angelicum), Rome

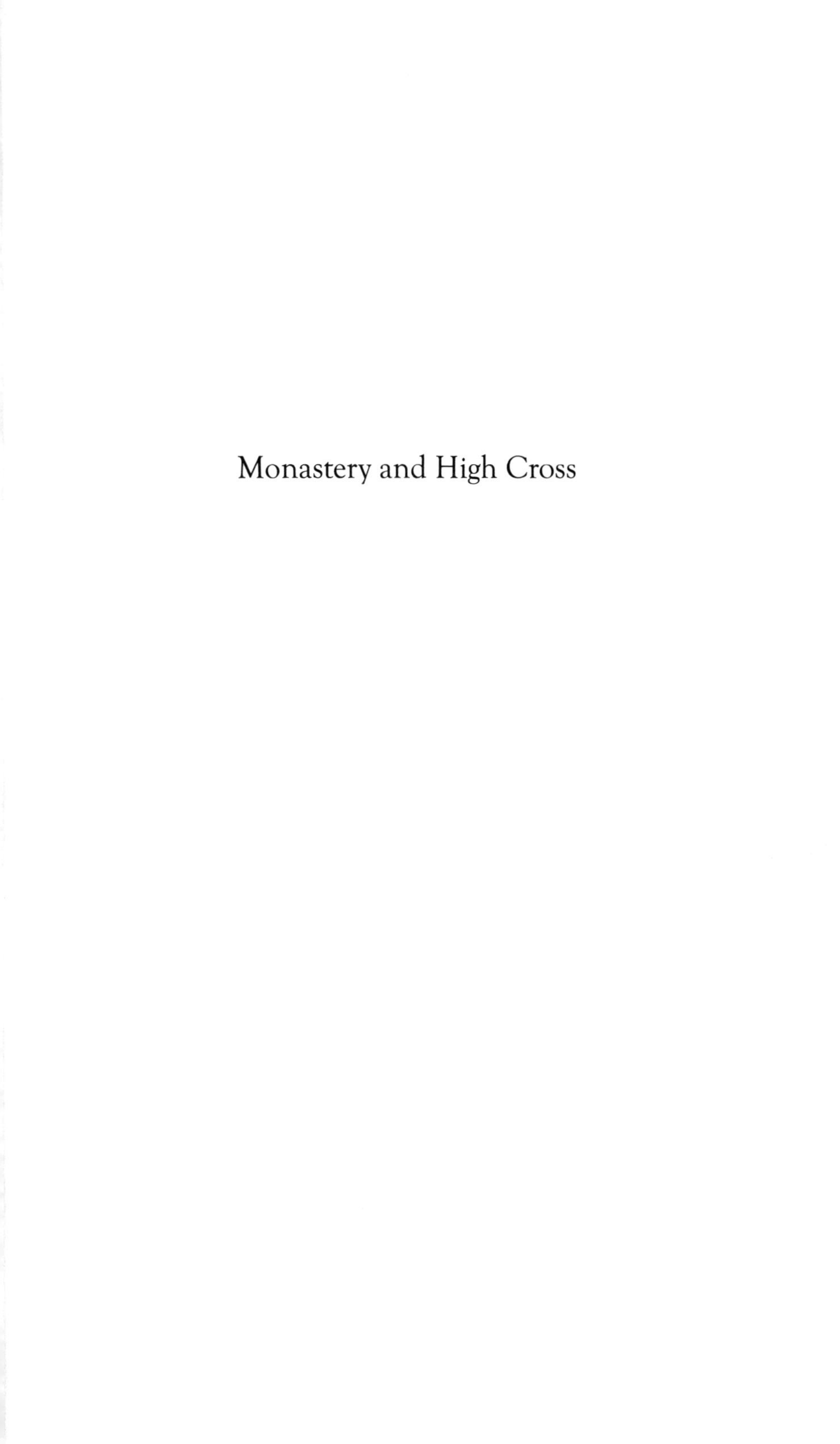

Monastery and High Cross

CONNIE MARSHNER

MONASTERY *and* HIGH CROSS

The Forgotten Eastern Roots of Irish Christianity

SOPHIA INSTITUTE PRESS
Manchester, New Hampshire

Cover design by Updatefordesign Studio.

On the cover: Celtic cross (58841433) image by mdmoinulhasan786 / www.freepik.com; Egyptian hieroglyphs (2720580) image by www.freepik.com.

Sophia Institute Press
Box 5284, Manchester, NH 03108
1-800-888-9344
www.SophiaInstitute.com

Sophia Institute Press® is a registered trademark of Sophia Institute.

paperback ISBN 979-8-88911-158-0

ebook ISBN 979-8-88911-159-7

Library of Congress Control Number: 2024932576

First printing

Tiolacadh.

Do mo theaghlach agus dóibh siúd a bhfuil grá acu dom.

Contents

Appendices

Praeteritio

In writing this book, which is an expansion of my dissertation for my Master of Arts degree in Gaelic Literature at University College Cork, I have grieved that I have not been able to do the justice to my topic that it deserves. I have been able to do only secondary research, combing through mountains of books and articles that other people have written, and pursuing footnotes to forgotten sources. In order to do original research, I would have needed command of ancient Arabic and Greek and Latin, Old and Middle Irish, and probably some other languages as well. Life simply did not prepare me for that.

I hope that what I have found will help my readers to see ancient Ireland with new eyes, and also to see the Church with deeper understanding. And I hope that, just perhaps, this book may pique the interest of future scholars who will be able to do more justice to the topic than I have and may inspire others to further develop the discipline of Hiberno-Coptic studies.

Buíochas

I want to thank Dr. Pádraig Ó Macháin of the Roinn na Nua-Ghaelige at Coláiste na hOllscoile Corcaigh for the Master of Arts in Gaelic Literature program. His love of Gaelic literature shines through and is contagious, even though I only ever saw him on the Internet.

I want to express my gratitude to Andrew Armstrong, Stephen Pilon, Mickey Krebs, and all the staff at St. John the Evangelist Library at Christendom College for their patience and help. Without SJE this work would not have been possible. I really didn't move in, my friends, even though I was there so many days when you opened and when you closed! The Irish studies resources of the library are the best there are south of the Shenandoah.

Agus, cinnte, buíochas agus grá mór do m'fhear céile William.

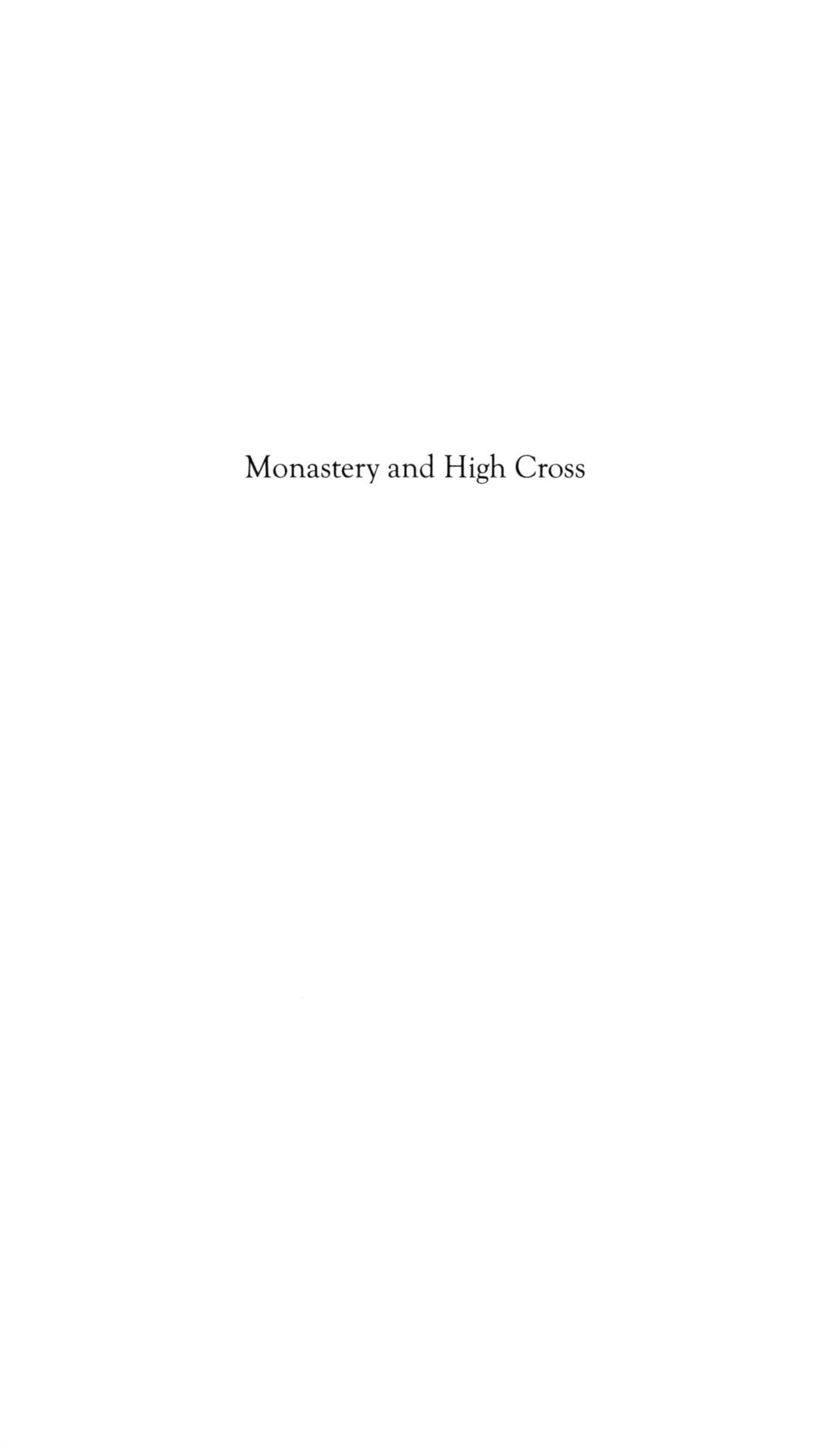

Monastery and High Cross

Introduction

On July 20, 2006, Eddie Fogarty was operating a peat-digger in a bog in Faddan More, County Tipperary. He saw something odd fall out as he scooped up a bucket of peat. The words *in valle lacrimarum*—"in the valley of tears," from Psalm 84—were just visible amidst the peat. Fogarty quickly covered the gooey pile with a damp cloth. Doing so preserved the 1,200-year-old manuscript he had just discovered.

Now known as the Faddan More Psalter, this was the first early medieval manuscript to be found anywhere in the world in the last two hundred years. Sections of it are still legible to those who can read Irish majuscule, and it is on display in the Irish National Museum after years of meticulous conservation.

The cover was largely intact, having been made from a single piece of leather. Inside the cover was papyrus from Egypt. To find a book made the same way, conservators had to go to the binding of the Nag Hammadi codices in Egypt, fourth-century Gnostic Gospels that had been discovered in 1945.

Book scholars already knew that "the majority of extant early medieval manuscripts that have come down to us in their original bindings (and this is a minute percentage of what existed originally) also display distinct technical features of the Coptic and Byzantine tradition."[1] Scholars had long speculated about the possibility of direct contact between Egypt and Ireland. The Faddan More Psalter confirmed it.

Egyptian papyrus lining a book in an Irish bog? Coptic bindings on medieval manuscripts? Egyptian monks in Ireland?

What's going on here?

What's going on is tangible proof that monks from the Egyptian desert came to Ireland in ancient times, bringing with them not only the art of bookbinding but also their monastic traditions, art, architecture, and patterns of devotion. Their presence is not mentioned by St. Patrick or later chroniclers, and it is known there were Christians in Ireland before St. Patrick arrived in the fifth century, so it is not unreasonable to surmise that they could have come as early as the fourth century.

Ireland's golden age saw the creation of the oldest vernacular literature in Europe: poems and prose recorded in magnificently decorated and illuminated manuscripts in unique scripts; an amazing collection of biblical and exegetical literature; the first codification of Church law and of secular law; a pedagogy in Latin that set the standard for Europe for centuries; a unique hagiography; unique art in metal and stonework, and more.

New research is showing that some of what has been considered uniquely Irish actually may have its origin in Egypt and elsewhere in the Middle East, where Christianity began. This is the story of those origins, those traditions, and the Faith we still share.

[1] John Gillis, *The Faddan More Psalter: The Discovery and Conservation of a Medieval Treasure* (Dublin: National Museum of Ireland, 2021), 124.

Chapter 1

The Gaelic World

Because it was not under Roman influence, as the Roman Empire fell into dissolution late in the fourth century, Ireland continued to flourish even as the rest of the world sank into what came to be called the Dark Ages. After all, Irish raiders wouldn't have been able to steal slaves from Britain if the Roman Empire hadn't been too weak to defend its colony.

The positive aspect of that isolation was that Ireland was able to maintain its own unique Gaelic social system with its own language, literature, religion, and culture. It continued on its own course, uninterrupted by conquest. The downside was that, because there was no Roman influence, there were no roads, no cities, and no central government in Ireland—the lack of which had ecclesiastical and political consequences.

Ireland had kings—about 150 of them! They weren't like what we think of when we usually hear the word *king*. Our idea of king comes from late medieval Europe, where the king ruled over a vast geographical area, and was a high and distant figure. He could order you killed, you had to kneel down before him, and you had to be afraid of him. It wasn't that way in Gaelic Ireland. There, kingdoms were not much bigger than extended families, called *tuatha*. The king wasn't somebody to be afraid of; in fact, he was probably your third cousin. That mattered when Christians began to write about God. The use of the word *king* occurs frequently. It's used with fondness, and without the note of fear.

Your loyalty was to your *tuath*, your family, your tribe. The intensely local nature of these kingdoms was to have tragic consequences later: the tribes were never able to successfully organize a central governance system in order to repel invasion from that larger kingdom across the Irish Sea, which had one king with a central government and a well-organized military drafted from the entire country.

But we're talking now about an older Ireland—one into which a spoiled and lazy (by his own admission!) sixteen-year-old boy, the son of a Roman deacon in Britain, was suddenly thrust when Irish slave traders raided his village. There probably were Christians already in Ireland when the lad arrived. Some of them may have been captured slaves like himself; others may have come from Gaul. Later chapters will investigate architecture, archaeology, and art and make the case that some Christians came from the Eastern Mediterranean world: Egypt and Constantinople and Armenia.

Though it be a blow to Irish pride, it's most likely that the Faith first would have come to Ireland from Britain. Here's how that would have happened:

Remember that the infant Church was a Greek Church. Six hundred years before Christ, ancient Greece had established a colony in southern Gaul, Massalia (today known as Marseilles). It was the only place in Gaul where Christianity was known in the third century, the westernmost place on earth.

St. Irenaeus, who is a saint in both the Eastern and Western Churches, brought the Faith to Gaul. He was a Greek from Smyrna, in Turkey. He had studied under St. Polycarp, who had heard the preaching of the Apostle, St. John the Evangelist. That means that he had a living memory of Jesus Christ—in other words, his faith was undiluted. During the persecution of Marcus Aurelius, Irenaeus fled to Lyon in Gaul. He happened to be in Rome in the year 177 delivering a message from the priests of Lyon to Pope Eleutherius when persecution came to Lyon and the bishop was martyred. After he returned home, Irenaeus was chosen as the second bishop of Lyon, and thereafter he devoted himself to combating heresies and evangelizing Gaul.

St. Nilus of Sinai

The Irish called it white martyrdom, "a man's abandoning everything he loves for God's sake."[2] The Greeks called it *xeniteia,* and it was a model of monastic life. A model of how seriously *xeniteia* was taken in the early days of the church is St. Nilus of Sinai, who died in either 430 or 451. He was a layman in Constantinople who had St. John Chrysostom as a spiritual director. He and his wife were so moved by the call to be closer to Christ that they agreed to separate; he and their son went into a monastery, while his wife and daughter entered a women's monastery. His monastery was raided by Saracens, his son sold into slavery. His son was purchased by the bishop of Elusa in Palestine, who made him doorkeeper of the church, where his father eventually found him. The bishop ordained them both,

[2] The same ancient homily refers to green martyrdom, which means by fasting and labor to free oneself from evil desires; red martyrdom was the endurance of death for Christ's sake. See John Ryan, S.J., *Irish Monasticism: Origins and Early Development* (Dublin: Talbot Press, 1931), 197.

and together they spent the next forty years living in a cave in Sinai, writing letters defending Chrysostom, countering Arianism, and trying to convert pagans.

Since time immemorial there had been an active tin trade between the Mediterranean and Cornwall, so it's very likely that traders stopped by Marseilles on their way to Britain and left behind not only Roman coins but also Christianity. There is the ancient tradition that the "wealthy merchant" (see Mark 15:43 and Luke 23:50) Joseph of Arimathea was the first to bring the good news to Britain: as a tin trader, he would have traveled that route regularly. One charming British tradition holds that on one of his journeys he brought the boy Jesus along with him on the voyage. Another tradition, which survives in some renditions of the Arthurian legend, is that he brought the Holy Grail to Britain after the Resurrection.

Even into the middle years of the seventh century, this trade route was still going strong and Egyptians were still coming to Cornwall to buy tin. In the *Analecta Bollandiana* 45 of 1927, the story of such a voyage is told in the life of St. John the Almoner, patriarch of Alexandria: a vessel with twenty thousand bushels of wheat from Egypt was storm-tossed to a Cornish port that was experiencing famine. A barter was arranged, and wheat was exchanged for tin—which was found on later examination to be silver, not tin.[3]

[3] Joseph H. Crehan, "The Liturgical Trade Route: East to West," *Studies: An Irish Quarterly Review* 65, no. 258 (Summer 1976): 87–99, jstor.org/stable/300900e05, 89–90.

In any event, Christianity was present in Britain from very early. Tertullian, writing in his *Treatise against the Jews* in 208, said that there were "places among the Britons unapproached by the Romans but subdued to Christ."[4] In 231, Origen, a Greek of Alexandria and Palestine, wrote: "The power of Our Lord and Savior is with those who in Britain are divided from our world,"[5] and in 246, he mentioned distant nations who were only partly converted, including Britain. By 304, the Britons had their first martyr, St. Alban, whose martyrdom is well-documented.

Tertullian's statement is intriguing. The Romans had "approached" most everyone in Britain south of Hadrian's Wall. Could the "Britons unapproached by the Romans" actually be a reference to the Irish? Or could it be a reference to the Celtic area of Cornwall?

In any case, there's no question that Britain got the Faith from Gaul, and that it took hold there. There is also linguistic evidence: Old Irish has several words of Latin origin and Christian significance that show by their modifications that they were derived not directly from Latin but through the medium of British speech.[6]

Just one year after Emperor Constantine issued the Edict of Milan, which allowed the Church to come out of hiding by making her as legal as all the other cults in the empire, he called a council of all bishops of the Western Empire at Arles, in southern France. Three bishops from Britain attended that council.

[4] Tertullian, *Treatise against the Jews*, 7, quoted in Charles Hole, *Early Missions to and within the British Islands* (London: Society for Promoting Christian Knowledge, 1888), 12.

[5] Quoted in Hole, *Early Missions*, 17–18.

[6] James F. Kenney, *The Sources for the Early History of Ireland* (New York: Columbia University Press, 1929; Dublin: Pádraic Ó Táilliúir, 1979), 160.

They were so poor that they needed to beg for free lodging—but they were there.

Although there is some evidence that the Pelagian heresy was present in the islands, overall, the early British Church remained orthodox in its belief. In 358, St. Hilary of Poitiers wrote that British bishops were among those who had escaped the Arian heresy. A few years later, no less than St. Athanasius gave Britain's bishops the seal of his approval in 363: "Their sentiments I know from actual investigation," he wrote, "and from their own letters."[7] Word of the Church in Britain reached even St. John Chrysostom, who was in Antioch in 387 when he wrote: "Even outside our world, the very British Islands beyond this sea and in the ocean itself have felt the power of the word, as testified by the Churches and altars they have erected."[8]

Note that Chrysostom referred to plural "British Islands." The phrase can be taken to include Ireland, because at that time, and for a few centuries to come, the areas we know today as Britain, Ireland, Wales, and Cornwall all functioned as one for most purposes. What we today call Scotland was then populated by pagan Picts, but the western coast of modern Scotland and the northeastern coast of Ireland (County Antrim) were beginning to take shape as the Gaelic Kingdom of Dal Riada (*Argyll* is a corrupt form of *Earra-Ghàidheal*, Old Irish for "Coast of the Gaels"). The phrase "Celtic Mediterranean" is sometimes used to describe the sharing of people, language, commerce, and ideas among those areas.

By the time of Chrysostom in 387, then, the Faith was present in Ireland. Note that Chrysostom did not say that the islands were entirely converted, only that there was a foothold and that

[7] Quoted in Hole, *Early Missions*, 22.

[8] Ibid., 22.

churches had been erected. But what were Ireland and its pagan Celts like before Christianity arrived?

Celts and Druids

The Celts were a collection of Indo-Europeans who at one point held sway all across Europe and were united by their Celtic language and Druidic religion. They came from central Europe, where the oldest archaeological evidence of the Early Iron Age Hallstatt culture that thrived from 1200 B.C. to 450 B.C. was found in 1824 near a salt mine south of Salzburg, Austria. The Late Iron Age La Téne civilization on the shores of Lake Neuchatel in Switzerland flourished from 450 B.C. to 50 B.C., and was discovered in 1857.[9] The objects found at the site near Lake Neuchatel are notable for their curvilinear designs and stylized animal and bird forms—which appear later on in Irish art.

Scholars debate when the Celts first arrived in Ireland, and whether they came as invaders or peaceful settlers. Regardless, we know that there were four different waves of migration, the first beginning as early as 700 B.C. The last wave was the Gaels, and they are believed to have arrived about 100 B.C.

Julius Caesar fought Celts, whom he called Gauls and Britons, and attempted to exterminate them. By modern times, they had all been pushed to the "Celtic fringe": what now includes Brittany, the Isle of Man, Wales, Cornwall, northern Scotland, Ireland, and a bit of Galicia in Spain. Nowadays those places still have some musical traditions in common, which are shared with the music of their descendants in North America and around the world.

[9] Christiane Eluére, *The Celts: Conquerors of Ancient Europe* (New York: Harry Abrams, 1993), 14.

P's and Q's

The Celtic language segmented into the Goidelic/Gaelic, known as Q-Gaelic, and the Brythonic/Welsh, or P-Gaelic. Which explains, in case you're interested, why Scottish and Manx speakers (Q) can understand Irish (Q), but Welsh speakers (P) cannot. You have to mind your P's and Q's if you want to learn Gaelic!

In Ireland and Britain, the Celtic religious leaders were the Druids. The Druidic religion did not allow writing—everything of importance had to be committed to memory. It required twelve years of study in order to become a poet, time that was spent memorizing a huge quantity of tales and poetry: the Book of Leinster lists 250 main stories and one hundred secondary tales that had to be memorized. The word for poet was *filidh*, which had overtones of prophecy, since *filidh* would lie down in the dark to receive the inspiration for their poetry. *Filidh* had an honor-price just below that of a king, which indicates the high regard in which they were held. A bard was a lower-level poet, who was worth half the honor-price of a *filidh*. Bards had power nonetheless, because poems gave immortality to their subjects: if a poet wrote that you were unjust, or unkind, or stingy, that's how you would be known for the rest of history!

There was a zero-toleration policy for error in the memory training. So, what the poets remembered and what was later transcribed by monks once Gaelic began to be written down can be relied upon as accurate. Gaelic literature dates from about A.D. 600, when monks first began writing down the Irish tales, until about 1200, when the Norman invasion outlawed Gaelic in favor of English and disrupted the patterns of patronage.

With a start date of A.D. 600, however, it is worth noting that Gaelic literature is the oldest vernacular literature in Europe. Most people are surprised to learn that. Then again, our American culture's perceptions of Ireland's culture were ultimately created by English writers who despised the Irish, and by Americans who caricatured them on stage and screen.

Most of our knowledge of the Celts comes from the Roman historian Posidonius, who lived 135 to 50 B.C., and Strabo, a Greek who lived 64 B.C. to A.D. 24. This knowledge, thus, comes from Britain, where the Romans tried to suppress Druidism in their efforts to conquer Britain. Whether Druidism was the same in Ireland cannot be known. Posidonius wrote very detailed descriptions of the human sacrifices over which the Celts presided—an aspect of Druidism that is often conveniently overlooked by those seeking to revive that strand of paganism. Pliny (†A.D. 79) wrote of the Druids' love of both mistletoe and human sacrifice. Tacitus described a battle in Wales in which they covered their altars with the blood of the losers, and then read the entrails of their victims. Obviously, practices like these that were contrary to the law of God had to be suppressed as Christianity prevailed, but other aspects of native culture were absorbed by Christianity in Ireland.

Part of the success of the conversion of Ireland was the Christians' respect for the native literature. Although some Church Fathers urged the elimination of pagan traditions and lore as part of the conversion process, St. Patrick knew that the Faith was strong enough to absorb it. He accepted or indeed *baptized*—ancient lore and pagan feasts. Christian monks were able to write down those tales because the conversion of Ireland was gradual, and bards were still around when monasteries were established, and they could repeat them to scribes. It is not possible to know whether all of them were written down. It is entirely possible that particularly salacious or violent passages would have been quietly dropped. Given the existence of 250 monasteries in Ireland by the seventh century, most of which would have had *scriptoria*, it's possible that most got recorded but then forgotten, as poets had to become plowmen in order to survive. If much ancient Gaelic literature is lost today, it is not the fault of early Christianity: later invasions and the destruction of monasteries and churches destroyed mountains of literature.

Druidism had an origin story: Brigid is the name of the goddess who is said to have created Ireland. It had a trinity of gods: Dagda, sire, harp-player, and poet; Lugh, his son who brought the sun; and Ogma, the god of eloquence and poetry. The first writing system in Ireland, *Ogham* (pronounced "ahm"), is named after Ogma.

The Celtic tales and myths have endured in the popular mind. The tales of Cuchullain, the Hound of Ulster, and Queen Maeve of Connacht, who went to war over a white bull, are part of what is known as the Ulster Cycle. Finn McCool is a bumbling giant in contemporary children's books, but his original tales are known as the Fenian Cycle, in which Fionn Mac Cumhaill is a doer of great deeds.

The Cycles and other tales are full of blood and gore, deceit, lying, shape-shifting, wife-stealing, plunder, and murder. It is noteworthy, however, that often characters meet their doom when they fail to be courageous, generous, loyal, or beautiful—or when they fail to keep a *geis*, or taboo, that has been imposed on them.

Also noteworthy is that often heroes use words, chants, music, and prayers to accomplish their wonders. The number three was sacred. Celts believed in an afterlife. The Druids in Gaul believed that "souls and the cosmos are indestructible, but that sometime fire and water will overpower them."[10]

Hmm ... life after death, trinitarianism, keeping a *geis*, words and prayers to accomplish wonders. This sounds familiar. Could this be an example of *prefigurement*, a providential pre-evangelization, paving the way for Christianity?

By all accounts in the conversion of Ireland, there was only one red martyr, St. Patrick's chariot driver. Conversion was nearly bloodless—something that cannot be said of any other country in the world—but it was not rapid. To judge by the written laws and penitentials of the monasteries, Druids were still active as late as the seventh and early eighth centuries. It's clear that, as the priestly and learned class of paganism, some of them became the priestly and learned class of Christianity as well. This intellectual transition helped to ensure the continuation of ancient ways.

In Search of the "Celtic Church"

Yet there is factual basis for saying that early Christianity in Ireland was unique. It was—but not necessarily in the way that it is often represented.

It is true that early Irish Christianity was different from what we are familiar with today. Hymns and poems from ancient Ireland strike the modern reader as refreshingly original. They contain beautiful imagery, emphasizing the discovery of God in nature and profound personal connection to the Divine. The celebration of the Eucharist—to the extent we know about it from surviving sixth- and seventh-century documents—was very different from the

[10] John Carey, "Saint Patrick, the Druids, and the End of the World," *History of Religions* 36, no. 1 (August 1996): 42–53, 45.

post–Council of Trent, post–Vatican II liturgy that most Latin-Rite Catholics know.

There is no evidence before the fifth century, and only fragments from afterwards survive. What is known for sure, however, is that throughout Britain and Ireland there was a diversity of rites for celebrating the liturgy. It wasn't until 1172, at the Synod of Cashel, that the Roman Rite of the day was definitively adopted. If a synod had to be held to adopt the Roman Rite, you can be sure that there were others floating around. Indeed, written records confirm that fact. When Augustine was sent to Kent (later Canterbury) in 597 to convert Saxon king Ethelbert, he found a diversity of liturgical practice. He wrote to Pope St. Gregory the Great about how he should regard the diversity, and Gregory's reply was, in today's parlance, "Don't sweat the details."

Eventually, of course, Rome's way came to dominate, but for centuries the pre-Norman Irish Church was marked by its diversity from Rome liturgically and otherwise.

With all the chaos in Ireland of the Viking invasion in the ninth century, the Norman invasion in the twelfth, and the Elizabethan invasion in the seventeenth, countless documents and manuscripts disappeared or were destroyed, and the ancient liturgical diversity was forgotten. When those early documents were discovered by Protestant scholars, they were used to make the case that the forced protestantization of Ireland was not really so bad. After all, Ireland really hadn't been all *that* close to Rome. This was the birth of the notion of a "Celtic Church."

The idea of a "Celtic Church"—though not the term—began with the work of Church of Ireland archbishop James Ussher (1581–1656). Ussher wrote in his 1639 *Britannicarum Ese* that, in the early medieval period, the churches in the British Isles were distinct from each other, and from Rome. Ussher was one of the first graduates of Dublin's Trinity College (founded 1591), a serious scholar whose work on Ignatius of Antioch stands up well today. His observations were accurate, though his interpretation was colored by the anti-Catholic bias of his times.

Two hundred years later, another scholar named Frederick Edward Warren (1842–1930) took up Ussher's theme. He, too, was an Anglican clergyman, and he served as vice president of St. John's College, Oxford. He revived the idea of a Celtic Church with his translations and explanations of the sixth- and seventh-century documents he discovered. In 1881, he published *Liturgy and Ritual of the Celtic Church*, a critical edition of the Stowe Missal, the Antiphonary of Bangor, and other surviving liturgical fragments from Cornwall, Wales, Scotland, and Ireland.

Warren was the first scholar in modern times of ancient Irish culture, for which he deserves great credit. He was a true pioneer in what today is known as Irish studies, and his work still frames the conversation on the subject. Warren did have an axe to grind, however: he wanted to prove that the "history of the Celtic Church, both in these islands and on the continent, exhibits its occasional proofs of its independence of, and hostility to, the claims of Rome."[11] Warren believed that history was on the side of the Protestants, and he used the lack of what he recognized as Roman flavor in the most ancient Irish religious documents to support his case.

Warren's premise made it into most history books. No less a perceived authority on English history than Winston Churchill wrote in 1956 that "the Celtic churches received a form of ecclesiastical government which was supported by the loosely knit communities

[11] F. E. Warren, *The Liturgy and Ritual of the Celtic Church* (Oxford: Clarendon Press, 1881), 40.

of monks and preachers, and was not in these early decisive periods associated with the universal organization of the Papacy." "[The Irish Church] was monastic in its form, and it traveled from the East through Northern Ireland to its new home without touching at any moment the Roman center."[12]

To be sure, there's some truth in what Warren and Churchill say. There were definitely differences between the early Church in Ireland and the later Church, either Roman or Anglican, that Warren would have observed. And Christianity did not initially come to Ireland from Rome, but from other routes—though all the evidence suggests that it came via Munster, the southernmost province of Ireland, rather than through Ulster, in northern Ireland. Another scholar has made a case for early Gaulish missions in north Connacht and north Leinster, documenting geographic pathways for the possible transmission of the Gallican liturgy, about which more later.[13]

Churchill does not mention that, as soon as Rome became aware of Christians in Ireland and was able to act, a bishop named Palladius was sent to Ireland in 431.

What were those differences? Where did they come from? Do those differences mean that the Faith in Ireland was not really Catholic? Not at all. In fact, the steadfastness of the Irish Church to orthodox doctrine, and its respect for the See of Peter, was always its hallmark. Even Warren acknowledged as much.

At the same time that Warren and Churchill were pointing out evidence of a lack of conformity between the early Irish Church

[12] Winston Churchill, "A History of the English-Speaking Peoples, Part 1: The Birth of Britain," *Life*, March 19, 1956, 93.

[13] Charles Doherty, "The Basilica in Early Ireland," *Peritia* 3 (1984): 303–315.

and Rome, Catholic controversialists were fully vested in defending Rome, and asserting a Roman provenance for everything—whether or not it was justified.

Even as recently as the 1960s, most Catholics had never heard of the Eastern rites, after all. It wasn't until 1995 when Pope St. John Paul II urged the Church to "breathe with her two lungs"[14] that most Catholics became aware that our Church was not Roman in origin. The result was a considerable body of new writing, both academic and popular, which was supported by varying degrees of research and of accuracy of interpretation and was sometimes used as weaponry in sectarian warfare. Fortunately, recent scholarship has been able to strip away some of the preconceptions and misconceptions.

For Further Reference

Carey, John. "Saint Patrick, the Druids, and the End of the World." *History of Religions* 36, no. 1 (August 1996): 42–53.

Churchill, Winston. "A History of the English-Speaking Peoples, Part 1: The Birth of Britain." *Life*, March 19, 1956.

Crehan, Joseph H. "The Liturgical Trade Route: East to West." *Studies: An Irish Quarterly Review* 65, no. 258 (Summer 1976): 87–99. jstor.org/stable/30090005.

Doherty, Charles. "The Basilica in Early Ireland." *Peritia* 3 (1984): 303 315.

Eluére, Christiane. *The Celts: Conquerors of Ancient Europe*. New York: Harry Abrams, 1993.

Gillis, John. *The Faddan More Psalter: The Discovery and Conservation of a Medieval Treasure*. Dublin: National Museum of Ireland, 2021.

[14] John Paul II, Encyclical Letter on Commitment to Ecumenism *Ut Unum Sint* (May 25, 1995), no. 54.

Hole, Charles. *Early Missions to and within the British Islands.* London: Society for Promoting Christian Knowledge, 1888.

John Paul II. Encyclical Letter on Commitment to Ecumenism *Ut Unum Sint.* May 25, 1995.

Kenney, James F. *The Sources for the Early History of Ireland.* New York: Columbia University Press, 1929; Dublin: Pádraic Ó Táilliúir, 1979.

Ryan, John, S.J., *Irish Monasticism: Origins and Early Development,* Dublin: Talbot Press, 1931.

Warren, F. E. *The Liturgy and Ritual of the Celtic Church.* Oxford: Clarendon Press, 1881.

——. *The Liturgy and Ritual of the Celtic Church.* 3rd ed. Edited by Neil Xavier O'Donoghue. Piscataway, NJ: Gorgias Press, 2010.

Chapter 2

The Church of St. Patrick

Of course, the Christianity in Ireland was different from the Christianity in western Europe. Why do I say "of course"? A side trip into Church history will put the Church into the context of the fourth and fifth centuries.

To get into the spirit of things, first set aside some distinctions that matter nowadays. Go back to the early, early days when there was only one way to be a follower of Jesus Christ. There was no "Orthodox" or "Catholic"—let alone "Protestant." There was no "Eastern" or "Western" or "Oriental." Those distinctions were just beginning to come into existence at different places right around the time St. Patrick was arriving in Ireland.

What's more, the Christianity that came first came to Ireland in the time period known as Late Antiquity did not at all look like the Christianity in Rome of the High Middle Ages, because Christianity began in the Middle East. The first apostolic sees were Rome, Constantinople, Alexandria, Antioch, and Jerusalem. The first intellectual center of the Church was the Catechetical School of Alexandria: St. Augustine was from Hippo in Algeria, and the defender against the early heresy of Arianism was St. Athanasius, bishop of Alexandria.

The first liturgies and prayer customs were based on what the apostles would have known from the Jewish Temple. The only language of the Church was Greek until 395, when Emperor Theodosius split the imperial capital between Rome and Constantinople. St. Jerome, who died in A.D. 420, first translated the Greek and Hebrew texts of Scripture into Latin. Latin, which had been the dominant political and legal language of the Western Roman Empire, began morphing into local languages—Spanish, or French, or Italian—after the Romans left.

The first four hundred years of the Church were preoccupied by settling Christological questions. Who *was* Jesus Christ? And who was Mary, His Mother? Well into the fifth century, Christians were preoccupied as they sorted through the controversies of Arianism and Nestorianism. Notice that those questions were settled not in Rome, but in Alexandria, Nicaea, or Constantinople. Rome simply was not the center of Christian scholarship in those days.

The roots of later distinctions were intellectual as well as geographic. Generalities generally are not good, but this one might be helpful: the West was practical and legalistic, while the East was mystical and idealistic. Rome was the center of law and administration, and Tertullian, a North African lawyer, brought Roman legal thinking and terminology into theology. He was concerned with order, discipline, moral issues, jurisdiction, and government. The East focused on the Person and nature of Jesus Christ, and how individual souls may draw nearer to Him—mind and body, heart and soul. Eastern Christianity applied its intellectual power to defeat heresies that threatened revealed truth about God. Origen, a theologian of Alexandria, forged links between Christianity and the philosophy of the Greeks, articulating that Jesus united divine nature with human nature, so that by communion with the divine, we humans might rise to be divine. St. Athanasius of Alexandria expressed it in the fifty-fourth chapter of his work *On the Incarnation*: "God became man so that man might become God." St. Augustine said it in a sermon too: "God became man so that man might become God."[15]

At risk of oversimplifying, it could be said that on the macro level, for the next five hundred years, the West (Rome) was of necessity mainly occupied with converting and civilizing barbarians, and governing western Europe to a greater or lesser degree. Constantinople mainly had to fight off barbarians and deal with its chaotic ruling families. Thus, Rome and Constantinople gradually grew apart for centuries without anybody having the bandwidth to notice very much.

Bishop Palladius was sent to Ireland by Pope Celestine in 431; Patrick came later. Note that 431 was the year of the conclusion of the Council of Ephesus, the third ecumenical council, the one that put the final kibosh on the heretic Nestorius. This great ecclesiastical drama had been consuming Christianity for about a hundred years. Politically, in 431 the empire and its ordered society were rapidly crumbling, and barbarians (many of whom had already been converted to Arian Christianity) were entering the empire en masse. For Europe, surviving while incorporating massive new populations was the first order of business.

In the fifth, sixth, seventh, and eighth centuries, imposing rules on *anybody* was low on Rome's list of priorities, because the Church was still in the process of getting herself organized. By the sixth century, Constantinople had become the center of

[15] Augustine, *Sermo 13 de Tempore*, quoted in "St. Augustine: God Became Man So That Man Might Become God," *Te Deum Laudamus!* (blog), January 3, 2009, *PL* 39, 1097–1098, https://te-deum.blogspot.com/2009/01/st-augustine-god-became-man-so-that-man.html.

Christian thought. It possessed an unbroken tradition of Christianity in both Church and state. Historians call the period from 537–752 the "Byzantine Papacy." Not only was Constantinople the home of the most competent theologians and leaders, but also the Byzantine emperor—that is, the Roman emperor in his new Eastern capital, the *Nova Roma*: Constantinople—had the right to approve the selection of a pope before he could be consecrated! Most Catholics don't realize that there were eleven Greek and six Syrian popes before the year 753.

Rome Borrowed from Constantinople

Liturgical trade routes are two-way streets.

A book by Andrew Ekonomou, *Byzantine Rome and the Greek Popes,* makes the case that "Constantinople had influenced Gregory far more than he ever admitted" — in other words, that it was through the agency of Pope St. Gregory the Great, he who is famous for Gregorian chant, that some of the things most loved in the Roman Rite were added — as direct borrowings from Constantinople. A school for chant was one of the things he borrowed!

Prior to Gregory's day, the Alleluia was sung at Mass only between Easter and Pentecost. He changed that, and he was criticized for "byzantining" the Mass — but he responded by saying he had taken the practice not from Constantinople but from the church of Jerusalem. That sounds like the argument in the *Ratio de Cursus* to me!

Rome did not celebrate solemn Easter Vespers until after the middle of the seventh century — even though it had long been performed in Constantinople. It was Pope Gregory the

Great who brought the custom over from Constantinople.[16] He introduced to the Roman calendar feasts of the Blessed Virgin that had hitherto been observed only in the East.

Andrew Ekonomou is a Byzantine history scholar with a more varied biography than most academics: a former state prosecutor in Georgia, he is senior counsel at the American Center for Law and Justice. He holds a Ph.D. in Byzantine history from Emory University.

In short, for the first nine centuries, Rome was primarily occupied with getting the Church organized. Additionally, it had to sort out its relationship with the kings and emperors of emerging Europe (e.g., who was going to choose the pope: the cardinals or the Frankish emperor?), with Constantinople, with other Italian city-states as they arose and claimed power, and, by the seventh century, it had to focus on repelling Islam from Europe. A great deal of ground had to be covered before the path was laid to becoming the Church that would dominate the world of the Renaissance, from which we can draw clear lines to the Church of today.

In these times of uncertainty and change, as the end of the world was (believed to be) bearing down fast, innovation in the Church was to be avoided. Any such changes would mean separation from the truth as it had been received from Christ and the apostles. Conserving the past meant staying as close as possible to Christ, to the apostles, and to the true Faith.

[16] Andrew J. Ekonomou, *Byzantine Rome and the Greek Popes* (Lanham, MD: Lexington Books, 2007), 165.

The Irish Difference

Irish Christians shared many of the same concerns as their fellow Christians in Rome and Constantinople, yet there were marked differences. The Faith had first been carried to the island by people seeking to achieve communion with God. Ireland's first evangelists were mystical and idealistic—very much "of the East," and probably came from the Egyptian desert. Uncovering their legacy is what this book is all about.

So, yes, the Church in Ireland was different from the Catholic Church that people would have known in the seventeenth century or later. And, no, that's not a problem.

Many of the Church's institutions we take for granted were in the early stages of their organic evolution during the period of Late Antiquity (formerly called the Dark Ages). Take, for instance, canon law. It simply didn't exist for the first twelve centuries *anno Domini*. Instead, the Church was governed at the "micro" level by bishops, abbots, and priests.

That explains a lot. For instance, today, for Mother Teresa of Calcutta to become a canonized saint, her cause needed to be advanced and promoted through a series of "offices," or departments, in the Vatican. The process of canonization evolved gradually: Pope Alexander III (1159–1181) began claiming for the Holy See the process of making a saint. It wasn't until Pope Sixtus V (1585–1590) that the Roman Curia—the Holy See's bureaucracy—got the job.

St. Malachy became the first Irish-born saint to go through the bureaucratic process and be formally canonized by Rome. That was in 1190! (A cynic might note that, around the same time, Rome was consolidating its control over the Church in Ireland. Giving the natives their own official saint was perhaps helpful in winning the locals over to the new system.) St. Olan the Egyptian, whose holy well has been venerated in County Cork since the fourth century, was grandfathered into the new system. Pope Urban VIII (1623–1644), while forbidding the cult of non-beatified or non-canonized persons, made an exception for those regarded as saints for at least a hundred years.

The Easter Fire — Gift of the Irish?

There is no debate that today's custom of the new fire at Easter traces back to Ireland, and there is no debate that its origin was Jerusalem, where the tradition of the new fire at the Church of the Anastasis has been known since the fourth century, thanks to Egeria, and was probably old then. Though that practice was limited to the Holy City, it could have been known in the monastic universe that conversed with the desert — but it was unknown in Rome as late as the eighth century.[17]

So when St. Patrick kindled that Easter fire, he was following the tradition of Jerusalem. The question is: Did Patrick know he was doing that, or did the circumstances of his evangelistic encounter prompt him to reinvent it? In any case, Patrick is the proximate cause: from Patrick it went throughout Europe and into the universal Church.

Msgr. L. Duchesne in 1927[18] wrote that it was customary for the Irish as early as the sixth century to kindle great fires at nightfall at Easter Eve. "It appears from the correspondence

[17] Archdale King, *Liturgy of the Roman Church* (Milwaukee: Bruce, 1957), 195.

[18] Msgr. L. Duchesne, *Christian Worship: Its Origin and Evolution; A Study of the Latin Liturgy up to the Time of Charlemagne*, 5th ed., trans. M. L. McClure (London: Society for Promoting Christian Knowledge, 1927), 250–251, last quotation from n. 1.

between St. Boniface and Pope Zacharias that these fires were lighted not from other fires, but from flints." In other words, they were really new fires. This custom appears to have been peculiar to the British or Irish, and to have been conveyed, through the Anglo-Saxons, to the Continent by missionaries of the eighth century. Thank you, St. Columbanus! "There is no trace of it in the ancient Merovingian books. It was not known, moreover, at Rome." "In the Mozarabic Missal now in use, there is, as in the Roman Missal, a blessing of the fire at the beginning of the Easter Vigil. The fire is obtained from a flint and steel."

Yet there are scores—if not hundreds—of saints in Ireland from many earlier centuries who never went through the "official" process, simply because the "official" process did not exist! That doesn't mean that these men and women were not saints, of course. Surely they were holy men and women deserving of reverence. Some of them may have performed miracles before or after their deaths, and were proclaimed saints by the people or the bishop in the area, because that's how it was done in those early days. Many of these ancient Irish saints are recognized both by Catholics and Orthodox.

By contrast, while major ancient martyrs are remembered across Europe, many of the local saints are being forgotten today. In Ireland, saints tended to be "owned" by the local laity. (Witness the abundance of holy wells and shrines all around Ireland with the names of saints, and the plethora of saints' names in Irish geography.) These ancient saints have tended to be remembered and invoked by local people in Ireland, despite occasional clerical disapproval of their "backward" devotion. Sadly, memories are now fading in modern, secular Ireland of some of the ancient local saints as trendy new housing developments invent new names that could come from anywhere in the English-speaking world. Interestingly, however, a Russian Orthodox bishop told me recently that devotion to local saints continues to be a custom in Eastern Christianity.

A similar organic evolution occurred with the Divine Liturgy, called in the earliest days of Irish Christianity the "Offering," now known as "the Mass" in the Western Church. The way the Eucharist was celebrated at Pascha (Easter) in Jerusalem in the fourth century was meticulously documented at the time by a Spanish nun named Egeria. Today the Melkite Greek Catholic and the Antiochian Orthodox Paschal liturgy resemble those descriptions better than anything else in the world. When St. John Chrysostom, bishop of Constantinople, wrote down the Divine Liturgy—the set of procedures for celebrating the Eucharist—in the fourth century, he wrote down what had already been in use in Constantinople for centuries. Because it was written down, it went around the world and became the baseline, if you will, for the universal Church. As the Church moved westward into continental Europe, the way the Eucharist was celebrated changed. The liturgy of late antique Ireland, as will be discussed in chapter 7, is a case study of this organic evolution.

St. Patrick the Legend

There is no doubt that St. Patrick was real, even though no historical document mentions him until the seventh century—two hundred years after he lived. The extravagance of later hagiography, however, makes it very difficult for scholars to sort out fact from fiction in the story of Ireland's patron saint. Current scholarship accepts a date of death for St. Patrick around 492.[19]

[19] Gearóid MacNiocaill, *Ireland before the Vikings*, The Gill History of Ireland, vol. 1 (Dublin: Gill and Macmillan, 1972), 22.

The earliest source of information about St. Patrick is the *Vita sancti Patricii*. It was written by Muirchú moccu Machtheni, a monk in the province of Leinster, in the seventh century, under the patronage of Bishop Aedh of Slébte. Around the same time, Tírechán, a bishop from north Connacht, also wrote a biography about St. Patrick, the *Collectanea*.

Both Muirchú and Aedh had attended the Synod of Birr in 697. That Synod had been called to reconcile differences that had developed between two factions of the Church in Ireland. Muirchú's faction was known as the *Romani*, who wanted to introduce innovation in order to follow Rome. The others, called the *Hibernenses*, were content to follow traditional liturgy and customs.

No complete copy of the *Vita* exists. There are three incomplete copies in Europe, and one in Ireland, where the *Vita* is included in the larger *Book of Armagh*, which is reliably dated to 807. The *Collectanea* is also in the *Book of Armagh*, which was copied in the ninth century. Sometime in the tenth century, an anonymous hagiographer wrote the *Vita tripartita sancti Patricii*, which further expanded the Patrick myth. The *Vita tripartita* portrays Patrick casting curses on people and wresting promises from God that the Irish will have advance warning of the end of the world.

The *Vita* is considered the first biography, though it falls more into the category of hagiography. The two genres are different types of writing altogether. Muirchú at least acknowledges that, by writing two hundred years after the fact, he relied on the opinions and guesses of others. To say he embellished his story would be an understatement.

Patrick's own writing contrasts with all the later hagiographic myth-making texts. It is simple and straightforward. He speaks from the heart without literary devices (as better-educated Latin writers would have done). He writes about prayer and God's answering prayers. Muirchú, on the other hand, tells fantastic tales and invents miracle stories—for instance, that the whole country was converted instantly after Patrick confronted the king at Easter. Another miracle story says that Coroticus was turned into a fox because he did not repent as Patrick called on him to. The tale we may have heard as children about Patrick and his companions shape-shifting into deer so that the evil king Laoghaire would not see them comes from hagiography, not from Patrick himself.

Some scholars maintain that the creation of the cult of Patrick was a deliberate tactic in the ecclesiastical politics of the seventh century. There were some power struggles going on between the Irish system of monasteries and the Roman demand for dioceses. (Remember: not having been under Rome, Ireland was not organized the way the Roman Church was.) By the seventh century, Armagh was striving to be recognized by Rome as the primatial see of Ireland and created propaganda to support its claim. The bishop was claiming jurisdiction over all Ireland, in opposition to the monastic system in which monasteries were under the authority of their own abbots.

The problem was that Armagh did not have the relics of St. Patrick, so it had to resort to propaganda. What better way to establish the claim than by raising the status of Patrick, saying he had confronted the high king and built a church in Armagh? Yet here, too, there was a problem: Patrick never mentions a relationship to Armagh. He never mentions any place by name in his writings. In any case, the propaganda campaign was successful: fourteen centuries later, both the Catholic and the Anglican archbishops of Armagh consider themselves the direct successors of St. Patrick.

Hagiography—with its amazing miracles performed by saints and exquisite tortures detailed for martyrs—can be fun to read. Still, we must realize that it's not the same as historical biography.

If we give the impression that such tales must be taken literally, we may create major obstacles to another's faith. God certainly does give some of His servants miraculous powers, probably more often than our materialistic age gives credence to. Nevertheless, He does so only rarely. Miracle stories may have strengthened the faith of some peasants in ancient days, but in the current scientific age it beggars belief that Patrick and his companions were turned into deer so that they could walk across the field, or that St. Brigid hung her cloak on a sunbeam, as her hagiography tells. As far back as 1790, Edward Ledwich, a pioneer scholar of ancient Ireland and author of the first *Antiquities of Ireland*, was driven to deny the very existence of St Patrick entirely on the grounds that "so fantastic a person was incompatible with either history or common sense."[20]

One of the hagiographies has Patrick casting snakes out of Ireland. Snakes, I'm sorry to say, never existed in Ireland. Ireland had broken off from the rest of the European landmass during the last Ice Age; when things warmed up again, reptiles couldn't get there. On the other hand, snakes are often a literary image for evil. So, perhaps the story of driving out the snakes can be read as symbolic of driving out paganism. That's hagiography for you.

Patrick the Man

The identity and chronology of St. Patrick are matters of considerable controversy among scholars. For one thing, there is no corroboration of his work, either in contemporary British or European historians, nor in any church records. No evidence has been found of Patrick's being sent by Rome, whereas there is a record

[20] Cited in Robert E. McNally, "St. Patrick: 461–1961," *Catholic Historical Review* 47, no. 3 (October 1961): 309, jstor.org/stable/25016896.

that Bishop Palladius was sent from the continent of Europe by Pope Celestine in 431 *ad Scottos in Christus credentes*—"to the Irish believing in Christ." (At that time, *Scottos* meant Irish, as Caesar had used the term. Only later did the term come to be applied to the residents of the northern part of Britain.)

To make things worse, Palladius is also called Patricius in some sources, giving rise to the "two Patrick problem" that has bedeviled scholars for more than a century.

So, it's better to be an "originalist" and stick to what Patrick wrote about himself.

According to one hagiography, Patrick was born on March 17, 461. This seems plausible, given what little we *do* know about Patrick, though in other hagiographies his date of death is given as March 17. His *Confession* and *Letter to Coroticus* are dated to the fifth century, and are considered the beginning of Irish history and literature. The *Confession* is Patrick's own memoir, written in poor-quality Latin, and the *Letter* is his excommunication of a slave raider, Coroticus, who had stolen some of his new converts. In the *Confession* he spends some time defending himself against attacks from somebody, presumably a bishop—but who, and why, and what charge, nobody knows.

Early in the twentieth century, Heinrich Zimmer raised the question of how St. Patrick, whose own education was very poor, could have caused within a hundred years his adopted land to be known for its extraordinary learning. Kuno Meyer took up the question, focusing on St. Patrick's tirade: "You rhetoricians who do not know the Lord, hear and search who it was that called me up, fool though I be, from the midst of those who think themselves wise, and skilled in the law, and mighty orators, and powerful in everything." Meyer defended St. Patrick by pointing out that St. Patrick was inveighing against pagan scholars from Gaul who were living in Ireland in his lifetime: "It is clear now that Patrick here refers to pagan rhetors from Gaul resident in Ireland, whose arrogant presumption, founded upon their superior learning, looked with disdain and derision upon the unlettered saint."[21] Those rhetoricians could have arrived in Ireland after fleeing the oncoming barbarians in France. Having trained in the Roman educational system, they would have scorned Patrick's rustic Latin.

What's important is that everyone agrees that the oldest surviving documents from early Christian Ireland are Patrick's writings.

The only manuscript copy of the *Confession* in Ireland is included in the *Book of Armagh*, a vellum manuscript of 222 leaves, which was written between 807 and 808 and is now preserved at Trinity College in Dublin. That version of the *Confession* is incomplete. The entire *Confession* and *Letter to Coroticus* are in manuscripts in Perrone, France, in the *Perrona Scottorum* monastery, which Irish monks founded in the seventh century.

The *Confession* is very readable, and many editions are available today. It shows Patrick to be a simple man of profound faith, filled with the Holy Spirit, passionate about Holy Scripture, believing that the Bible is unchangeable truth, and that the Day of Judgment was not far off.

The basic story is well-known: He was kidnapped from his home in Britain by slave traders around age sixteen and became a shepherd on the hills of Ireland, nobody knows where. Most likely he was surrounded by pagans, though some of his fellow slaves may have been Christian captives. The Lord looked upon him and told him in a dream that a ship would take him away to freedom.

[21] Kuno Meyer, "Learning in Ancient Ireland," *Irish Review* 2, no. 21 (November 1912): 457.

He arose and walked three days to where he found a ship, which indeed took him away. Later, he had another dream in which the Irish people called him to return. And so he did.

His description of himself is humble. He had paid little attention in school, he admits, and had little use for religion until he found himself on that hillside tending animals for his master. God was preparing him for the future: he learned the language and the culture, and he learned about Druidism; it is believed that Miliucc, his master, was a Druid high priest.

He started praying a hundred times a day—which he did for the rest of his life. "After I arrived in Ireland, I tended sheep every day, and I prayed frequently during the day. More and more the love of God increased, and my sense of awe before God. Faith grew, and my spirit was moved, so that in one day I would pray up to one hundred times, and at night perhaps the same. I even remained in the woods and on the mountain, and I would rise to pray before dawn in snow and ice and rain. I never felt the worse for it, and I never felt lazy—as I realise now, the spirit was burning in me at that time."

After seven years of captivity he heard the voice of the Lord telling him to escape and where to go, and he obeyed without hesitation. He tells how he got to where he was going (but he doesn't name the place)—and then he skips ahead. He doesn't mention where he studied or who taught him or who ordained him, or when, either as a priest or as a bishop. Even the name of his hometown, which he gives in the *Confession*, cannot be traced today. The bandit Coroticus cannot be found in historical documents either, though the terrorism for which Patrick reproaches him was common at the time.

When he arrived in Ireland to convert it, he found little evidence of Christianity: "Daily I expect for myself either murder, capture, or slavery. Once I was seized by enemies who longed to kill me. They took from me all I had, and bound me in iron," he wrote. Often he felt homesick, "like a stranger and an exile for the love of God."

Yet he traveled the country and converted the people, and established monasteries for men and for women. How did he do it? Patrick would probably be the first to tell you that it was not Patrick but God who deserves the credit for anything.

Bishop Secundinus, called St. Sechnall in Irish, died in 448 and may have been one of the first bishops of Armagh. He wrote the hymn "Audite Omnes Amantes," found in the seventh-century *Antiphonary of Bangor*, which includes this stanza about St. Patrick:

Constans in Dei timore
Ed fide immobilis
Super quem aedificatur
Ut Petrum ecclesia
Cuiusque apostolatum
A Deo sortitus est
In cuiusportae adversum
Inferni non prevalent.

Constant in the fear of God
And with unwavering faith
On which it is built
Like Peter the church
The apostleship of each,
He was chosen by God
Against whose gates
Hell does not prevail.

Enough said.

The Church Patrick Found—and Founded

God can write straight with crooked lines, it is often said, and St. Patrick is a case in point.

Patrick had not learned good Latin and had not advanced in the study of Roman rhetoric. No doubt his inattentiveness to his tutor was a worry to his parents who wanted him to pursue a career in the Roman political or ecclesiastical system. (As I mentioned earlier, his father was a deacon, his grandfather a priest, and for both jobs one needed education.) But his lack of learning became an advantage to Patrick as an evangelist: he could speak clearly and simply, without the complex rhetorical devices that the better educated (such as his contemporary, St. Augustine) felt compelled to use.

Uniquely in Christendom, Ireland was converted without bloodshed. That is worth pondering a moment. How could that have been, since the Gaels were certainly inclined to fighting?

With Patrick, we should give the credit to God, but it's also true that Patrick's years of slavery had prepared him as nothing else could have. He already loved the people and had forgiven them for the slavery they inflicted on him. He knew the Irish language, which would have won him respect. He may even have encountered people he had known during his days as a slave.

Perhaps the conversion was made a bit easier because difficult concepts were already familiar, given the (significant, though limited) similarities between Irish paganism and Christianity, which I already discussed. Perhaps there was also a nascent Church in Ireland when he arrived. Some of them may have been captured slaves, as Patrick had been. Some may have been traders or sailors who had settled in Ireland. And some of them may have been monks from Egypt. And thereby hangs our tale.

Monasteries vs. Dioceses

What did St. Patrick's Church look like in the next hundred years?

For centuries, it was believed (or perhaps assumed) that, as Patrick laid the foundations for the Irish Church, he also laid the foundations for a diocesan structure, as preferred by the Roman Church. Yet the Church that Patrick helped to found within a hundred years became distinctly *monastic*, rather than diocesan, in its organization.

After all, monasticism in the sixth century was sweeping the whole Christian world. In many nations, such as Ireland, monks were the first (or at least the principal) evangelists. And with no prior history of Roman organization, how would the Irish have had the experience and skills to form a dioceses? Further, to be a bishop of a diocese, one needs a city in which to have a "chair"—and there were no cities in early Ireland. Interestingly, to this day the Irish word for city, *cathair*, is similar to the word for chair, *cathaoir*.

Monasteries were very successful in Ireland from the beginning. The earliest monks seeking solitude would not have had trouble finding it. As their sanctity attracted followers and monasteries grew, the nature of ancient Irish, or Brehon, law would have helped.

In Brehon law, there was no primogeniture. Upon the death of a chieftain or king, his property did not go to his eldest son. Rather, the *dearbhfhine*—four generations of relatives and descendants—would assemble together and decide how to dispose of his property. If the king had been persuaded by St. Patrick or another missionary to grant some land for a monastery, upon the king's death the family would have to decide the future use of the land.

If monks had ingratiated themselves with the local community (improving farming, caring for the poor, etc.), the *dearbhfhine* might well decide, "Let's keep the monastery. And let's send Eoghan to run it." So Eoghan would become the abbot, combining an administrative role with clerical orders. Eoghan's son might be the family's choice to be the next abbot, and so on. In fact, some monasteries did become family enterprises over generations. And, due to their connection to Ireland's most powerful families, they became political tools of certain kings and clans. Some monasteries grew quite large and established daughter monasteries, until a whole system of related monasteries, known as a *parochia*, came to exist by the seventh century—at which point there was a movement to reform the monasteries and make them less worldly. Kathleen Hughes is an articulate exponent of this interpretation.

Irish history is subject to revisionism no less than any other history, and the current fashion is to posit that the model actually was more diverse: that there were dioceses as well as monasteries—just as there were elsewhere in the Western Church in the early medieval period. This academic dispute is interesting, but it is merely academic. Chapter 5 on monasticism and its origins will explore in depth the desert origins of monasteries. Everyone agrees that by the sixth century Irish monasteries—which began as *díserts*—had expanded and grown into communities that were known throughout the world (which is to say Europe at the time) as the go-to place for learning. A few of the largest ones were home to thousands of souls—not all monks, but all within the monastery's purview.

Saving Civilization

By the seventh century, Ireland had become the Isle of Saints and Scholars, because its monasteries were known throughout the world as the conservers and preservers of Western civilization and learning. Within a couple of generations of Patrick's death, schools across Europe were led by Irish monks. Not only ecclesiastical Latin was studied, but also the classical Latin and Greek of

Virgil and Homer. Eventually, the students of the monks who had evangelized the Anglo-Saxons were called upon by Charlemagne to educate the court of his Holy Roman Empire.

How did it happen that, just two generations after poorly educated St. Patrick of the rustic Latin, the learning of Western civilization came to be distilled in the westernmost outpost of Europe?

Kuno Meyer, a Leipzig-trained Celtic philologist, wondered in 1912 how Irish monks acquired this learning so fast. Could they have skipped across to Gaul to study for a few years? he wondered. Meyer noted that intellectual traffic would have been in the opposite direction, considering what was going on in Gaul in the fifth century. He based this opinion on the work of Heinrich Zimmer (1851-1910), a pioneer of Celtic studies at the University of Berlin, who had discovered previously forgotten writings from the fifth century.

"How can I compose six-foot verse," wrote one Sidonius Apollinaris in Gaul, "when I am surrounded by seven-foot barbarians?" Sidonius was a Gallo-Roman aristocrat senator who eventually became the bishop of Clermont. In 470, he lamented that owing to the terrible devastations of the barbarians, he could only call to mind "one person at Treves (near modern Luxembourg)—Arvogastis was his name—able to speak and write Latin in its full purity." In other words, there were no Latin scholars any more in the Low Countries. They were gone.

Zimmer found confirmation in the writing of Virgilius Maro Grammaticus, a Gaulish grammarian and scholar of the sixth and seventh centuries. Virgilius wrote in Old Irish as well as in Latin, and his Latin grammar was widely known to Irish medieval scholars.[22]

[22] Zimmer, quoted in Meyer, "Learning in Ancient Ireland," 451–452.

He minced no words in his view of the barbarians who were entering the Roman Empire:

> The Huns, who were infamously begotten, i.e., by demons, after they had found their way by the guidance of a hind through the Maeotic marshes, invaded the Goths, whom they terrified very much by their unexpectedly awful appearance. And thanks to them, the depopulation of the entire Empire commenced, which was completed by the Huns and Vandals and Goths and Alans, owing to whose devastation all the learned men on this side of the sea fled away and betook themselves to transmarine parts, i.e., to Hibernia or withersoever, and they brought about a great advance of learning to the inhabitants of those regions.[23]

Zimmer took this to refer to Ireland, because the word used is *transmarine*—that is, across the water. If Virgilius had meant Spain, or Iberia, it would not have required a trip across the water from Gaul. And for sure, the flight to Ireland of scholars would have brought about a great advance of learning to the inhabitants of those regions! However, it should be remembered that Latin itself also died a natural death as a vernacular: as historian Peter Brown points out, pure Latin was the language of the Roman bureaucracy. As the bureaucracy disappeared after 410, the language gradually merged with the local tongues.

Could Gaulish scholars have fled to Ireland? Why not? There was regular trade between Gaul and the southern Irish province of Munster. Such emigration would help explain the spread of the Gallican liturgy in Ireland—of which more in chapter 7.

[23] Meyer, "Learning in Ancient Ireland," 452.

So, those who love classical learning can thank Ireland. Meyer noted that[24] "while the Council of Carthage decreed that no bishop should read the books of the Gentiles; while Augustine and Ennodius laid it down that the liberal arts were but the handmaids of theology, the Irish continued to study and love the classics for their own sake. . . . The Irish Christian scholars having thus received classical learning at a time when it was still the natural study of every educated person were not like their Continental brethren troubled by any scruples as to the unfitness of that literature for the Christian, by that 'lurking uneasiness of conscience which haunted the Continental monk who loved his Virgil.' " This openness to classical writing might help explain why Irish monks were also open to their own classical tales and sagas.

Technically, Kuno Meyer's hypothesis remains without further documentation, and therefore must be considered unproven. As Timothy O'Neill, a University College Cork professor and one of the world's leading scholars of ancient manuscripts, told me: "He presented a logical argument but the solid backing of source material to prove the points raised is lacking."

Other sources corroborate the hypothesis, however. One source notes that in the year 550, a shipload of fifty landed in Bangor, in Ulster. The Venerable Bede, in writing about the ravages of the Plague of 664, notes that the Irish generously accepted refugee scholars from Britain: "Many of the nobles of the English nation, and lesser men who also had set out thither, forsaking their native island either for the grace of sacred learning or a more austere life. And some of them indeed soon dedicated

[24] Kuno Meyer, *Learning in Ireland in the Fifth Century and the Transmission of Letters: A Lecture Delivered before the School of Irish Learning in Dublin on September 18th, 1912*, 458–459.

themselves faithfully to the monastic life.... All these the Irish willingly received, and saw to it to supply them with food day by day without cost, and books for their studies, and teaching, free of charge."[25]

Indeed, there is no hard proof of these migrations, no matter how logical it may be to suspect their existence. There are no passports from the fourth, fifth, and sixth centuries. By their fruits, however, perhaps, they may be known.

For Further Reference

Bede. *The Ecclesiastical History of the English People*. Oxford World's Classics. Edited by Judith McClure and Roger Collins. Oxford: Oxford University Press, 1969.

Bradshaw, Brendan. "The Wild and Woolly West: Early Irish Christianity and Latin Orthodoxy." In W. J. Sheils and Diana Wood, *The Churches, Ireland and the Irish: Papers Read at the 1987 Summer Meeting and the 1988 Winter Meeting of the Ecclesiastical History Society*, 1–23. Oxford: Blackwell, 1989.

Darcy, R., and William Flynn. "Ptolemy's Map of Ireland: A Modern Decoding." *Irish Geography* 41, no. 1 (2008): 49–69. DOI: 10.1080/00750770801909375.

Duchesne, Msgr. L. *Christian Worship: Its Origin and Evolution; A Study of the Latin Liturgy up to the Time of Charlemagne*. 5th ed. Translated by M. L. McClure. London: Society for Promoting Christian Knowledge, 1927.

Ekonomou, Andrew J. *Byzantine Rome and the Greek Popes*. Lanham, MD: Lexington Books, 2007.

[25] Bede, *The Ecclesiastical History of the English People*, ed. Judith McClure and Roger Collins (Oxford: Oxford University Press, 1969), 3, 27.

Monastery and High Cross

Hughes, Kathleen. *The Church in Early Irish Society*. Ithaca, NY: Cornell University Press, 1966.

King, Archdale. *Liturgy of the Roman Church*. Milwaukee: Bruce, 1957.

Mac Niocaill, Gearóid. *Ireland before the Vikings*. The Gill History of Ireland, vol. 1. Dublin: Gill and Macmillan, 1972.

McNally, Robert E. "St. Patrick: 461–1961." *Catholic Historical Review* 47, no. 3 (October 1961): 305–324. jstor.org/stable/25016896.

Meyer, Kuno. "Learning in Ancient Ireland." *Irish Review* 2, no. 21 (November 1912): 449–459.

Sullivan, Sir Edward. *The Book of Kells*. 2nd ed. New York: Crescent Books, 1986.

Chapter 3

Travel and Archaeology

Far from being a remote and backward isolated fringe of civilization, as it was presented by those who wrote English history from the seventeenth century onward, ancient Ireland was a full participant in the commerce and culture of the whole Christian world from the earliest days.

True, Ireland did not have large towns, let alone cities, until after the ninth century, when the Vikings who came to raid stayed to trade. True, there are no Roman ruins to be discovered underneath Dublin. Nonetheless, Ireland is a rewarding place for archaeologists to work. An ever-expanding inventory of archaeological evidence offers proof of connection between Ireland and the Christian East.

Four Thousand Years of Archaeology

Only in recent years has Ireland begun pouring cement on top of history. Ireland's centuries of poverty and oppression meant poverty and deprivation for the people who lived there — but from an archaeologist's perspective, it meant the preservation of ancient artifacts. The lack of growth meant that new buildings were not constructed. In Rome today, an archaeologist has to dig through layers of cities to get to the most ancient remnants of human habitation — but in Ireland, a single backhoe can get back four thousand years. When the M3 roadway from Navan to Kells and the N52, the Kells Bypass, were constructed, archaeologist Fintan Walsh found forty-three sites along just those two roadways that went back that far.

Mediterranean-to-Ireland Travel in Ancient Days

You might be saying to yourself at this point, "Connie, are you crazy? Aren't we talking about the Dark Ages when nobody went anywhere more than five miles from where they were born? Isn't it ridiculous to think penniless monks went thousands of miles from home?"

To which I say, "Hang on to your hat!"

Please: begin by realizing that the so-called Dark Ages were not all that dark. The idea that Late Antiquity and the medieval period were ignorant and superstitious was a spin put on history at the time of the Enlightenment—you know, the French Revolutionary period—by people who wanted to discredit religion and with it the Age of Faith that was the medieval age.

This common misapprehension may have been behind the statement by historian Norman Baynes, when he wrote in 1929, "Can we assume that Syrians in Gaul after 450 remained in contact with their native East?" and answered, "I myself cannot believe that ships and traders alike were customarily passing between Italy and Merovingian Gaul."[26] In 1929, Baynes didn't believe

[26] Cited in Crehan, "The Liturgical Trade Route," 88.

that even trade between Italy and France continued—so the notion that Ireland remained in contact with the Mediterranean was indeed far-out.

But in 1929, many of the discoveries that I'm going to tell you about hadn't been made yet. But we should cut Baynes some slack. It seems that he himself came to amend his view: in 1948, Baynes edited an English version of *Analecta Bollandiana* 45, which included a narrative of a voyage in the middle of the seventh century by Egyptians coming to Cornwall for tin.[27]

As recently as 1965, the late Joseph Raftery, archaeologist and former president of the Royal Society of Antiquaries of Ireland, repeated Baynes's 1929 statement when he said that "too much is read into too little," and that "there is no valid reason, as far as I can see, to assume that there were any contacts at all between the island in the west and the faraway eastern Mediterranean, separated by some thousands of miles."[28]

In fact, there are mountains of evidence of contacts between the little island on the western fringe of Europe and the great centers of civilization in the Mediterranean. I don't know what the state of research was fifty years ago, and I mean no disrespect to older generations of scholars. But today the evidence of intercourse between Ireland and the East in the ancient days is abundant.

In 1959, liturgical historian Archdale King reported that an Ogham inscription on a stone near St. Olan's Well in Aghabulloge, County Cork, was interpreted to read, "Pray for Olan the Egyptian."[29] Ogham wasn't used much after the fourth century,

[27] Ibid., 89.

[28] Joseph Raftery, "Ex Oriente . . . ," *Journal of the Royal Society of Antiquaries of Ireland* 95, no. 1/2 (1965): 193–204, jstor.org/stable/25509589, 199.

[29] Archdale King, *Liturgies of the Past* (Milwaukee: Bruce, 1959), 229.

so we can be sure that that is one old stone! The local parish and holy well still bear his name. Where would the idea come from since time immemorial that an Egyptian named Olan needed to be prayed for? And that he was a saint? There probably was an Egyptian named Olan, and the folks who didn't travel more than five miles from home in their lifetime thought he was remarkable and therefore remembered him with respect.

From Ireland to Jerusalem by way of Egypt was, in fact, a common pilgrimage route for centuries after Christianity became legal. Around the year 825, the Irish monk Dicuil wrote travelogues, including a surviving one about his visit to Egypt en route to Jerusalem, with no indication that the route was in any way novel or unfamiliar. In light of the transfer of written materials in earlier centuries, it is clear that the route was well-traveled.

There is abundant historical evidence both older and younger than the days of Rome. There's the account of the voyage recorded in chapter 15 of Bede's *Ecclesiastical History*, completed in 731, by Bishop Arculf of Gaul, who was on his way home from Jerusalem, Alexandria, and Constantinople, probably in 681, when his ship was carried by a storm to Iona, where he was welcomed by the monastery and stayed to teach Abbot Adomnán how to draw the holy places of Jerusalem.

Memorable Trips through Ancient Holy Lands

In the nineteenth century, a manuscript was discovered that was the diary of a Spanish nun named Egeria who had traveled the Jerusalem-Egypt pilgrimage route around the year 380. Her description of the Easter liturgy in Jerusalem remains a definitive record of liturgical practice, and she describes monasteries in the desert. The diary was republished in 2018 as *The Pilgrimage of Egeria* by Liturgical Press, edited by McGowan and Bradshaw.

In 1994, Scottish historian/journalist William Dalrymple undertook to follow the path of a journey by monk John Moschos in the sixth century, from Mount Athos to Constantinople to Syria, visiting the great monasteries along the way. He discovered that some of the monasteries were still surviving then, and he wrote about them with deep respect. His journey — through a civil war in Turkey and through the ruins of Beirut — is recorded in his book *From the Holy Mountain: A Journey among the Christians of the Middle East,* and is one of the best travelogues ever. The ISIS war in Syria may have since destroyed some of what he observed. Bonus: Dalrymple had studied Hiberno-Saxon art, so he has an eye for insular artistic connections! This was published in 1997 by Holt.

More recent findings in archaeology also have overtaken Raftery's view. In light of new knowledge, says archaeologist Amanda Kelly, "we can redress the then-reasonable denial of 'any contacts at all between the island in the west and the faraway eastern Mediterranean, separated by thousands of miles.' "[30] Emerging research was continuing to challenge Raftery's conclusion, even before the discovery of the Faddan More Psalter.

[30] Amanda Kelly, "The Discovery of Phocaean Red Slip Ware (PRSW) Form 3 and Bii Ware (LR1 Amphorae) on Sites in Ireland—an Analysis within a Broader Framework," *Proceedings of the Royal Irish Academy: Archaeology, Culture, History, Literature* 110C (2010): 35–88, www.jstor.org/stable/41473662, 73.

Ancient History

In 2001, classicist professor Philip Freeman wrote that contact began before the Roman period, with Bronze Age double-axes and faience beads of Aegean and Egyptian manufacture, and a Barbary ape skull of the last few centuries B.C., unearthed five kilometers southwest of Armagh, Northern Ireland, at the site of Navan. The Barbary ape is a native of North Africa; its presence in Navan proves that some kind of trade routes connected Ireland and the western Mediterranean even in pre-Roman Britain.[31]

Ireland was known in classical literature from the middle of the first century B.C. The River Boyne was an established route in the High Imperial period of Rome; it is included in Ptolemy's *Geographia*, where it is cited as "Buvinda."[32] Brugh na Bóinne, the sacred mound at Newgrange, a Neolithic tumulus, has yielded coinage from Emperors Domitian (81–96) to Arcadius (383–408). Agricola, who conquered Britain for Rome and died in the year 93, must have had a good reason to fortify the English coast facing Ireland in the latter half of the first century A.D. He assured his son-in-law Tacitus that "a single legion and a few auxiliaries would be sufficient entirely to conquer the country and bring it into subjection."[33] Tacitus did not follow that suggestion; however, both he (†ca. 120) and Ptolemy (†ca. 170) mention voyages by

[31] P. Freeman, *Ireland and the Classical World* (Austin: University of Texas Press, 2001), 3.

[32] R. Darcy and William Flynn, "Ptolemy's Map of Ireland: A Modern Decoding," *Irish Geography* 41, no. 1 (2008): 53–54, DOI: 10.1080/00750770801909375.

[33] Tacitus, *Life of Agricola*, chap. 24, cited in Eleanor Hull, "Observations of Classical Writers on the Habits of the Celtic Nations, as Illustrated from Irish Records," *Celtic Review* 3, no. 9 (July 1906): 62–76, 64.

merchants, which may account for the first- and second-century archaeological material at Newgrange and elsewhere.[34]

Agricola's fortifications seem to have been successful: there is no archaeological evidence of Irish settlement in Britain before the fifth century, around the time that a certain Patricius was abducted from somewhere in North Britain.[35] Elva Johnston, a late antique history professor at University College Dublin, opines that Palladius's mission to Ireland in 431, as recorded in Prosper of Aquitaine's *Chronicle*, may have been just another form of Roman frontier management[36] as the fading empire was struggling to keep order.

Connections between Ireland and the Byzantine world are ancient. In 2006, Amanda Kelly, now an assistant professor of archaeology at University College Dublin, had been studying Roman-Byzantine sites in the Eastern Mediterranean when she had the opportunity to direct some excavation in Ireland. She was surprised when "both fields, rather unexpectedly, converged.... Phocaean Red Slip Ware and Bii amphorae sherds found in County Meath can be accurately and exclusively attributed to a center in Asia Minor." Kelly concludes that "in light of this knowledge ... we can redress the then-reasonable denial of 'any contacts at all between the island in the west and the faraway eastern Mediterranean, separated by thousands of miles.'... In the fifth and sixth centuries, someone in Ireland was drinking expensive wine, using expensive oil, and obtaining them via a network 'from Gaza to Garranes.'"[37]

[34] Freeman, *Ireland and the Classical World*, 70–71.

[35] Lloyd Laing, "The Romanization of Ireland in the Fifth Century," *Peritia* 4 (1985): 261–278, 274.

[36] Elva Johnston, "Religious Change and Frontier Management," *Eolas* 11 (2018): 104–119, jstor.org/stable/10.2307/26605110, 116.

[37] Kelly, "The Discovery of Phocaean Red Slip Ware," 73.

Archaeologist Harold Mytum of the University of Liverpool concurs: although pottery from the Mediterranean is archaeologically detectable, he says, "it is likely that the art-historical evidence ... gives a correct picture, albeit a fuzzy one, of the web of contacts which Ireland maintained directly and indirectly with many parts of the Christian world."[38]

J. N. Hillgarth, a longtime professor of history at the Pontifical Institute of Mediaeval Studies at the University of Toronto, notes that Eastern Mediterranean pottery found in the British Isles is mainly on fifth- or sixth-century sites, and that a shift began around 600 of the main trade route from the East, from the old line leading to Marseilles to a new orientation from North Italy over the Alps and up the Rhine. "There seems no doubt, however, that ships from the Mediterranean although probably in smaller numbers, continued to reach the British Isles in the seventh century. We know this from the contemporary Greek Life of St John the Almoner of Alexandria who died in 616 and from the unhappy experiences of Arculf in the 680's"[39] as well as from archaeological evidence.

People other than traders could travel on merchant vessels, of course. From early on, Irish pilgrims visited Jerusalem, the Levant, and Egypt: the Royal Irish Academy holds a manuscript travel guide for Irish pilgrims to Scetis in the Nitrean Valley of Egypt, an area famous for its monasteries.[40]

[38] Harold Mytum, *The Origins of Early Christian Ireland* (London and New York: Routledge, 1992), 79.

[39] J. N. Hillgarth, "Visigothic Spain and Early Christian Ireland," *Proceedings of the Royal Irish Academy: Archaeology, Culture, History, Literature* 62 (1961–1963): 167–194, www.jstor.org/stable/25505106, 178.

[40] Aziz S. Atiya, *History of Eastern Christianity* (Notre Dame: University of Notre Dame Press, 1968), 55n1.

Christian heresies and arguments could have provided a reason for churchmen of the East to flee to the peaceful shores of Erin. Nestorianism, for example, bitterly divided Christians for many decades before it was condemned at the Council of Chalcedon in 451. Notably, Theodore of Mopsuestia, the mentor of Nestorius, was known widely in Ireland.[41] Emperor Justinian did not restore Byzantine control in North Africa and southern Spain until the sixth century, and with the rise of Islam two centuries later, historian Fr. P.J. Corish concurred that "it may well be that some refugee monks of the eastern tradition actually made their way to Ireland as Islam drove west from Egypt in the seventh century, reaching Tripoli in 644, crossing the straits of Gibraltar in 711, and thrusting deep into France within the next generation."[42]

Possible religious migrations to Ireland did not end until the Vikings came: The iconoclast controversy raged throughout the Levant from the mid-600s until 842 in varying degrees of intensity, dividing churches and governments, causing the destruction of monasteries and churches and the murder of their inhabitants. In the summation of English historian Marina Warner, the iconoclast controversy "was responsible for a surge of western interest in the eighth century when many Byzantines, including clerics, came to the west, fleeing persecution."[43]

41 Martin McNamara, "De Initiis: Irish Monastic Learning 600–800 AD," *Eolas* 6 (2013): 4–40, jstor.org/stable/10.2307/26193960, 34.

42 Patrick J. Corish, "The Christian Mission," in *A History of Irish Catholicism*, vol. 1 (Dublin: Gill and Macmillan, 1972), 10.

43 Diane Peters Auslander, "Gendering the 'Vita Prima': An Examination of St. Brigid's Role as 'Mary of the Gael,'" *Proceedings of the Harvard Celtic Colloquium* 20/21 (2000/2001): 187–200, n. 11 on p. 192 to Marina Warner, *Alone of All Her Sex: The Myth and Cult of the Virgin Mary* (New York: Knopf, 1976), 108–109.

The Monks Were Right to Fear the Vikings

In 2018, a study was done in Iceland of the DNA of ancient Icelanders whose skeletons were found in burial sites across the island. These are skeletons from a thousand years ago — around 1118 — in other words, during the era of the Viking raids on Ireland. In the skeletons there was an even split of Norse (Norway and Sweden) and Gaelic ancestry, mainly Norse men and Irish women. Not that there was ever much doubt what became of women who were kidnapped by the Vikings: they became the mothers of half the population of Iceland.

At the end of the seventh century, Theodore of Tarsus was appointed archbishop of Canterbury (668–690). He had no prior connection to Britain, having come from Cilicia, east of the Bosphorus. In the words of that preeminent scholar of Late Antiquity, Peter Brown, Theodore came "from a world that owed nothing to the Latin West. . . . [He] belonged to a generation of extraordinary Greek scholars on the run. Many sought to flee the advance of the Arabs by settling in the extreme western end of the East Roman Empire, at Rome and Carthage. They were men of ascetic vocation, used to being 'strangers.' They moved all over the East Roman world from one monastery to another. They were the nearest equivalents, in the Mediterranean world, to their contemporaries in the British Isles—the great Irish 'pilgrims' and *sapientes*, men of wisdom, such as Columbanus."[44]

[44] Peter Brown, *The Cult of the Saints: Its Rise and Function in Latin Christianity* (Chicago: University of Chicago Press, 1981), 368.

Literary Archaeology

Armenia was specifically known in Ireland, as literature shows. The *Lebor Gábala Érenn*, the *Book of Takings*, a compilation of early tales about the invasions and origins of Ireland that was written down around the eleventh century, declares the origin of the Sons of Míl to be from Armenia. According to legend, the Sons of Míl (later known as the Milesians) were the final race to invade Ireland, sailing via Spain. They had wandered the earth for generations before. One of their ancestors helped to build the Tower of Babel; others stayed a while in Scythia and in Egypt. The *Lebor Gábala* traces the ancestry of the Sons of Míl back to Noah, with the intention of creating a high and noble ancestry for Ireland, so its historical value is somewhat limited—but the point is, Armenia was known and held in high regard, or else the authors would not want to be identified with it.

The *Táin Bó Cúailnge*,[45] the tale of the Ulster Cycle known as the Cattle Raid of Cooley, is believed to go back to at least the seventh century, though it wasn't written down until the eleventh. When the *Táin* was recorded in Old Irish, it would have been written as the *filidh* had recited it to the monks. In the tale, CúChulainn traveled as far as Sléibe Armenia, according to Fergus Mac Róig, his friend. Armenia was a great empire at the time, and the Irish knew about it. To have visited was a bragging point to CúChulainn.

Poetry and tales were important entertainments among the Gaels. A wealthy man might commission a manuscript to be made

[45] The *Táin Bó Cúailnge*, or the Cattle Raid of Cooley, sometimes called Ireland's *Iliad*, is the saga of the war between Ulster and Connaught instigated by the jealousy of Queen Maeve. The Ulster champion was CúChulainn. The best modern translation is by Thomas Kinsella.

for him and his family, and he would instruct the scribe to include in it some of the stories he wanted to hear over and over again. A few of these manuscripts have managed to survive. The Book of Lismore, also known as the Book of Mac Carthaigh Riabhach, written in the mid-fifteenth century, is one of the lucky ones. It has 198 surviving leaves. Half are religious, including lives of St. Patrick, St. Brigid, and other Irish saints. The other half are secular material, such as tales of Charlemagne, the *Travels of Marco Polo*, and tales of Fionn Mac Cumhaill, among others.

The *Tenga Bithnua* is also found in the Book of Lismore. This unique piece may have been considered religious, or perhaps the fantastical nature of the narrative was recognized and it was considered a tale. In any case, the text of it mentions Armenian women on the sixth day of Creation. *Tenga Bithnua* means "evernew tongue"; its literary conceit is that of a dialogue between St. Philip the apostle and Hebrew sages. (Philip's tongue was cut out nine times and miraculously restored each time, hence the title.) Here's what's fascinating: the tale is based on a lost piece of Egyptian apocrypha as well as on the Acts of Philip, a piece of apocrypha that is otherwise unknown in Latin Christendom.[46]

Church Archaeology

Conventional archaeological evidence also supports the existence of similarities, and therefore of possible connections, between Ireland and the East. "To conserve" means to hold on to the past, and few institutions were more conservative than monasteries. Innovation

[46] Stephen C. E. Hopkins, "John Carey (trad.), *The Ever-New Tongue: The Text in the Book of Linsmore*," Memini Travaux et Documents, OpenEdition Journals, https://journals.openedition.org/memini/1478.

was frowned upon, because innovating in ecclesiastical matters might lead to error or even heresy—which might, in turn, endanger salvation. Therefore, elders, or fathers, were respected. What the monastery's founder taught would be preserved and handed down exactly as he had taught it. A church built in the sixth century would be built with the skills and design of a church built in the fifth century or earlier, because that is the method—probably the *only* method—the artisans would have known. A manuscript illuminated in the seventh century would have incorporated techniques and designs passed down from master to pupil for many years. This faithfulness to predecessors is how the texts of Holy Scripture have survived, of course.

Ireland had more than 250 churches by the year 800—more than England or any comparable area on the Continent. Most architectural remains seem to be of very small dimensions, however. How to explain this, when presumably there would have been large numbers of Mass-goers?

First, understand that, while unusual in modern Western Christendom, small buildings were the norm for churches in the ancient East. Where the climate is temperate, apart from cities and imperial centers very small churches are usual; in early centuries of Christianity, the liturgy was celebrated in a small space just large enough for the holy table, two necessary side tables (the necessary furniture behind an iconostasis in an Eastern church today), and the celebrants and acolytes, while the congregation gathered outside, where Communion was distributed to them.

This is the practice to this day in the annual Croagh Patrick pilgrimage, where thousands gather outside while Mass is said in a small chapel (called an oratory) at the top of the mountain. St. Patrick is said to have spent forty days fasting on that mountain in County Mayo, perhaps because it was already a pagan ritual site, and Christian pilgrimages have taken place there ever since. Archaeologists have found glass beads that may date back to the third century B.C. In 1995, archaeologists on Croagh Patrick found ruins of numerous huts and the foundations of a stone structure they call an oratory that has been carbon-dated to as early as A.D. 430, making it the earliest church building yet excavated in Ireland.

Frederick Edward Warren, the scholar and Church of England pastor who wrote the earliest critical editions of important surviving liturgical works of the British Isles, was one of the first to note the architectural similarities between the East and ancient Ireland:

> Both in Greece and Ireland the smallness of the churches is remarkable. They never were, in fact, basilicas for the assembly of large congregations of worshippers, but oratories, where the priest could celebrate the divine mysteries for the benefit of the laity. It is not only at Mount Athos, and other places in Europe, but also in Asia Minor, that we find the method of grouping a large number of small churches together, seven being the favorite number and one often attained.[47]

It is possible that some of those ruins considered "huts" on Croagh Patrick were actually small churches. There are the ruins of seven churches on Inis Mór, the largest of the Aran Islands. Skellig Michael also has the remains of seven churches.

In 1955, Irish architectural historian Harold Leask described a church in Rahan, County Offaly, thus: with "two small chambers flanking the chancel to the north and south, and entered from it

[47] Warren, *The Liturgy and Ritual of the Celtic Church*, 49, quoting architectural historian James Fergusson, *Illustrated Handbook of Architecture*, vol. 11 (London: J. Murray, 1855), 915.

through two small, round-headed doorways." He noted that "these little rooms may be the *porticus* known in the Eastern Church as the *diaconicon* and *prothesis*; the first for use of the clergy as a sacristy, and the second to receive the offerings of the faithful. They were also features of churches of the fifth and sixth centuries in Syria and North Africa ... and they appear, curiously, in some English churches built in the seventh century."[48]

Let's be more precise about these three spaces. The "Holy Place" is everything behind the iconostasis. The *diaconicon* is the small room on one side (ideally the south) of the Holy Place where the vestments are stored. The *prothesis*, meanwhile, is on the other side (ideally the north) and is where the sacred vessels are stored. The *diaconicon* contains the sink that drains directly into the ground for the water used to wash the holy things. These customs did not all carry forward into the Roman Church, but this ancient floor plan has surprising utility today: the altar boys vest in a room separate from where the priest prepares for Divine Liturgy.

Leask also noted that the Rahan archway is assigned to the seventh or eighth century. Moreover, the palmette motive and the curious bulbous form of the colonette bases also appear "in the chapel of the palace of Ani in Armenia, and datable, it is said, to the early seventh century at the latest. Since Armenian clerics dwelt for a time not very far away from Rahan in the seventh or eighth century, the importation of these motives is attributed directly to them and to that period."[49] There's Armenia again, in seventh-century Ireland!

[48] Harold G. Leask, *Irish Churches and Monastic Buildings*, vol. 1, *The First Phases and the Romanesque* (Dundalk, Ireland: Dundalgan Press, 1955), 90–91.

[49] Ibid., 90.

Catholic liturgical scholar Fr. John W. Hunwicke considers the evidence clear that the liturgical building was intended to house only the celebrant bishops and priests during the Missa Fidelium, the congregation, and probably the deacon, remaining outside except when (and if) they entered to receive the Lord's Body and Blood. The Stowe Missal and other Irish texts retain diaconal formulae that may have been used outside the building while the sacerdotal liturgy continued inside.[50]

In other words, the building itself would have been the sanctuary while the congregation stood outside the building, perhaps under an awning arrangement. Some texts suggest that people received Communion in order of rank, perhaps in the order in which the confractions of the eucharistic bread were arranged.

The *Riagáil Phátraic* is a law tract written in Old Irish, possibly in the eighth century. While St. Patrick's name is ascribed to it, he could not be the actual author. What is clear, however, is this: it was a binding document. The bishop is required to make sure there is "an offering of the body of Christ on each altar." In other words, Mass every Sunday and major solemnities was required, along with other devotions.

Thinking along these lines has caused some to suggest that the "Mass rocks" found around Ireland and long thought to be where fugitive priests celebrated Mass during Penal Days were in fact relics of holy places long before the seventeenth century. By way of evidence, Hunwicke notes that a Mass rock in Cahirciveen, County Kerry, has a cross inscribed on it and is dated to around the year 600.

[50] J.W. Hunwicke, "Kerry and Stowe Revisited," *Proceedings of the Royal Irish Academy: Archaeology, Culture, History, Literature* 102C, no. 1 (2002): 1, www.jstor.org/stable/25506158.

Other archaeological studies support this claim. Two early monastic settlements that had been scientifically excavated and published by 2002 give evidence that between the fourth and seventh centuries the churches consisted of wooden buildings, including what are now called "oratories" that measured ten feet six inches by eight feet and ten feet by six feet six inches.[51] Later stone successor buildings were as small as eight feet by six feet and nine feet by seven feet.[52] In other words, they were about large enough for a main altar, a preparation table, a priest, a deacon, and an acolyte or two. Historically, many medieval Byzantine churches were no more than thirty feet long, and even today most Eastern congregations and buildings are intentionally small by Western standards.[53]

Understanding the evolution of the Mass (as it is known in the West today) explains how this may have worked. Lots of people would gather to hear the Word, but far fewer people received Communion. This is in keeping with the practices of the Byzantine Church during the life of St. John Chrysostom, whose Divine Liturgy became the remote ancestor of the Mass as it is celebrated today in the West, and is used in Eastern Catholic and Eastern Orthodox Churches to this day almost as Chrysostom wrote it. Chrysostom, notably, did not create that liturgy—he merely organized and recorded what had been the practice for centuries before him of the celebration of the Eucharist.

Once Christianity was legalized, the reading of Scripture and litanies of petition—known as the Liturgy of the Word—was open

[51] Ibid., 3.

[52] Ibid., 4.

[53] Robert Taft, S.J., *Between East and West* (Washington, D.C.: Pastoral Press, 1984), 45.

to all, pagan and Christian alike. After the readings and petitions, in Chrysostom's liturgy, the priest says: "The doors! The doors!" These words are preserved in the modern Byzantine liturgy, though they have no contemporary import. Originally, however, this was an instruction to the deacons: clear the room of everybody who is not worthy to partake of the holy mystery of the Eucharist. In other words: pagans, catechumens, penitents, and anyone not allowed to receive Communion must depart now! And the liturgy would pause while the deacons enforced the command. There's no evidence that that particular custom came to Ireland, but it does explain how small churches could have been sufficient: many more were welcome to hear the Word than were welcome to receive the Eucharist.

In early Church days, many believers put off being baptized until they were near death, so of course they would have to leave before Communion. In those days, too, the sacrament of Confession as we know it did not exist. (See chapter 5 to understand the role of Irish St. Columbanus in developing this sacrament). Public Confession was reserved for major public sins like adultery and murder, and priests would often assign extreme penances, such as banishment from Communion for several years, since absolution could not be given but once in a lifetime. Thus, the number of people to receive Communion at an ordinary Mass could indeed have been very small.

St. Basil the Great, who died in 379, wrote in his Letter 93 that he received Communion four times a week. Liturgical scholar Robert Taft, S.J., noted that from the fourth century onward, the teaching about Communion began to change, and gradually Communion became more an act of personal piety and less a communal celebration of the death and Resurrection of the Lord. For that reason, too, fewer of the faithful received regularly as time went on. Pope Nicholas I (ca. 800–867), he who incorporated the *filioque* clause into the Creed of the Latin Mass, wrote that it was the custom to receive Communion daily only during Lent.

The point is that small churches could have worked because those standing outside could hear the readings (outdoors was quiet in the days before engines) and could drift away before the consecration and Communion, when a much smaller group would stand near the entrance to the church to receive Communion. In a monastery itself, the communicants may have been fewer, and even though monastic settlements could contain thousands of people, the Communion customs would have been the same.

Devotion to the Eucharist

Despite—or perhaps because of—infrequent reception of the Eucharist, the ancient Irish were strongly devoted to the Eucharist, as another archaeological find reveals. This finding relates to the custom of *chrismals*.

For a period of time, the chrismal was a very popular private devotion for priests in Ireland and in their daughter church in Anglo-Saxon Britain—one in which the Irish were perhaps ahead of the rest of Europe. A chrismal was a small phial, worn around the neck on a thong of leather, that originally may have contained holy oil and a fragment of the Holy Eucharist for administering Baptism or Extreme Unction, but that came to be used to carry the Eucharist continuously on one's body. Elsewhere in Europe relics of martyrs were carried around the neck—but Ireland had no martyrs! The Irish penitentials are rife with penances for losing a chrismal, or being negligent with it. The prayers of blessing of a chrismal in an eighth-century text calls it a "new tomb for the Body of Christ"—powerful evidence of how firm was the belief in the transubstantiation—even if the word was not yet used.

This custom of carrying the Eucharist on one's person is not proper today, as Father O'Donoghue notes. But "the concept of keeping the Host as a devotional practice, as opposed to the need to keep it for the sick and dying, was one of the elements in the birth of mainstream Western eucharistic devotion."[54] In other words, the Irish devotion to the Body and Blood of Jesus Christ is considered by Church historians to be a stepping stone to the development of the tabernacle, and the more developed liturgical worship of the Eucharist that we know today.

Reservation of the Blessed Sacrament: Gift of the Irish?

The *oratio periculosa*, a prayer in the Stowe Missal, reveals that by the seventh century Irish were isolating a moment of consecration in the liturgy centuries before the rest of the Western Church did so. "It does seem that Ireland is ahead of many other regions in assigning the consecration to this particular moment of the liturgy," comments O'Donoghue,[55] who also observes that Jungmann sees a "very lively sentiment in the Irish-Celtic tradition for a definitive meaning of the words of institution" long before a similar doctrine developed in the West.

This devotion to the Real Presence as manifested in this liturgical practice may be connected to the early development

[54] Neil Xavier O'Donoghue, "Insular Chrismals and House-Shaped Shrines in the Early Middle Ages," in *Insular and Anglo-Saxon Art and Thought in the Early Medieval Period*, ed. Colum Hourihane (University Park, PA: Princeton University Index of Christian Art, 2011), 91.

[55] Neil Xavier O'Donoghue, *The Eucharist in Pre-Norman Ireland* (Notre Dame, IN: University of Notre Dame Press, 2011), 73.

under the influence of Irish monks in areas of reservation at a high altar. In 1945, Dix wrote,[56] "There is no single certain case of an altar being used in any way as the place of permanent reservation known from anywhere in Christendom before A.D. 800.... The first instance of reservation at a high altar comes from Anglo-Saxon England, in Ethelwold's poem on the monastery Church of Lindisfarne, which can be dated precisely in A.D. 802.... Outside England, however, there is no trace of reservation at the altar in the West until the later ninth century, and then only in regions which had been influenced by Anglo-Saxon and Celtic missionaries and monks."

It may not be boastful to say that the Irish helped invent the tabernacle. Dom Gregory Dix (1901–1952), an Anglican liturgical scholar, was unable to find documentation of any case of an altar being used as a place of permanent reservation of the Blessed Sacrament until the ninth century—and that in a poem by Anglo-Saxon Ethelwold about the monastery church of Lindisfarne, which can be dated precisely to A.D. 802. Lindisfarne Abbey had been founded in 634 by St. Aidan, who came from Iona, which had been founded by the Irish monk Columba. Until the Viking ravages, Lindisfarne was a center of learning and a source of Irish evangelization of the Anglo-Saxons. Dom Dix found no evidence of reservation at the altar elsewhere in Europe until the later ninth century, and then beginning in regions that had been influenced by Irish and Anglo-Saxon missionaries and monks.

[56] Dom Gregory Dix, *The Shape of the Liturgy* (London: Dacre Press, 1945), 28–29.

Church Decoration

It is not possible to be certain how the interior—or indeed the exterior—of those structures was decorated, since most of them were wooden. However, there is evidence that some walls were decorated in what today would be considered Byzantine style.

Cogitosus, a monk of Kildare and author of the first biography of St. Brigid in 650, noted that at St. Brigid's Monastery in Kildare, the "church was adorned with painted pictures, and the party wall within it defining the sanctuary was decorated and painted with figures and covered with rich hangings." What could a "party wall defining the sanctuary" be if not a wall between the sanctuary and the congregation—which, if decorated with saints, becomes an iconostasis? "Another stone church faced with plaster at Whithorn, the first Christian church in Scotland, built by St. Ninian in 379, might have had, painted onto the plaster, representations of some of those saints who were invoked in the Litany."[57]

Michelle Brown, professor emerita of medieval manuscripts at the University of London, added more evidence of Byzantine-style decoration of churches in her observation of a seventh-century monastery in Leicestershire, England: "The monastic church at Breedon-on-the-Hill houses what may be the remains of a carved Byzantine-style iconostasis screen with Virgin and Apostles, and architectural friezes inscribed with Syrian lion-hunts, centaurs and workers in the vineyard."[58] This blending of pre-Christian Celtic, Germanic, and early Christian (i.e., Eastern Mediterranean) art

[57] Hunwicke, "Kerry and Stowe Revisited," 3.

[58] Michelle P. Brown, "Strategies of Visual Literacy in Insular and Anglo-Saxon Book Culture," in *Transformation in Anglo-Saxon Culture: Toller Lectures on Art, Archaeology and Text*, ed. Charles Insley and Gale R. Owen-Crocker, 71–104 (Barnsley, UK: Oxbow Books, 2017), www.jstor.org/stable/j.ctvh1dhhq.9, 79.

is a subject unto itself; suffice it to note that there is evidence of Byzantine influence in a church likely to have been built by missionaries from Ireland as late as the 800s. Remember that, until recently, art, like architecture, was a conservative art, which built upon the teaching and skills of its predecessor and changed only gradually.

Books: To Have and to Hold

Frederick Warren was the first to note the similarities between Ireland and Egypt in the leather satchels used since ancient days to protect and cover books: "There are before the writer at this moment," he wrote, "the leather satchel of the Irish Missal belonging to the C. C. C. Library, Oxford, and the leather satchel of an Aethiopic MS. of about the same date belonging to St John's College, Oxford. They resemble each other so closely in texture and design that they might be thought to have come from the same workshop."[59] Perhaps the craftsmen of the younger satchel had indeed been trained by craftsmen of the older satchel.

On the east coast of Scotland, about a mile north of Arbroath, a short distance north of Dundee, is a stone slab depicting two monks carrying leather book satchels around their necks and holding staffs in their hands. The slab is in the church of St. Vigeans, named after Irish abbot Féchán, who founded a monastery there and died of the plague in the mid-seventh century.

After the leather book-satchel, the next level of protection for a very valuable book was a metal cover, a *cumhdach*. Twentieth-century liturgical historian Archdale King, a skeptic of the Ireland-Egypt link, had to admit that both Egypt and Ireland made metal book shrines to further protect precious manuscripts. He also

[59] Warren, *The Liturgy and Ritual of the Celtic Church*, 54.

acknowledged that "St. Patrick's bell," dating from the fifth century, "appears to have been made in imitation of the Coptic bells," and that "waggon-vaulted roofs in Irish churches may well have been suggested by those of ancient Egypt."[60]

The earliest extant book shrine dates back to around the year 600 and is part of the Coptic Treasure of Archbishop Abraham of Harmonthis in the Coptic Museum in Cairo. So, if Egyptian monks were indeed working in monasteries in Ireland, they would have known how to make book shrines. The transfer of technology was fortuitous: *cumhdaigh* (the plural of *cumhdach*) have given protection to many ancient books. The Book of Dimma, for instance, was found in 1789 "among the rocks of the Devil's Bit Mountain in the county of Tipperary, carefully concealed and perfectly preserved" because of its *cumhdach*.

In Ireland, as in Egypt earlier, as books were honored for the power conveyed from within them, they became objects of veneration in and of themselves, and were adorned accordingly, both in the East and in Ireland. Rightly were these called *shrines*. Michelle Brown, the medieval manuscript specialist, wrote that "ivories or bejeweled metalwork plates attached to wooden binding boards are found on Byzantine, Coptic, Armenian, Irish, Anglo-Saxon, Carolingian, and Ottoman books.... In Coptic Egypt and Ireland metalwork shrines ... also occurred."[61]

The designs on some early Coptic bindings resemble the cross-carpet pages of the books they hold. The metal Lough Kinale book-shrine likewise carries a design resembling insular carpet pages.[62]

[60] Archdale King, *The Rites of Eastern Christendom*, vol. 1 (Rome: Tipografia Poliglotta Vaticana, 1947), 374–375.

[61] Brown, "Strategies of Visual Literacy in Insular and Anglo-Saxon Book Culture," 97.

[62] Ibid., 99.

That *cumhdach* that was found at the bottom of Lough Kinale, County Cavan, in 1986 is believed to pre-date other *cumhdaigh* in museums; it could be as old as the seventh century, though the eighth century is more likely.

The St. Cuthbert Gospel made in Wearmouth-Jarrow in Northumbria in the 690s was also made in the Coptic manner. This Gospel was found in 1104 inside the saint's coffin when his relics were translated to a new shrine in Lindisfarne. Burying someone with the Gospel as a pillow was (and is) a Coptic custom: the earliest extant complete Coptic Psalter, for instance, now in the Cairo Coptic Museum, had been placed as a pillow under the head of a teenage girl around the year 400. Michelle Brown speculates that "an older analogy for both might be the ancient Egyptian practice of interring the Book of the Dead with the deceased to aid their passage into the afterlife."[63]

Reference in the Book of Leinster to Egyptian monks buried in Ireland intrigues scholars; the history of political and religious upheavals in the Levant gives plausible explanation why there might have been Egyptian monks in Ireland. Archaeology hints strongly to possible connections between Ireland and the Mediterranean.

Some more tangible elements are two that are modern icons of Ireland: high crosses and illuminated manuscripts. They, too, have their roots in the East.

For Further Reference

Atiya, Aziz S. *Coptic Encyclopedia*. New York: Macmillan, 1991.

——. *History of Eastern Christianity*. Notre Dame: University of Notre Dame Press, 1968.

[63] Ibid.

Auslander, Diane Peters. "Gendering the 'Vita Prima': An Examination of St. Brigid's Role as 'Mary of the Gael.'" *Proceedings of the Harvard Celtic Colloquium* 20/21 (2000/2001): 187–200.

Brown, Michelle P. "Strategies of Visual Literacy in Insular and Anglo-Saxon Book Culture." In *Transformation in Anglo-Saxon Culture: Toller Lectures on Art, Archaeology and Text*, ed. Charles Insley and Gale R. Owen-Crocker, 71–104. Barnsley, UK: Oxbow Books, 2017. www.jstor.org/stable/j.ctvh1dhhq.9.

Brown, Peter. *The Cult of the Saints: Its Rise and Function in Latin Christianity*. Chicago: University of Chicago Press, 1981.

Corish, Rev. Patrick J. "The Christian Mission." In *A History of Irish Catholicism*, vol. 1. Dublin: Gill and Macmillan, 1972.

Darcy, R., and William Flynn. "Ptolemy's Map of Ireland: A Modern Decoding." *Irish Geography* 41, no. 1 (2008): 49–69. DOI: 10.1080/00750770801909375.

Dix, Dom Gregory. *The Shape of the Liturgy*. London: Dacre Press, 1945.

Freeman, Philip. *Ireland and the Classical World*. Austin: University of Texas Press, 2001.

Hillgarth, J. N. "Visigothic Spain and Early Christian Ireland." *Proceedings of the Royal Irish Academy: Archaeology, Culture, History, Literature* 62 (1961–1963): 167–194. www.jstor.org/stable/25505106.

Hopkins, Stephen C. E. "John Carey (trad.), *The Ever-New Tongue: The Text in the Book of Linsmore*." Memini Travaux et Documents. OpenEdition Journals. https://journals.openedition.org/memini/1478.

Hull, Eleanor. "Observations of Classical Writers on the Habits of the Celtic Nations, as Illustrated from Irish Records." *Celtic Review* 3, no. 9 (July 1906): 62–76.

Hunwicke, J. W. "Kerry and Stowe Revisited." *Proceedings of the Royal Irish Academy: Archaeology, Culture, History, Literature* 102C, no. 1 (2002): 1–19. www.jstor.org/stable/25506158.

Johnston, Elva. "Religious Change and Frontier Management." *Eolas* 11 (2018): 104–119. jstor.org/stable/10.2307/26605110.

Kelly, Amanda. "The Discovery of Phocaean Red Slip Ware (PRSW) Form 3 and Bii Ware (LR1 Amphorae) on Sites in Ireland—an Analysis within a Broader Framework." *Proceedings of the Royal Irish Academy: Archaeology, Culture, History, Literature* 110C (2010): 35–88. www.jstor.org/stable/41473662.

King, Archdale. *Liturgies of the Past*. Milwaukee: Bruce, 1959.

Laing, Lloyd. "The Romanization of Ireland in the Fifth Century." *Peritia* 4 (1985): 261–278.

Leask, Harold G. *Irish Churches and Monastic Buildings*. Vol. 1, *The First Phases and the Romanesque*. Dundalk, Ireland: Dundalgan Press, 1955.

McNamara, Martin. "De Initiis: Irish Monastic Learning 600–800 AD." *Eolas* 6 (2013): 4–40. jstor.org/stable/10.2307/26193960.

Mytum, Harold. *The Origins of Early Christian Ireland*. London and New York: Routledge, 1992.

O'Donoghue, Neil Xavier. "Insular Chrismals and House-Shaped Shrines in the Early Middle Ages." In *Insular & Anglo-Saxon Art and Thought in the Early Medieval Period*, ed. Colum Hourihane, 79–90. University Park, PA: Princeton University Index of Christian Art, 2011.

——. *The Eucharist in Pre-Norman Ireland*. Notre Dame, Indiana: University of Notre Dame Press, 2011.

Raftery, Joseph. "Ex Oriente …" *Journal of the Royal Society of Antiquaries of Ireland* 95, no. 1/2 (1965): 193–204. jstor.org/stable/25509589.

Taft, Robert, S.J. *Between East and West*. Washington, D.C.: Pastoral Press, 1984.

Walsh, Fintan. *The Road to Kells: Prehistoric Archaeology of the M3 Navan to Kells and N52 Kells Bypass Road Project*. Dublin: Wordwell Books, 2022.

Chapter 4

The High Cross, from Armenia to Ireland

A piece of papyrus, an ape head, and pottery shards may be the only archaeologically detectable proof of ancient Irish intercourse with the Mediterranean, but the study of early Irish art opens up vast new evidence of Eastern Christian influence in Ireland.

The high crosses of Ireland! Scarcely a travel book about Ireland is published without a high cross somewhere in the artwork on its cover. Rightly is the high cross an apt symbol for Ireland, because there is nothing anywhere else in the Christian world that can compare to it. Rightly have these—the highest artistic monuments of their day—been called "prayers in enduring stone." From church steeples to gravestones, the high cross, whose distinctive artistic form is usually called the Celtic cross, is beloved throughout the Irish diaspora.

But new research reveals that the true origins of the Irish high cross lie in far-off Armenia.

"It appears likely," wrote the late Hilary Richardson, a preeminent pioneer archaeologist and scholar of insular medieval Irish art, "from the evidence available that the free-standing stone monuments of Early Christian Ireland preserved a tradition which had originated in the eastern Christian world."[64]

Illuminated manuscripts are universal images of ancient Ireland. With their unique script, and their intricate curvilinear artwork and glowing colors, painstakingly and lovingly painted on calfskin vellum, they inspire awe in anyone who sees them. They were the highest artistic achievement of Late Antiquity during which they were made. There is nothing in the world like them. A whole genre of "Celtic art" has been inspired by the curvilinear shapes and interlaced animals common to them. The font that graces the walls and menus of Irish pubs around the world is often called "Kells," in homage to the magnificent seventh-century illuminated manuscript that sets the standard for all other manuscripts, the Book of Kells.

And yet the art of illumination was, in fact, passed down to Ireland from Egypt.

Writing was brought to Ireland by the first monks, and it was in Latin. By the seventh century, vernacular Gaelic had come into its own as the ancient tales were written down. Thus, Irish Gaelic (Gaeilge) has the oldest vernacular literature in Europe. Gaelic poetry and hymns to the Mother of God still amaze the world with their striking images and the freshness of their vision.

But some of the images in those poems come from Egypt or Constantinople.

Archaeological evidence—wine jars excavated in southwest Ireland and also in southwest Britain—shows that trade continued after the end of the Roman Empire, especially with Gaul,

[64] Hilary Richardson, "Observations on Christian Art in Early Ireland, Georgia and Armenia," *Proceedings of the Royal Irish Academy* 87, section C (March 1987): 129.

Spain, and North Africa. Along with amphorae, would not manuscripts, plain ones or decorated ones, have come on ships? Along with the texts, would not have come ideas, symbols, and artistic inspirations?

From Stone Slabs to High Crosses

Following the disintegration of the Roman Empire there was no monumental work anywhere in western Europe, either in architecture or in sculpture: the building of monuments simply ceased. It was at opposite ends of the Christian world—Transcaucasia (Armenia) in the east and Ireland in the west—that monuments were created again.

But before we go to Armenia, we must take a detour to the most ancient of Irish stone monuments: stone slabs.

The freestanding cross first appears in Ireland in the seventh century. It was preceded in time by stone slabs. Slab stones seem to have been the prior expression of Irish art. Throughout Ireland are thousands of slabs of stone, many of them inscribed with primitive carvings.

Some of the stones are carved with a *chi-rho*, or *chrismon*. This is one of the most ancient Christian symbols, formed by superimposing the Greek letter *chi* over the letter *rho* (the first two letters of *Christos* in Greek). Variant designs have appeared from time to time. In 1972, Irish archaeologist Ann Hamlin found the first *chi-rho* carved on a stone in northeast Ireland. She had examined *chi-rho* carvings on stones around Ireland and England and noted that the simpler "monogram" form of the *chi-rho* was a fifth-century evolution of the older "Constantinian" form, used in a Romano-British context, an example of which had not been found in Ireland before. She speculated that the origin of this stone may have been the influence of Scotland, but was confident more would be found in time.[65] However, in 1998, L. W. Hurtado, the founder of the Centre for the Study of Christian Origins at the University of Edinburgh School of Divinity, found the same simplified symbol going back to the second century in Coptic[66] and Armenian sources. This raises the possibility that Egyptian monks might have been in Ireland as early as the third century!

Another feature of the stone slabs whose roots are lost in the mists of antiquity is the utilization of the *orans* posture: elbows close to the body, palms up, hands outstretched. *Orans* figures appear first in the catacombs of Rome. The *orans* was the correct posture for newly initiated persons at the beginning of Christianity: as baptizands came up from the water after being immersed, and entered the eucharistic area for the first time, Tertullian (ca. 155–220) wrote, "You spread out your hands for the first time."[67] The contemporary understanding is that such was the customary posture for prayers of praise and intercession—as distinct from penitence, which was on the knees. In his treatise *On Prayer*, 14, Tertullian wrote "We ... not only lift them up, but also spread them out, and modulating them by the Lord's passion, in our prayers also press our faith in Christ."[68] Modulating the hands by the Passion seems to refer to the outstretched arms of Christ on

[65] Ann Hamlin, "A Chi-Rho-Carved Stone at Drumaqueran, Co. Antrim," *Ulster Journal of Archaeology* 35 (1972): 26, http://www.jstor.org/stable/20567707.

[66] As used in this book, "Coptic" should be read as "Egyptian Christian."

[67] Kilian McDonnell and George T. Montague, *Christian Initiation and Baptism in the Holy Spirit: Evidence from the First Eight Centuries* (Collegeville, MN: Liturgical Press, 1991), 99.

[68] Tertullian, *Corpus Christianorum* 1:265.

the Cross. Significantly, that is also the *cros-figell* posture formerly thought to be unique to Irish monastic prayer and penitence.

The *orans* posture is common in both eastern and western early Christian art in the first four or five centuries. Toward the end of that time period it appears on Gallo-Roman sarcophagi, where it represents a soul in Paradise.[69] It also appeared in Ireland, perhaps as early as the fifth or sixth century, and as late as the ninth. What changed in Ireland was the clothing of the person depicted.

In 1970, medievalist Helen M. Roe wrote of the discovery of three carved stones: a nude (except for a loincloth) orant figure on a slab in a churchyard at Staholmock, County Meath, and two clothed ones at Dunshauglin, County Meath, and Conwal, County Donegal, all sites of religious foundations that seem to date back to the fifth and sixth centuries.[70]

Between first illustrations of the orant figure and what seemed to be the latest appearance of that posture, Roe noted changes in iconographical detail that she attributed to "growing influence of Syrian and Coptic artists to whom classical nakedness was abhorrent." Syro-Palestinian formulas came to be adopted in the mid-sixth century, by which time crucifixion scenes are clothed. "From the eighth century onward, the majority of Crucifixions on the High Crosses show Christ fully clothed."[71]

In other words, somehow the new Syro-Palestinian standards in religious art were communicated to Ireland in the sixth century.

The Church of Jerusalem celebrated the discovery of the True Cross by St. Helena on September 14 in 335, by dedicating

[69] Helen M. Roe, "The Orans in Irish Christian Art," *Journal of the Royal Society of Antiquaries of Ireland* 100, no. 2 (1970): 212–221, jstor.org/stable/25509749, 215.

[70] Ibid., 212.

[71] Ibid., 217–218.

churches built by Emperor Constantine at Calvary and at the Holy Sepulchre, and the feast rapidly spread to Constantinople—and stayed there until Pope Sergius, who came of an Antiochian family in Sicily, placed the feast on the Roman calendar in 720.

Irish high crosses existed well before Sergius's new feast, however, so the impulse behind them can be attributed to the older tradition, rather than to the papal decree. Crosses were first put up in Armenia and in Georgia in the fourth century, to mark the acceptance of Christianity, a symbol of the triumph of the new religion.[72]

So crosses in Ireland could possibly date to before St. Patrick. In Waterville, County Kerry, there is a cross carved with an alpha and omega, very ancient Christian symbols from the East. Some scholars consider the Waterville cross to be from the sixth century and "probably the earliest such stone in Ireland." But another scholar considers that same cross to be "associated with the very earliest, possibly pre-Patrician church."[73]

During the seventh century, the freestanding "Celtic cross," as it is known today, began to appear. Made mostly from the eighth to the twelfth centuries in Ireland and western Scotland, the cross is carved on all four sides, and it has a unique design of steps at the base, a ring at the juncture of the arms, and a capstone in the shape of either a beehive hut or a chapel.

Where does all that come from? What is the origin of the Irish high cross? Where did the monks get the idea?

[72] Richardson, "Observations on Christian Art," 137.

[73] Hunwicke, "Kerry and Stowe Revisited," 14, footnote: "Sheehan (1990, 162 and 164) felt that a cross from near Waterville, carved with alpha and omega (cf. Treatise, para. 3) dated from the sixth or seventh century and was probably the earliest such stone in Ireland. Herity (1995, 314), reaching a similar conclusion, considered that it was 'associated with the very earliest, probably pre-Patrician church.' "

From Transcaucasia to the Emerald Isle

Art historians have concluded that Irish high crosses seem to have Armenian ancestry. Sculpture in stone was never of great importance in Byzantium, and the practice disappeared in the West after the end of the Roman Empire—so here again, Transcaucasia and Ireland, the two most remote fringes of the former empire, are uniquely similar. In 1967, Françoise Henry pointed out the "similar ancestry" between the Irish high cross and crosses in Svanetia in northwest Georgia and Armenia.[74]

Armenia!

Well, why not? Armenia was a major Christian nation and Ireland was au courant with the rest of the world. At its peak, Armenia's boundaries extended from the Caspian Sea to the Black Sea. It was evangelized by apostles Bartholomew and Jude Thaddeus in the first century. It became the first nation in the world to adopt Christianity as its official religion in the year A.D. 301, back when Christianity was still illegal in the Roman Empire. In Armenia, St. Gregory the Illuminator, who convinced the king to convert to Christianity, was famous for putting up crosses early in the fourth century as a symbol of the triumph of Christianity.

Interestingly, Ireland had no native tradition of building in stone, or even of using cut stone. Significantly, no archaeological dig of prehistoric Celtic Ireland has yielded any evidence of any tradition of carving in stone at any time.

From the Bronze Age to the early Christian era, standing stones—stones set upright in the ground—were a feature of the Irish landscape. Sometimes they were arranged in circles, as at Stonehenge

[74] Françoise Henry, *Irish Art in the Early Christian Period to 800 A.D.* (Ithaca, NY: Cornell University Press, 1965), 199.

in England. More than 600 of them can be found in Cork and Kerry alone.

About 350 standing stones in Ireland are inscribed in Ogham, as are some on the Isle of Man and in Wales and Cornwall—all Celtic areas. In Wales the Ogham is sometimes accompanied by Latin inscriptions written in Roman characters, but in Ireland the carvings are in Ogham only—which indicates that they are older. Generally, these stones mark boundaries and burial sites.

Ogham was the first effort at writing Irish, a system of notches and lines representing letters, which is believed to have begun as early as the first century and ended around the fourth, with the coming of Christianity. Ogham stones are still being discovered occasionally—a big stone would often find later use as a gate post or in the foundation of an old barn.

Ogham inscriptions were surface decoration on the stones, but nothing that changed the shape of the stone. In other words, those stones were not carved. It is a significant difference.

Hilary Richardson, the archaeologist and preeminent scholar of insular medieval art, was the first holder of the Royal Irish Academy's exchange fellowship with the former U.S.S.R. Academy of Sciences in 1985. While there, she pursued archaeology in the Caucasus Mountains, a region that had been closed to the West for seventy years. Since she was already extremely knowledgeable about Irish art, she found connections that nobody else could have found. In 1996, she published her finding of a "common denominator" between the Celtic cross and Armenian votive stelae dating between the fifth and seventh centuries.[75] *Stele* is the word for a stone monument that is higher than it is wide, and covered in carving or relief.

[75] Richardson, "Observations on Christian Art," 130.

Here's an interesting coincidence: the inner sides of one stele adjacent to a fifth-century basilica at Odzun in the Lori province of Armenia have ornamentation with the apostles in pairs in panels on the west face. The South Cross of Castle-dermot, County Kildare—one of the oldest high crosses—has exactly the same images! "In Transcaucasia," wrote Richardson, "there had also been a megalithic culture with dolmens and standing stones in the prehistoric past. In Armenia the setting up of stone pillars is found in the Bronze Age.... At the beginning of the Christian Era in Armenia and Georgia stone was in common use as a building material and techniques were already sophisticated."[76]

History of the Cross as an Image

For the first three hundred years of Christianity, the cross was an underground and hidden symbol. The True Cross was discovered in Jerusalem by St. Helena in 326, and the Church of the Holy Sepulchre was built shortly thereafter. That church was dedicated on September 14, and that date became the feast of the Exaltation of the Holy and Life-Giving Cross. The event spurred the beginning of Christian art using the cross. The feast itself didn't make it to the West for a few centuries: it was first proclaimed in Rome by Pope Sergius (687–701), who came from an Antiochean family, though he had grown up in Sicily. That, interestingly, is about the same time that the high crosses in Ireland became abundant.

[76] Ibid., 129.

In modern times, Armenia, Georgia, and Azerbaijan together make up the region known as Transcaucasia. The area is abundant with fifth-, sixth-, and seventh-century carvings—which are similar to the sculpture of Ireland and of the areas influenced by Ireland, especially northern Britain where Irish monks evangelized the Anglo-Saxons in what was then known as Northumbria.

Indeed, beginning in the fifth century, these stelae became widespread in Transcaucasia. These have important characteristics in common with the Irish cross: a large cubic stone base into which a shaft is inserted and a capstone on the top. Frequently stelae are carved in relief on all four faces, and the base may be carved as well—just as some high crosses are carved in relief on all four faces, and the base as well. Irish capstones are either dome-shaped like beehives or look like miniature churches, which is exactly how Solomon's Temple is represented in Folio 202 of the Book of Kells.

For instance, the front of a seventh-century stele from Haridj, now in Erevan, Armenia, has a figure of Christ blessing very similar to the attitude found on the eighth-century Ruthwell Cross in Dumfriesshire, Scotland (formerly Northumbria).[77] That cross is dated reliably to about 680, a time when Irish missionaries were active in western Scotland. "This might not cause surprise were it not for the fact that there is a total lack of any comparable material to be found elsewhere in Christendom," Richardson notes.[78]

[77] Ibid., 132.
[78] Ibid., 129–130.

That these Armenian art conventions appear in Ireland and nowhere else strongly suggests that the artists went from one place to the other.

Carvings on the High Cross

So, did the erection of crosses in Ireland, as earlier in Armenia, also proclaim the triumph of the new religion? Possibly. The timing might work: by the seventh century, paganism was still present but waning in Ireland.

The high cross in the ruined monastery of Clonmacnoise in County Louth is the piece of art that defines the genre. It is called Muiredach's Cross because an inscription on the base reads: "Say a prayer for Muiredach, who had this cross made." There were two Muiredachs who were abbots of the monastery, and a king whose site included the monastery, all in the eighth century.

The eighteen-foot-tall solid sandstone Muiredach's Cross is covered with carvings: the east face has pictures from the Old Testament, the west face has pictures from the New Testament. That geographical orientation is followed in other high crosses as well.

The non-Biblical carvings on the faces and sides of many high crosses hearken back to the Eastern Desert. The high crosses were built in monasteries, and the subjects of their carvings indicate this. Many images portray the founder of monasticism: St. Anthony of the Desert, who appears on many stone crosses—though, significantly, it has been noted by art historians that he does not appear in Roman or Gallic art of the period. This fact points strongly to Egypt as a tradition of origin for monasticism in ancient Ireland: honor is always paid to fathers in the Faith.

Another visual evidence is the frequent use of two other monastic fathers, St. Anthony and St. Paul the First Hermit. The meeting of St. Anthony and St. Paul in the wilderness is depicted in an icon at St. Anthony's Monastery, which still stands in the eastern desert of Egypt—and also appears on at least eighteen Irish high crosses.[79]

"Ireland is one of the few areas outside Egypt and Italy where these figures are known to have been portrayed at this period," notes archaeologist Peter Harbison.[80] The Ruthwell Cross portrays Paul and Anthony face-to-face, holding bread between them, standing up. Another cross with the same image is the Moone Cross in Kildare.

Rev. Neil Xavier O'Donoghue, today's foremost scholar of early Irish Christian liturgy, observes that the many instances of the Paul/Anthony subject on high crosses constitute the vast majority of all the first-millennium artistic portrayals of this scene. The image directly connects Irish monasticism to the Desert Fathers, as it portrays an incident in the *Life of St.Paul the First Hermit*, as written by St. Jerome.

The story is that it was revealed to St. Anthony the Great that he was not the first monk, as he thought he was, so he went farther into the desert. There he met the hermit, Paul, and stayed with him until he died. Before Paul died, however, together they visited a spring to share some bread. They disputed as to who should do the honors of breaking the bread: Paul said Anthony should, according to the rules of hospitality; Anthony said Paul should, because of his senior age. Eventually they compromised and decided that each would seize the loaf on the side nearest to himself and pull, and keep what came off in his hand. That is the scene on the high

[79] Helen M. Roe, "The Irish High Cross: Morphology and Iconography," *Journal of the Royal Society of Antiquaries of Ireland* 95, no. 1/2 (1965): 226, https://www.jstor.org/stable/25509591.

[80] Peter Harbison, Homan Potterton, and Jeanne Sheehy, *Irish Art and Architecture* (London: Thames and Hudson, 1978), 60.

crosses—a story of holy friendship, and also a reminder of humility and deference between brothers in the Lord. In the story, Paul and Anthony divide the bread thus, and then drink some water, and pass the night in a vigil of praise together.[81]

For sure, the story came from the Egyptian Desert. Did the artistic inspiration come from the East? It's hard to deny that it did: the iconography of the Armenian and Irish crosses is too similar to be coincidence. Identical subjects are carved on both Armenian monuments and the Irish crosses. Scenes of Scriptures that tell of God's help or prefigure the life of Christ (the sacrifice of Isaac, Daniel in the lion's den, the three holy youths in the fiery furnace, and so on) often appear in both places. Interestingly, these Scripture passages are readings connected with the feast of the Exaltation of the Holy and Life-Giving Cross to this very day in the Eastern Church!

Artists draw from what they were taught—or at least, until modern times, they did. Here is one more echo of Egypt in the high cross. On several high crosses, Clonmacnoise, Durrow, and Kells, Christ is shown standing with two long-handled implements held across His chest. On Muiredach's Cross, it is a cross and a flowering rod. That's an odd pose for Christ; it doesn't appear anywhere else. But take a quick look in the Egyptian pyramids. There can be found images of Osiris, the god of the dead, standing with a crook and a flail over his shoulders, held so that they cross on his chest.

Its themes and decoration are from the East. But what about the actual structure of the cross itself—its engineering, so to speak?

The design concept of the Irish high cross is unlike any other cross originating anywhere in the world. It is not an evolution from

[81] O'Donoghue, *The Eucharist in Pre-Norman Ireland*, 194.

a carved stone slab but is quite a "separate conception," to use the words of Hilary Richardson.

The research of another Irish scholar establishes that the artistic inspiration comes from Jerusalem.

Before such academic disciplines as "Gaelic Literature" or "Irish History" existed, people who were interested in ancient things and studied them seriously were called *antiquarians*. There were a few of them in each century since the seventeenth, and modern Irish history is deeply in their debt. Helen M. Roe was such a one. Born in 1895, she was an educated woman of the English gentry, receiving an MA degree in 1924 from Trinity College. While traveling in Europe after serving as a nurse in World War I, she became interested in medieval art. She devoted the rest of her life to exploring and writing about Ireland's ancient art, becoming the first woman president of the Royal Society of Antiquaries of Ireland.

She traced the design of high crosses all the way back to renderings of Constantine's Crux Gemmata, a bronze reliquary in the shape of a cross, studded with jewels and pearls, containing a relic of the True Cross. Constantine was said to have raised it on Golgotha in the fourth century. Its image was embossed on glass or silver phials that were taken around the world as souvenirs from a pilgrimage to Jerusalem.

What Helen Roe found convinced her that the inspiration for the Irish high cross originated with an artist in Jerusalem. She emphasized that, even while she documented the dependence of the Irish works on the Jerusalem art forms, "in fact, it cannot be too strongly stressed to how great an extent the Irish expressions of such foreign exemplars became, in the truest sense, original and native."[82]

[82] Roe, "The Irish High Cross," 223–225.

Art historians have noted that very few representations of the Crucifixion have survived anywhere before the eighth century. (Until that time, it simply wasn't a symbol popularly used among Christians.) There is one exception, however: in the souvenirs that pilgrims brought back from Jerusalem. The surviving examples that we have of such souvenirs, mostly from the sixth and seventh centuries, are small vessels with two hands that held chrism or perhaps some consecrated wine, which people would bring back with them. In those early days the custom of carrying the Eucharist in the form of bread on one's person in a chrismal was common; these ampullae might have held the Eucharist in liquid form.

These ampullae include representations of the Crucifixion and the Resurrection in the same image.

The souvenirs that Helen Roe studied included thirty-two small silver phials, whole and fragmentary, that are preserved at the library at Bobbio, Italy. Bobbio was the site of the great monastery founded by St. Columbanus around the year 612, which became famous for its library. Some of the souvenirs portray the encounter of the myrrh-bearing women with the risen Christ at the tomb; others have images of the Church of the Anastasis built above the Holy Sepulchre.

Columba? Columcille? Copyright Law?
Columban? Columbanus?

The names are confusing and the men are different. But the stories are true.

First, Columba is Columcille. And Columban is Columbanus. Columba is what the Scots call Columcille, and Columban is what the Brits call Columbanus.

Columba means "dove," so Columcille is "dove of the church." Columba (521–597) founded the monastery at Iona, off the southwest coast of Scotland, beginning the Hiberno-Scottish mission. It became one of the most important monasteries in the world.

Throughout history Irish monks were known for their travels. In doing so, they were following another Egyptian teaching: *xeniteia,* or in Latin, *peregrinatio,* later called "white martyrdom."

A thousand years after it happened, the story was written down about how Columba's white martyrdom came about. Columba visited St. Finnian, who had been his teacher, and during the night he copied a Psalter (legend says it was the Cathach). When he was leaving the monastery, Finnian asked for it back. Columba maintained that since he copied it, it was his. They went to the king, Diarmat mac Cerbaill, who ruled, "To every cow its calf, to every book its copy." The first case of copyright law to hit the courts! This much is documented.

Columba was a man of fiery temperament, and he wouldn't accept the king's ruling. He is said to have instigated a rebellion by the Uí Néill (O'Neill) clan against the king, in which he himself took up arms in the battle of Cúl Dreimhne. His punishment was to leave Ireland and never see it again, about which he wrote two famous poems.

In any case, he made good on his punishment, and Iona became a center of Gaelic culture and Irish monasticism for three centuries, and is hailed as the birthplace of Christianity in Scotland. Í is the name of Iona in modern Gaeilge, but when Adomnán wrote the biography of Columba, he called the island Ioua — which a transcription error turned into Iona!

In insular miniscule the letters *u* and *n* can easily be confused by a tired monk.

Columbanus (543–615) was a different man entirely. He was educated at Bangor, in modern County Down, and with twelve followers left Ireland about 590 to convert most of western Europe. He founded monasteries across Europe, notably Luxeuil Abbey, and was expelled from Merovingian France because of his scolding of Queen Brunnhilda of Austrasia about the immorality of her children, and he ended up in Bobbio, in Italy, where he founded that famous center of medieval scholarship.

The souvenirs do not show Christ crucified. Instead, as the conqueror of death, His portrait on the shield of victory is raised *above* the cross, which is usually in the form of a mystical Tree of Life. It is a visual summary of the teaching of the early Fathers about Christ, the Word made flesh, who rose from the dead and trampled down death by His death.

Roe found twenty phials all of the same subject. Seventeen followed the same formula, and fourteen were almost identical. But three of them had a variation and were obviously cast from the same mold. That variation is a stauroteca on the cross.

A *stauroteca*, usually found on reliquaries, is a star-studded shield containing Christ's portrait. The image is not placed above the cross but is centered directly on the *transom*, the members of the cross-head extending above and beyond its rim. It is not a crucifixion scene, but instead the cross is shown in triumph with raised dots around its edges to represent the pearls of the Crux Gemmata, and the star-studded sky above reduced to tiny bosses (bumps).

When Roe found this, she wrote triumphantly:

> Here then for the first and only time known to me in Christian art is the Trophy of the Cross shown as though free-standing, the shield neither above nor resting on the crossing but enclosing the centre of the intersection ... the prefiguration of the form which in Irish hands became the characteristic, free-standing ring-headed High Cross.... This premiss once granted, the special features of the Irish monument fall neatly into place: the massive quadrangular base of two or more steps, an architectural expression of the ascent to Golgotha with the concept of the hill itself; the delicate running decoration of the ring arcs recalling the garlanded shield-rim; the four little volutes, whether set on the ring or at the intersection of arms and shaft, a last reminiscence of the star-filled cosmos; the house-cap with ornate roof, gables and sides, the simulacrum of the Holy Sepulchre.[83]

Helen Roe lived long enough for another new discovery to vindicate her long-held conviction. Just before she died, an Egyptian textile from the fifth or sixth century was discovered—and it represents the Crux Gemmata—and it is a Celtic cross.[84]

The textile was acquired by the Minneapolis Institute of Art in 1983. This is the oldest known example of a large Latin cross with a ring surrounding the arms in what is now called the "Celtic" fashion. The woven cross has a stepped base with a slot to receive a projecting tenon at the bottom, which is the engineering mechanism of the Irish monuments.

[83] Ibid., 224–225.

[84] Roger Stalley, *Early Irish Sculpture and the Art of the High Crosses* (London: Yale University Press, 2020), 11.

One thing you won't find on Irish high crosses are sheep. Only on one cross, the Market Cross in Kells, is there a shepherd with sheep. This is surprising, since sheep and shepherds are common on fourth- and fifth-century sarcophagi in Gaul. You would expect them to appear, assuming that the art was designed by local artists, who naturally would tend to include images of animals familiar to them.

This omission may be a footnote to the huge Church controversy over religious images that was heating up in the seventh century. Iconoclasts were declaring that no images of Christ or the saints were acceptable, and were destroying icons. The Christian world was deeply divided by the controversy.

An ecumenical council, known as the Quinisext, was held in Trully in Constantinople in 692 to reiterate the canons of earlier councils, and also to institute some reforms. Theodore of Studios, who was the head of a huge monastery in Constantinople, was a leading reformer. He urged that, in iconography, Christ could no longer be represented symbolically as a lamb but could be depicted only as a man.[85] Rome was not at that council, though most of its canons were later accepted as valid. What is interesting is that this Byzantine teaching seems to have come to Ireland from a council of the Eastern Churches with the sculptors of the high crosses. That is why Christ appears as a man, but not as a lamb, on Irish high crosses.

Decorated Manuscripts

Along with high crosses, decorated manuscripts are the most widely recognized manifestation of the golden age of Gaelic civilization from the sixth century forward. They were the product

[85] Quinisext Council in Trully, can. 82 (Mansi 2, 977–980).

of monasteries, of which there were at least 250 across Ireland by the middle of the seventh century. Monasteries in Ireland came first, and daughter monasteries followed soon.

When the cenobitic (or solitary) life was giving way to the eremitic (or communal) life in monasteries, the impetus to live in mortification of the flesh continued. Leaving Ireland was the "white martyrdom" that a monk could impose on himself—or could be imposed on him as penance. Recall that Ireland was a tribal-based society, and a person's social and legal existence depended on his family connections—so leaving Ireland meant leaving not only everything one had known, but also leaving all security and status. Since there was no longer any opportunity for "red martyrdom"—dying for the Faith—many Irish monks sought to impose white martyrdom on themselves. Thus did they go to the coast of Scotland, where there were pagan Picts, and from thence southward into Northumbria, where there were pagan Anglo-Saxons, as Christianity had effectively died out when Rome vacated Britain. Irish monks were seeking the desert, but they founded monasteries. There was so much travel and evangelization and cultural cross-fertilization between Ireland and Scotland and Britain that the whole area and its shared culture of this period has been called the Celtic Mediterranean. The art of those regions collectively is known as *insular.*

Out of this era came the golden age of Gaelic literature and the illuminated manuscripts. The peak years of manuscript decoration were from 600 to 1200. Gospel books were naturally the most honored, and thus received the most ornate treatment. It's no surprise that the famous illuminated manuscripts are Gospel books; the Books of Kells, Lindisfarne, Durrow, and Dimma are particularly famous.

The Book of Kells is the most decorated and illuminated of all—"illuminated" meaning that real gold and silver were used in the decoration. Though named the Book of Kells, it is probable that the book was at least begun at Iona, St. Columba's monastery on an island off the west coast of Scotland. However, after repeated Viking raids, the monks fled to Kells. The coincidence of time with the Viking invasions makes the Book of Kells one of the youngest illuminated manuscripts.

Its story encapsulates the history of Irish manuscripts in general. Because of the multiple invasions, the conquests, the eventual total colonization of Ireland, and the attempted extirpation of the Gaels and Catholicism, only about three hundred medieval Irish language manuscripts of any description still exist. An international study in 2022 by a team of scientists and manuscript scholars from five European countries and Taiwan found that an estimated three thousand Irish manuscripts have been lost. About two hundred prose tales survive, but that is because they were written in manuscripts two or three hundred years after the original tale was composed, and those copied manuscripts survived overseas.

How Did the Irish Write?

Between the years A.D. 600 and 900, manuscripts were produced in Irish monasteries in abundance. Until 1600, most manuscripts were written on calfskin vellum (only a handful written on sheepskin parchment survive).

Today we grab a piece of paper to write something — back then, you had to grab a calf! And process it for a couple of months at least! Then you had to come up with a quill, and a tip, and ink that would last — and then you had to write on a very bumpy surface. While you sat on a stool by a narrow slit in a wall, with maybe a candle, and probably shivered most of the time.

Writing was an onerous process, one that deserved the honor it received.

Most writing in Ireland was in Latin until about 1200, and the important books, such as Gospels, were written in a special large script invented by the Irish, which is called *insular majuscule.* If you open the Book of Kells, even if you're fluent in Latin, you have to work to read what you see.

For everyday writing and for writing in Irish, a simpler script, which was faster and took up less space, developed. This is called *insular miniscule,* and it is the basis of the familiar so-called "Celtic" script familiar today. It remained in use as long as manuscripts were copied, which they were until the nineteenth century.

The earliest surviving decorated Irish manuscript is the Cathach (*cath* means "battle" in Irish), a Psalter written around the year 600. Originally thought to have been written by St. Columba himself, it was honored as such with an ornate book shrine. It is not elaborately decorated, but the first letters of psalms are decorated in a swirling style reminiscent of the ancient Celtic La Téne art. It's called the Cathach, or "Battler," because it was enshrined and carried into battle in the hopes of ensuring divine favor. And it so happens that in Armenia, Gospel books were processed before armies as they marched into battle.[86]

Michelle P. Brown, professor emerita of medieval manuscript studies at the School of Advanced Study in London, sees a connection between the proliferation of manuscripts, Pope Gregory the

[86] Brown, "Strategies of Visual Literacy in Insular and Anglo-Saxon Book Culture," 98.

Great, and the Christian East. Gregory is known in Catholic circles for his liturgical reforms, and for his mandating the arrangement of the plainchant that bears his name to this day. Venerable Bede (672–735), the first historian of Britain, placed Gregory firmly in British tradition with the story of his famous pun. While walking through a Roman slave market, Gregory was struck by the beauty of some recently captured slaves. Their blue eyes and pale skin were striking to these swarthy Mediterraneans. Inquiring where they were from, the pope was told they were Angles. "More like angels," he is said to have remarked. Immediately he desired to convert these angels—a desire that came to fruition years later when he sent Augustine to Canterbury to establish a mission. Irish monks had already been busy converting the Anglo-Saxons, of course, but their customs were different from Rome's, and Gregory wanted conformity to Roman ways.

Before he became pope, at the time when the Lombards were approaching Rome, and Rome sought help from Constantinople to address the threat, young Deacon Gregory was sent as Rome's ambassador to Constantinople for six years. Byzantium had its own problems, and was unable to offer help, so his mission was technically unsuccessful. Perhaps it influenced his decision later on to focus on converting barbarians in western Europe. But his sojourn in the East, where icons were important devotional and catechetical aids, definitely gave him a firsthand view of the importance of imagery in building faith.

After he became pope in 609, Gregory provided stimulation to church art and to book arts. "In Rome the church and book arts were stimulated around 600 by Pope Gregory the Great, whose own approach to images and icons was informed by that of St. Catherine's, Sinai, and Byzantium," Brown writes. "Gregory's perception of the didactic and contemplative function of images may have owed much to those of pre-iconoclastic Byzantium and the Christian Orient, which in turn informed those of early Christian Britain."[87]

Out of Egypt

Images borrowed from the East became stone carvings, which in turn inspired manuscript illumination. The oldest known illuminated manuscripts in the world are the Garima Gospels of Ethiopia; the latest research suggests that they were written and illuminated in the fourth century, using iconography drawn from pagan Egyptian art.[88]

The art in decorated manuscripts is powerful evidence that monks in Ireland had Egyptian teachers. The Cathach, the oldest of them all, utilizes red dots decorating some initial letters. This is a technique borrowed from Egypt. Another initial shows a fish or dolphin holding a cross, a motif familiar in Coptic Egypt. Red dots appear on the garments of the evangelists in the Book of Kells as well.

Archdale King, a liturgical scholar whose histories of the liturgies of the East and West are still regarded as definitive studies, noticed as long ago as 1947 that the interlacing in Celtic ornamentation strongly resembles the ornamentation found in Coptic churches of Old Cairo.[89]

Interlacing is a distinctive element of design in insular art, in both manuscript and carving. Interlace is ornamentation with intertwining ribbon patterns that weave around a letter or even a whole page. These intricate designs fold over on themselves along

[87] Ibid., 81.

[88] "Garima Gospels," *Encyclopedia of Art History*, http://visual-arts-cork.com/history-of-art/garima-gospels.htm.

[89] King, *The Rites of Eastern Christendom*, vol. 1, 374.

the border of a page, intertwine with other long ribbons of a different color, and sometimes turn into animals at one end. It is immediately recognizable as Irish—or Anglo-Saxon, because Irish missionaries took it to the Anglo-Saxons and they made it their own. The great illuminated manuscripts have interlaced initials and decorations, and full pages of it, called carpet pages. That decorative technique crosses over from vellum to stone: ribbon interlace appears on the Fahan Mura slab near Columba's monastery in Derry. That slab is incised with a cross filled with broad ribbon interlace—and a seventh-century inscription in Greek uncials!

Today art scholars agree that the interlace that is a key element in ornamentation in insular illumination "may have been inspired by the art of Coptic Egypt" as "fifth- and sixth-century Coptic manuscripts and textiles display a system of ribbon interlace that bears a striking resemblance to the earliest type found in insular manuscripts."[90]

Illumination, of course, requires color. Obtaining the color points to yet another tangible connection to the East: manuscript colors that have lasted more than a thousand years did not come from dyes available in the local forests of Erin. Who would have known the craft except those who had learned it from those who went before them—parents and grandparents, perhaps, or older monks, whose own ancestors may have decorated the pyramids? To acquire the ingredients would require a trade network across the known world.

Lapis lazuli, the source of the finest blue ink in manuscripts, came from a mine in the northeast of modern-day Afghanistan.[91] Other blues came from the indigo plant, which is native to tropical

[90] Polly Cone, ed., *Treasures of Early Irish Art: 1500 B.C. to 1500 A.D.* (Dublin: Royal Irish Academy, 1977), 58–59.

[91] Bernard Meehan, *The Book of Kells: An Illustrated Introduction to the Manuscript in Trinity College Dublin* (London: Thames and Hudson, 1994), 88.

climates. A substitute for gold was orpiment, called *auripigmentum*, which is arsenic trisulfide. That is found in the vicinity of volcanos, making Turkey the most likely source, though gold was preferable for obvious reasons. Certain shades of red came only from the pregnant body of a miniscule Mediterranean insect that lives in only one type of oak tree, the *Kermoccocus vermilio*.

And we think global trade is a new invention! What bound these rare and expensive ingredients together into usable forms was just common, garden-variety egg white.

Could all this have happened without direct connections between Ireland and Egypt and beyond? True, the craft of binding manuscripts into a codex, or book, was known in ancient Rome; before then, vellum was stored in scrolls. But the same decorative arrangements of ribbons and crosses, and the same way the books were bound together in Egypt in the sixth century, possibly as early as the fifth century, and Ireland in the seventh century—this could not be accidental. This points to a direct connection between early Irish Christians and the monasteries of Egypt and its form of Greek Christianity.

The Cathach from the sixth century is the oldest surviving Irish manuscript, and incidentally the second-oldest Latin Psalter in the world. Because of its early date it is totally devoid of any Northumbrian or Anglo-Saxon influence that affected later art.

The Egyptian influence on the Cathach was first noted by Françoise Henry (1902–1982), a remarkable woman to whom Ireland owes a debt of gratitude. Henry was founder of the Department of History of European Painting at University College Dublin. She was French, and originally came to Ireland to study Irish carvings while writing her thesis. She saw the high crosses at Ahenny and was inspired by them. She earned her doctorate in 1932 on Irish carvings and rapidly became the world's leading expert on Irish art of the early Christian period.

In 1965, Henry wrote that the use of dots "is of Coptic origin and is found in paintings of the monasteries in the Egyptian desert. It passed into Byzantine art and though it is still not as common then as it will become later, it does occur in Byzantine manuscripts of the sixth century, such as the Dioscorides in the Vienna Library or the Gospel-book in the cathedral of Rossano in Calabria. It is difficult to establish how the Irish scribes came to know it."[92]

By 1977, Henry's opinion was conventional wisdom. G. Frank Mitchell, president of the Royal Irish Academy, wrote in the 1977 introduction to the *Treasures of Early Irish Art* international exhibit book that "Eastern Mediterranean influence also appears in the Cathach: another initial shows a fish or dolphin bearing a cross, a motif familiar in Coptic Egypt."

Gospel books frequently include portraits of the evangelists themselves. And those portraits frequently follow Egyptian models. The evangelists in the illuminated manuscripts of the Dimma Gospel (eighth-century, from Tipperary), the ninth-century Book of Deer from Scotland, and the St. John Gospel (eighth-century, in St. Gall, Switzerland) derive "ultimately from the early Christian figure of a standing evangelist carrying his book on veiled hands, as it appears on a Coptic painted book cover of the first half of the seventh century,"[93] wrote the late art historian Otto Karl Werckmeister.

Françoise Henry noted that in the Echternach Gospel, produced at Lindisfarne late in the seventh century but now in the

[92] Henry, *Irish Art*, 64.

[93] O. K. Werckmeister, "Three Problems of Traditions in Pre-Carolingian Figure-Style from Visigothic to Insular Illumination," *Proceedings of the Royal Irish Academy: Archaeology, Culture, History, Literature* 63 (1962–1964), https://www.jstor.org/stable/i25505109.

Bibliotheque Nationale in Paris, the way that St. Luke holds a cross in one hand and a flowering staff in the other is the posture of the Egyptian Osiris-judge in the Egyptian Book of the Dead from pre-Christian art in Egypt.[94] The same posture appears as Christ in judgment in the Book of Kells and on Muiredach's Cross.

Hidden Messages in Ancient Manuscripts

Not all ancient manuscripts, of course, were magnificently decorated and illuminated. Most of them were workhorses. Their job was to spread the gospel and make sure the liturgy was celebrated correctly. The copying of them was a full-time, year-in/year-out occupation for many monks.

Much of what the world knows about the Old Irish language actually comes from studying marginal notes in early Irish manuscripts written in Latin. It was tedious work, copying manuscripts in the cold, with only a candle for lighting, and the mind would wander. Occasionally a monk would write something in a margin, or at the bottom of a page, or between lines. These scribbles are known as *glosses*. In the library at St. Gallen, Switzerland, there are many such examples. It's a magnificent collection that has survived since the founding of the monastery by St. Gall, who may have been one of the twelve monks who traveled with Columbanus in 612. In the Stiftsbibliothek (monastery library) is a manuscript called the Codex Sangalliensis 904. Written around 850, it is a copy of Priscian's *Institutiones grammaticae*, the standard textbook for the study of Latin since about the year 500.

An unnamed monk may have been distracted while shivering as he copied the Latin grammar, and to remind himself not to

[94] Henry, *Irish Art*, 186.

indulge in self-pity, he may have paused to count his blessings, which he wrote out in his native tongue on the margin of a page.

> *Is acher in gaith innocht fufuasna faircae findfholt*
> *ni ágor réimm mora minn dond laechraid lainn óa lothlind*

> Bitter is the wind tonight it tosses the ocean's white hair
> I do not fear the coursing of a clear sea by the fierce warriors from Norway

That gloss tells posterity that the manuscript was written in Ireland, where a monk may well have feared a Viking invasion from a calm sea. Fear of those invasions sent many Irish manuscripts to Europe for that very reason; well over fifty complete or fragmentary Irish manuscripts are still extant in libraries across Europe.

Irish Script on Screen

If you find yourself intrigued by decorated manuscripts, treat yourself to an online visit to ISOS. ISOS, which stands for Irish Script on Screen, is a project of the School of Celtic Studies of the Dublin Institute for Advanced Studies. It is a website of high-resolution digital images of complete Irish manuscripts. Because of the Irish diaspora, manuscripts from Irish monasteries have found their way around the world. The Victoria State Library in Australia, the National Library of Scotland, and the British Library, as well as Irish institutions and universities, have shared their collections with this extensive project. The entire Book of Lismore has been digitized, and may be found on the website: www.isos.dias.ie.

Flabella and Communion Spoons

Another artifact that seems to have made its way to Ireland from the East is the liturgical fan, known as a *flabellum*. These are such ancient items that, to this day, flabella flank the papal throne for ceremonial occasions. In that case, they are huge things made of ostrich feathers and silk.

Both the antiquity and Egyptian origin of flabella are self-proven: flabella were found in the tomb of Tutankhamun.[95] They were very much present in ancient Irish Christianity: St. Columba's flabellum was revered as a relic until 1034, when it was lost overboard in a nautical journey.[96]

And they are very much present today in Eastern churches, where the flabellum frequently takes the form of a six-winged seraphim engraved on a gold disc and mounted on top of a long pole, sometimes with bells attached. Originally used to fan the holy offerings during the anaphora, to this day flabella are carried in the Great Entrance and at the Gospel reading in the celebration of the Divine Liturgy of St. John Chrysostom, representing the presence of angels. The fan is the distinctive insignia of the deacon and is given to him during his ordination.[97]

Flabella appear in the Book of Kells: On the *Virgin and Child* page, in the hands of angels, they "connect the incarnate Christ to the eucharist" and in the *Temptation of Christ* miniature, two are crossed over the chest of a half-length figure in a pose reminiscent of Osiris. They also appear on folios 27V and 129V in the Book of Kells, where they are in the background of the evangelists' symbols.

[95] Martin Werner, "The Madonna and Child Miniature in the Book of Kells: Part I," *Art Bulletin* 54, no. 1 (March 1972): 1–23, 11.

[96] Meehan, *The Book of Kells*, 48.

[97] King, *The Rites of Eastern Christendom*, vol. 1, 118.

Frederick Warren found flabella in the illustration of Evangelist Matthew in the Hiberno-Saxon Gospel at Treves also.

In 1881, Warren was baffled by the findings of cross-engraved bronze spoons among archaeological finds of religious items in Wales and Iona.[98] However, Eastern icons show Communion being administered with a spoon, as is still the custom. Newer archaeological evidence suggests that spoons may have been used all around the Celtic Mediterranean. In 1958, a schoolboy in St. Ninian's Isle, in Shetland, Scotland, discovered a box of treasures under a stone marked with a cross, which may have been the floor of a church at one time. Hilary Richardson considered it "quite probable that the spoon found in the St Ninian's Isle treasure, buried around 800 AD, fits into this category, as does the long-handled spoon on the cross in Killary, Meath, in the panel of the Baptism of Christ."[99]

Liturgiologists maintain that the eucharistic cup in the West was held and drunk from by the laity until around the ninth century (the huge, magnificent Ardagh Chalice is older still, so it may well have been used to distribute Communion). After that, Communion was given under both species by means of a spoon. Communion in the Stowe Missal seems to be distributed under both species, judging by the Communion chants. The Treatise on the Mass that is bound into the missal gives directions that would make it necessary for separate administration.

[98] Warren, *The Liturgy and Ritual of the Celtic Church*, 133–134.

[99] Hilary Richardson, "Derrynavlan and Other Early Church Treasures," *Journal of the Royal Society of Antiquaries of Ireland* 110 (1980): 95, http://www.jstor.org/stable/25508778.

Icons of the Virgin in the Book of Kells

There are echoes of the East throughout the Book of Kells as well. For instance, in the miniature of Christ enthroned, the cross above Christ's head is flanked by two peacocks. The peacock motif appears frequently in early Christian carvings and mosaics.

One of the most famous pages, folio 7V, in the Book of Kells is that of the Madonna, sometimes called "Mother and Child Enthroned." It has been described as "the earliest extant Madonna and Child illustration in a Latin codex"[100]—but it is not at all Latin in its concept. While it is unique early medieval Latin illumination, it shares much affinity with the East. The arrangement of Mary and Jesus together, their gestures, and the angels surrounding them can be found in early Coptic, Nubian, and Ethiopian art. Armenian Gospels have the same image as well. Full-page illustrations of the Virgin and Child appear in sixth-century Syriac books, and ninth-century Coptic ones show a nursing Virgin surrounded by adoring angels.

The figure of the Virgin and Child seated on a throne surrounded by attending angels appears frequently in Coptic art. It is a classic Hodegetria pose, in which the Virgin points to the infant Jesus. That pose is first seen in the depiction of the adoration of the Magi in the catacombs, and "it was in Egypt that the Hodegetria was separated from this scene at an early date, to develop its iconic character. This process began in Egypt because there the worship of the Virgin was widespread."[101]

[100] Werner, "The Madonna and Child Miniature in the Book of Kells: Part I," 1.

[101] Victor Lasareff, "Studies in the Iconography of the Virgin," *Art Bulletin* 20, no. 1 (March 1938): 46–47, https://doi.org/10.2307/3046561.

Niamh Whitfield, art historian and archaeologist who studied the dress of the Virgin on the page, noted that the Virgin's attire is that of an Irish queen—but the brooch is on her right shoulder. That's in the wrong place for an Irish queen. An ancient Irish law-tract suggests that women's brooches should be placed on the breast. In the East, however, the right shoulder was the correct place for a woman to wear a brooch.[102] This suggests that the artist may have been copying from an Eastern model.

Furthermore, the lozenge (elongated diamond) shape of the brooch is a classic Eastern way of affirming that this is truly the Mother of God holding the Child Jesus. The lozenge is an artistic symbol of Christ, frequently found on early Christian lamps, and also on a number of high crosses, such as the Moone Cross in Kildare. The opening phrase of St. John's Gospel—"in the beginning was the Word," or *Logos*—is confirmed artistically in the Book of Kells by the powerful image of a lozenge as the focus of the whole page of symbols.

Skeptics point out that the known Coptic examples tend to be, so far as is known, later than the Irish,[103] and that this invalidates these observations. But there is a reason why the Coptic examples would be more recent: the earlier ones would have been destroyed in the iconoclast wars and the Islamic conquest.

The destruction of sacred images first began under the Muslims, who conquered Egypt in 639. Then it continued for a century and a half under various Christian emperors, beginning with Emperor Leo in 726. Even if ordinary Christians were afforded a degree of

[102] Niamh Whitfield, "Brooch or Cross? The Lozenge on the Shoulder of the Virgin in the Book of Kells," *Archaeology Ireland* 10, no. 1 (Spring 1996): 20–23, jstor.org/stable/20562237, 22.

[103] Raftery, "Ex Oriente," 201.

toleration under Islam, the makers of sacred images—idolaters and blasphemers, according to Islamic law—would not have been well tolerated in Egypt.

Further east, the iconoclast wars among Christians brought persecutions and destruction. Those wars ebbed and surged until 842. A hundred years of war on monasteries, relics, and holy images can, as Ireland well knows, destroy a significant number of manuscripts and other artifacts. The Seventh Ecumenical Council (Nicaea II, in 787) proclaimed that icons should be allowed in churches, but it was sixty years later, in 842, that Empress Theodora actually restored icons to churches. After Nicaea, when Christian Coptic artists resumed work, they naturally would have followed their ancient traditions, which would have been as old as Christianity itself. Thus, surviving Coptic art may indeed have younger dates than the Book of Kells, but the revival of traditions that had survived war and conquest may explain why it would have been the same art.

Is that most quintessential Irish work of art, the Book of Kells, therefore, a product of Egyptian influence? The conclusion of insular art scholar Martin Werner after comparing Kells with Egyptian, Nubian, and Ethiopian treatments of the same three subjects is that

> we must conclude that the artists who created these three miniatures were inspired by the components of a single iconographically cohesive demonstration.... Should we, then, look to Coptic Egypt as the most likely home of this exemplar cycle? Despite certain lacunae, the existing evidence argues for the validity of this suggestion. Taken alone, arguments adduced from Coptic and Ethiopic miniatures are admittedly tenuous. Coupled with the testimony of related arts, both Coptic and foreign, they

become immediately persuasive.... *We must conclude that the Columban monks who created the chef-d'oeuvre of the Hiberno-Saxon school had before them, among others, a set of symbolic miniatures brought from Coptic Egypt.*[104]

The Diatessaron

In 1968, Carl Nordenfalk, then-director of the Swedish National Museum, boldly asserted that "insular illumination rested mainly on one pillar: a copy of an illustrated edition of Tatian's *Diatessaron* the existence of which would probably have escaped us forever, had not in the sixteenth century an Armenian patriarch, of blessed memory, brought an astonishingly faithful copy of a similar manuscript back to the West."[105] The *Diatessaron* is a second-century compilation of the four Gospels as a single narrative; it is believed to have been originally written in Syriac. The edition illustrated by Tatian bears striking resemblance to insular illumination.

Academia pushed back hard against Nordenfalk, and in 1973, he modified his original assertion that the *Diatessaron* had come to the British Isles at the time of the earliest Christian missions. "It seems more probable that in one way or another a copy of an illustrated Diatessaron reached Iona only about the time the Book of Durrow was made," he wrote[106]—in other words, around the year 700.

[104] Martin Werner, "The Madonna and Child Miniature in the Book of Kells: Part II," *Art Bulletin* 54, no. 2 (June 1972): 129–139, 137–138, emphasis mine.

[105] Carl Nordenfalk, "An Illustrated Diatessaron," *Art Bulletin* 50, no. 2 (June 1968): 140, www.jstor.org/stable/3048527.

[106] Carl Nordenfalk, "The Diatessaron Miniatures Once More," *Art Bulletin* 55, no. 4 (December 1973): 544, jstor.org/stable/3049162.

He told the art world how it may have happened. There was a certain Gaulish bishop named Arculf (or Arculph), who was returning from pilgrimage to the Holy Land when he was rerouted by storms to Iona:

> From Arculph's dictation, Adamnán wrote his book *De locis sanctis* which contains so much factual and legendary information about the countries along the Eastern coast of the Mediterranean, from Constantinople to Alexandria. When describing the churches in Palestine, Arculph drew plans of them on a wax table which Adamnán had transferred to the parchment as illustrations to his text, a direct indication of the fact that the art of book illumination was practiced in Iona in his time. For once, then, we have a real historical connection between a place where Hiberno-Saxon art flourished and the Near East, and it is extremely tempting to assume that the illustrated Diatessaron was among the books in Arculph's baggage. It is, of course, nothing but a hypothetical idea but one that could explain the striking resemblance between the Persian and the Hiberno-Saxon miniatures better than anything else.[107]

Other sources confirm the possibility of this narrative. Storms in the North Atlantic go without saying. The Venerable Bede confirms the rest in *The Ecclesiastical History of the English People*, chapter 5, section 15. Adomnán's guidebook became used throughout Europe and may have been the book that rescued sixty Irish hostages. In 686, King Finnachta of the southern Uí Néill asked Adomnán to obtain release of sixty Irish hostages who had been captured by the predecessor of Aldfrith of Northumbria. Aldfrith

[107] Ibid., 544–545.

had been a pupil of Adomnán; he presented the king with his book on Holy Places and returned laden with gifts and the sixty hostages.

"No Other Plausible Explanation"

The architecture and art that define ancient Ireland—small churches in groups of seven, some with decorated walls defining the sanctuary, *cumhdaigh* or book shrines, stone slabs with *chi-rho* inscriptions, high crosses decorated with Syro-Palestinian art formulas, illuminated manuscripts with colophons, artifacts of ancient liturgical practice—all have origins that can be traced to the Christian East. In the absence of printed manuals, how could these ideas and this craftsmanship have been transmitted other than by human beings who traveled to Ireland? Does all this constitute evidence that Egyptian monks in Ireland in the seventh century were more than metaphors?

Colophons

Speaking of glosses on manuscripts . . . a word about colophons. A colophon is an inscription, usually at the end of a manuscript, stating the date, the name of the scribe, and acknowledging the benefactor or monastery for whom the work was copied. Colophons occur rarely in Europe, but they are frequent in insular manuscripts, especially Irish ones. That is fortunate, as colophons serve as important keys to tracing Irish history because they document who was living when.

As it happens, colophons are common and detailed in Armenian books, where their use rendered the book an intercessory prayer for its patrons ... as they frequently did in Irish manuscripts.

Do all these threads, fragments, hints, similarities, and coincidences add up to proof of Eastern influence on insular Christianity?

Harvard University's James Doan summed it up thus in the Harvard Celtic Colloquium in 1982: "In conclusion, the relation between Irish and Hiberno-Saxon illuminations and Mediterranean art, including Early Christian, Byzantine, and Coptic paintings, carvings, and textiles, is as best tenuous. Certain iconographic parallels, however, *suggest no other plausible explanation.*"[108]

For Further Reference

Early Christian Insular Art

Cone, Polly, ed. *Treasures of Early Irish Art: 1500 B.C. to 1500 A.D.* Dublin: Royal Irish Academy, 1977.

Doan, James E. "Mediterranean Influences on Insular Manuscript Illumination." *Proceedings of the Harvard Celtic Colloquium* 2 (1982): 31–38. jstor.org/stable/20557117.

Hamlin, A. "A Chi-Rho-Carved Stone at Drumaqueran, Co. Antrim." *Ulster Journal of Archaeology* 35 (1972): 22–28. http://www.jstor.org/stable/20567707.

Hamlin, Ann. "The Archaeology of the Irish Church in the Eighth Century." *Peritia* 4 (1985): 279–299.

[108] James E. Doan, "Mediterranean Influences on Insular Manuscript Illumination," *Proceedings of the Harvard Celtic Colloquium* 2 (1982): 31–38, jstor.org/stable/20557117, 36.

Harbison, Peter, Homan Potterton, and Jeanne Sheehy. *Irish Art and Architecture*. London: Thames and Hudson, 1978.

Henry, Françoise. *Irish Art in the Early Christian Period to 800 A.D.* Ithaca, NY: Cornell University Press, 1965.

King, Archdale. *The Rites of Eastern Christendom*, vol. 1. Rome: Tipografia Poliglotta Vaticana, 1947.

McDonnell, Kilian, and George T. Montague. *Christian Initiation and Baptism in the Holy Spirit: Evidence from the First Eight Centuries*. Collegeville, MN: Liturgical Press, 1991.

Nordenfalk, Carl. *Celtic and Anglo-Saxon Painting: Book Illumination in the British Isles* 600–800. New York: Braziller, 1977.

Richardson, Hilary. "Derrynavlan and Other Early Church Treasures." *Journal of the Royal Society of Antiquaries of Ireland* 110 (1980): 92–115. http://www.jstor.org/stable/25508778.

——. "Observations on Christian Art in Early Ireland, Georgia and Armenia." *Proceedings of the Royal Irish Academy* 87 (1987): 129–137.

Roe, Helen M. "The Orans in Irish Christian Art." *Journal of the Royal Society of Antiquaries of Ireland* 100, no. 2 (1970): 212–221. jstor.org/stable/25509749.

Werckmeister, O. K. "Three Problems of Traditions in Pre-Carolingian Figure-Style from Visigothic to Insular Illumination." *Proceedings of the Royal Irish Academy: Archaeology, Culture, History, Literature* 63 (1962–1964): 167–189. https://www.jstor.org/stable/i25505109.

Book of Kells

Henry, Françoise. *The Book of Kells: Reproductions from the Manuscript in Trinity College Dublin with a Study of the Manuscript by Françoise Henry*. New York: Knopf, 1974.

Lasareff, Victor. "Studies in the Iconography of the Virgin." *Art Bulletin* 20, no. 1 (March 1938): 26–65. https://doi.org/10.2307/3046561.

Meyer, Kuno. "Learning in Ancient Ireland." *Irish Review* 2, no. 21 (November 1912): 449–459. www.jstor.org/stable/30062882.

Meehan, Bernard. *The Book of Kells: An Illustrated Introduction to the Manuscript in Trinity College Dublin*. London: Thames and Hudson, 1994.

Richardson, Hilary. "Lozenge and Logos." *Archaeology Ireland* 10, no. 2 (Summer 1996): 24–25. www.jstor.org/stable/20562263.

Werner, Martin. "The Madonna and Child Miniature in the Book of Kells: Part I." *Art Bulletin* 54, no. 1 (March 1972): 1–23.

——. "The Madonna and Child Miniature in the Book of Kells: Part II." *Art Bulletin* 54, no. 2 (June 1972): 129–139.

Whitfield, Niamh. "Brooch or Cross? The Lozenge on the Shoulder of the Virgin in the Book of Kells." *Archaeology Ireland* 10, no. 1 (Spring 1996): 20–23. jstor.org/stable/20562237.

High Crosses

Flower, Robin. "Irish High Crosses." *Journal of the Warburg and Courtauld Institutes* 17, no. 1/2 (1954): 87–97. www.jstor.org/stable/750133.

Roe, Helen M. "The Irish High Cross: Morphology and Iconography." *Journal of the Royal Society of Antiquaries of Ireland* 95, no. 1/2 (1965): 213–226. https://www.jstor.org/stable/25509591.

Stalley, Roger. *Early Irish Sculpture and the Art of the High Crosses*. London: Yale University Press, 2020.

Other

Nordenfalk, Carl. "An Illustrated Diatessaron." *Art Bulletin* 50, no. 2 (June 1968): 119–140. www.jstor.org/stable/3048527.

O'Donoghue, Neil Xavier. "Insular Chrismals and House-Shaped Shrines in the Early Middle Ages." *Insular & Anglo-Saxon Art and Thought in the Early Medieval Period*, edited by Colum Hourihane, 79–91. University Park, PA: Princeton University Index of Christian Art, 2011

Richardson, Hilary. "Derrynavlan and Other Early Church Treasures." *Journal of the Royal Society of Antiquaries of Ireland* 110 (1980): 92–115. http://www.jstor.org/stable/25508778.

Tertullian. *Corpus Christianorum* 1:265.

Chapter 5

Monasticism

Carved into the high cross at Ahenny, County Tipperary, is a figure of a solitary monk sitting under a palm tree. Was he the founder of that monastery, being shown in the warm climes of Paradise? Possibly; no name is given. Or does he represent all the monks who came to Ireland from Egypt?

In Aghaboe, County Cork, is an Ogham stone near a well. Its inscription says, "Pray for St. Olan the Egyptian." Nobody knows how old it is, and some scholars say Ogham writing began in the first century. Almost all agree that the stone predates St. Patrick by at least a century.

One thing is certain. By the sixth century, something truly amazing was happening throughout the Christian world: Irish Adomnán in Iona, an island off the coast of Scotland, was practicing the same kind of eremiticism as St. Isaac of Syria in the Arabian peninsula. Monasticism was sweeping the world.

The term *monasticism* has picked up baggage in popular culture, and so it may be a good idea to place the early Irish monks in their historical context. First, dispel any mental image of Ellis Peters's fictional Br. Cadfael in his cozy sociable herbarium at his magnificent twelfth-century Benedictine abbey on the edge of Wales.

Irish monasticism began a thousand or so years earlier, and monks in Ireland lived in cold, wet, rocky, isolated, storm-tossed places like Skellig Michael, leading a life of physical suffering, hardship, loneliness, hunger, and inward struggle.

It was exactly the life that they sought.

What Is Monasticism?

One of the books that most influenced how the English-speaking world sees early Christianity was Edward Gibbon's (1737–1794) *Decline and Fall of the Roman Empire*. In essence, this Enlightenment-era historian blamed the fall of the Roman Empire on the baneful influence of Christianity: "The clergy successfully preached the doctrines of patience and pusillanimity.... The remains of military spirit were buried in the cloyster.... The attention of the emperors was diverted from the camps to the synods." Not only were Christians too inclined to forgive enemies, but too many of them preferred monastic to public life, literally wasting their lives in pursuit of their mad ideals: "Their credulity debased and vitiated the faculties of the mind.... Superstition gradually extinguished the hostile light of philosophy and science."[109]

Gibbon's prejudice lingers on in our even more scientific and materialistic age. Furthermore, in our comfort-loving twenty-first century, the very idea of voluntarily living in solitude and physical discomfort is perceived as tantamount to insanity. But in the early centuries of Christianity, when dying for Christ and achieving Heaven were no longer possibilities because Christianity was now legal, men and women sought to live for Christ by dying to themselves.

[109] Keith Windschuttle, "Edward Gibbon and the Enlightenment," *New Criterion* 15, no. 10 (June 1997), https://newcriterion.com/issues/1997/6/edward-gibbon-the-enlightenment.

What motivated these saints? It was simple. In 321, Athanasius had written that "the Son of God became man so that we might become God."[110] How better to attain unity with God than to cast off all earthly attachments and pray continuously? Why pursue earthly possessions or comforts if by abandoning them one can be united to God? Instead of fleshly pleasures, they chose a lifelong battle against temptation in the hopes of achieving mystical union with God while still on earth.

By denying the world and the flesh, a man or a woman (for there were women in the Egyptian desert as well as the Irish *díseart*) sought to acquire nothing less than personal union with the almighty, eternal, ineffable, incomprehensible God. Dying to worldly pleasures, living in solitude, going hungry and thirsty, and battling demons was their way to acquire the most important thing in the world, the only thing worth having: salvation. Along the way they might have visions and see or be seen to perform miracles.

Monasticism swept through the entire Christian world from the third century onward. Thousands, if not millions, of men and women, from emperors and empresses to plowboys and milkmaids, heard its call and followed. Seen from the forty-thousand-foot view, it is fair to say that monasticism was so large a part of the Church in the fourth and fifth centuries that it can be credited with laying the groundwork for much of Western civilization. Caring for the needy, healing the sick, learning from the wise, and teaching the ignorant: these things that define Christianity had their origins in monasticism. A few words, therefore, about the beginnings of it, the Desert Fathers and their followers.

[110] Athanasius, *On the Incarnation*, 54, 3, quoted in *Catechism of the Catholic Church*, no. 460.

Christians weren't the first to flee into the desert. Manuscripts found in the Qumran caves indicate that the Essenes, a Jewish sect, pursued what was essentially a monastic life before Christ. Likewise, the persecutions by Nero and other emperors in the second and third centuries drove Jews and Christians alike into the desert to repent of their sins before they were called to red martyrdom, as many feared. After the legalization of Christianity, that trickle became a flood.

It seems counterintuitive: Now that persecution was over, why not resume their normal lives? When persecution could strike at any time, one might die a martyr's death at any time and attain Heaven; when one had to live surrounded by comforts and temptations, it was more difficult to be certain of salvation when the end of the world came, as was expected. Following Christ was more difficult now because life now meant you were expected to have possessions, and to marry, and to care for your wife and your children—all of which were temptations to not follow Scripture literally: How could you sell all you have and give to the poor, for example, if you were responsible for a wife and children?

In the words of historian Nora Chadwick, "the mysticism of the ancient East [penetrated] to the West, combined with the severe intellectual thought of the Greek Church, and disciplined into a coherent penitential system by the ascetics of the Egyptian and Syrian deserts. This mysticism [introduced] a new system of values with a cleavage in the spiritual life of the West.... The Christian could follow the old path of a good life in the world, or a total dedication of himself to the spiritual life."[111]

[111] Nora Chadwick, *The Age of the Saints in the Early Celtic Church* (London: Oxford University Press, 1961), 9–10.

Monasticism began in Egypt and spread north into Syria in the second half of the fourth century, so that "Syrian" influence should be considered indistinguishable from "Egyptian." There were differences from one center to another, but they shall be considered together as "Eastern." Since these people were both men and women, the term used for them collectively was *monachoi* ("singular people").

They sought God on their own terms, seeking simplicity, seeking to lay aside earthly cares, taking Scripture literally and not worrying about what to eat or what to wear. A monk would pass through three stages of spiritual growth, which were later described by John Cassian: first, gaining control of the flesh and fleshly desires for food and possessions; second, following Christ's teaching radically; and third, achieving the union of one's soul with that of Christ. Solitude was frequently the only way to achieve the third and final stage. That was the stage at which the monk might receive visions or perform miracles.

Fourth-century Egyptian papyri provide the first records of *monachoi* who had abandoned everything in order to live solitary lives in the desert. A hundred years later, *monachoi* numbered in the thousands throughout the entire Roman Empire and beyond.[112] In Upper Egypt was the Thebaid (near Thebes) with its communal living, of which Pachomius was the chief exponent, and in Lower Egypt were Anthony the Great and the cenobites of the Scetis-Nitria region, about which Cassian wrote. From Alexandria some monks went to Syria, which then became a "great province for

[112] "Monasticism," in G. W. Bowersock, Peter Brown, and Oleg Grabar, *Late Antiquity: A Guide to the Postclassical World* (Cambridge: Belknap Press, 1999), 583.

ascetic stars"[113] and a source of considerable liturgical influence. Palestine and Cappadocia also housed monasteries.

No doubt these *monachoi* were rugged individualists, but they shared Eucharist on Sundays, and their sharing of constant prayer is the ancestor of what today is known as the Holy Office. They were known for hospitality to visitors and strangers, as well.

A sense of urgency compelled them, and by design they traveled far.

The Scriptures talk about the imminence of judgment. In the second century, Irenaeus of Lyons stressed the imminent coming of judgment. In the fifth century, Patrick wrote that he was living in the last days; Columbanus wrote the same thing. By the seventh century, as Gaelic literature was flowering, it was a popular belief that the world was going to end in the year 800, six thousand years after creation, according to Irish computation.[114] It was necessary to live as if there were (literally) no tomorrow—and that meant doing everything humanly possible every waking moment to save one's soul.

Traveling far from home was part of dying to self. "The first of the glorious contests is *xeniteia*," wrote Egyptian monk Nilus of Sinai (†430). The third rung of St. John Climacus's *Ladder of Divine Ascent* is "Exile or Pilgrimage." The word comes into Latin as *peregrinatio*. The Irish tradition of *peregrinatio*, of monks traveling far from home just in pursuit of holiness, thus has its roots in Egypt. In the Old Irish seventh-century Cambrai Homily,[115]

[113] P. Brown, *The Cult of the Saints*, 82.

[114] Marina Smyth, "Monastic Culture in Seventh-Century Ireland," *Eolas* 12 (2019): 96, jstor.org/stable/10.2307/26763328.

[115] Text and translation of original by Stokes and Strachan, *Thesaurus Palaeohibernicus*, vol. 2 (Cambridge: University Press, 1903), 244ff.

the same idea is called white martyrdom, "a man's abandoning everything he loves for God's sake."

The Nile Flows into the Shannon

What began in the desert of Egypt did not stay there. Egypt is close to Palestine; by the fourth century, when Christians regularly made pilgrimages to Jerusalem, stops in Egypt became part of the tour. It's hard to imagine tourists standing and gaping at monks coming in and out of their caves and huts—and yet that's exactly what happened. And it was all thanks to the written word.

The St. Anthony whose image appears on so many Irish high crosses is St. Anthony of the Desert. He is considered the father of it all, particularly of the solitary kind of monasticism. St. John Cassian (ca. 360–ca. 435), a saint on the Orthodox, Roman, and Anglican calendars, is credited with bringing the Eastern monastic system to the West. He was a bilingual Latin and Greek speaker who lived twenty-five years in Bethlehem and then in Egypt, where he was formed in the monastic milieu before becoming the confidant of St. John Chrysostom in Constantinople.

Meanwhile, the Nestorian heresy, which denied the unity of Christ's human and divine natures, was on the rise and creating political disorder. As early as the late fourth century, Egyptian refugees were welcomed in Constantinople by Chrysostom when theological arguments turned violent in Egypt. But Chrysostom himself eventually was deposed, and Cassian ended up at Massilia (Marseilles) in Gaul in the mid- to late 410s.

Cassian laid the foundations for orderly life among the increasingly numerous, widely diverse, radically holy individualists who were living in caves and huts. In 420, based on his conversations with monks in Egypt, he wrote *The Institutes on the Monastic Life* to guide a friend to establish a monastery. It analyzed the spiritual growth that was needed for holiness—a sort of how-to manual for those seeking unity with God. He wrote in Latin, but the works were quickly translated into Greek and became universal. Cassian was a major influence on Sts. John Climacus and John of Damascus, important theologians of his day. Pope St. Gregory the Great used his explication of the Egyptian tradition of the eight principal faults as the foundation of his own teaching on the seven deadly sins. Hardly has there been any important saint that has not been influenced by Cassian ever since, from Benedict of Nursia to Ignatius of Loyola to John Henry Newman.

Alexandria, Egypt, was not a peaceful place in the fourth century. The center of Christian learning from the very beginning of the Church, by the beginning of the fourth century it was being torn apart, in some cases literally, by arguments about the divinity of Christ. Those who did not accept the Arian heresy were driven from Egypt. Athanasius, for instance, was banished in 336 to Trier, in today's Germany, and later made his way to Rome. When Emperor Julian became Julian the Apostate, he denounced ascetics, so they fled for their lives—to Gaul, Italy, Spain, and perhaps to Ireland.

Thanks to the written word and the Roman postal system, the monastic phenomenon swept the Christian world as letters and books crossed and recrossed the empire.[116] In 360, St. Athanasius, then patriarch of Alexandria, wrote his biography *Life of Anthony* in Greek, which was soon translated into Latin by St. Evagrius and spread through the West. In 419, the *Lausiac History* was written by Palladius, at the request of the Byzantine court, and spread through the East.

[116] Nora K. Chadwick, *Poetry and Letters in Early Christian Gaul* (London: Bowes, 1955), 227.

Pachomius (†348), who spoke only Coptic and was the leader of the monasteries in Upper Egypt, wrote the first rule. It is very significant that Pachomius's Rule, which became the foundation of Christian monasticism, insists that all members of the community learn to read.[117] Thus, monasteries from the beginning were centers of literacy, scholarship, and literary output. When Irish monasteries became known for their learning and studying, they were merely following the Rule of Pachomius.

Originally written in Greek, Pachomius's Rule was soon translated into Arabic, Armenian, Coptic, Syriac, Latin, and several other languages. St. Athanasius, patriarch of Alexandria, wrote the *Life of Anthony* between 356 and 362, and his book became the equivalent of a global bestseller in its day. In 395, seven monks from a monastery on the Mount of Olives went to see what was going on in Egypt, and *Historia Monachorum in Egypto*, ascribed to Rufinus of Aquileia, was written as a result. It too was a bestseller for centuries. The *Apophthegmata Patrem Aegyptorum* (*Sayings of the Desert Fathers*) began as an oral tradition in Coptic and, when written down, became another widely read and influential book.

How exactly any particular book made it to Ireland is unknown. What is not disputed is that "Irish scholars of the seventh century were remarkably well versed in earlier Christian literature."[118] They "had access to a surprising amount of patristic and canonical literature,"[119] and there were plenty of empty spaces in Ireland to be "deserts" in which holy men and women could abide.

[117] Chadwick, *The Age of the Saints in the Early Celtic Church*, 39.
[118] Smyth, "Monastic Culture in Seventh-Century Ireland," 94.
[119] Ibid., 96.

Adomnán's *Vita Columbae* (*Life of Columcille*) has remarkable parallels with the *Life of Saint Anthony*: both Anthony and Maedoc of Ferns were ferried by angels across rivers they were unable to cross, for instance, and angels dictated the Rule to St. Pachomius and also to St. Brendan of Clonfert.[120] Interestingly too, Columba's aversion to music has a parallel in the writings of the Egyptian desert.[121]

Christianity in Ireland: *Ad Scottos in Christum credentes*

Prosper of Aquitaine's *Chronicle* records that Palladius was sent to Ireland in 431,[122] so it is certain that by the time Patrick arrived, whenever that was, Christians were already present. All evidence suggests that an independent monastic system already had some kind of foothold.

Most scholars agree that southern Ireland probably had the greatest concentration of Christians, who had migrated from Britain or had been converted by contact with Britain. There was a problem, however: Pelagianism was running rampant in Britain at that time. That heresy denied the need for infant

[120] Gregory Telepneff, *The Egyptian Desert in the Irish Bogs* (Etna, CA: Center for Traditionalist Orthodox Studies, 1998), 37.

[121] Derwas J. Chitty, *The Desert a City: An Introduction to the Study of Egyptian and Palestinian Monasticism under the Christian Empire* (Crestwood, NY: St. Vladimir's Seminary Press, 1966), 72.

[122] Prosper of Aquitaine, Epitoma Chronicon (425–455), in Migne, *Patrologia Latina*, LI. Also in T. Mommsen, ed., in *Chronica Minora Saec IV–VII* (Berlin, 1892), https://archive.org/details/chronicaminorasa09momm and at https://daten.digitale-sammlungen.de/bsb00000798/images/index.html?id=00000798&seite=353.

Baptism, based on what it saw as the essential goodness of human nature and the freedom of the human will. It had been declared a heresy at the Council of Carthage in 418, but Pelagius was a Briton, so he had a following at home. In fact, semi-Pelagianism continued in southern Gaul and wasn't condemned until the second Council of Orange in 529.

Prosper also notes, in *Contra Collatorem*,[123] that the reason that bishop was ordained was to "make the barbarian island Christian," which some scholars currently understand as meaning to suppress the Pelagian heresy.[124] Other scholars maintain that Patrick was sent to try to discourage the growing power of monasticism, so that it could be replaced with the diocesan governance model. Pope Celestine, who died shortly after sending Palladius as bishop to Ireland, was particularly voluble in expressing his dislike of monasteries and monastic bishops.[125] The two goals are not mutually incompatible.

Ex Aegypto Transducta: Transplanted from Egypt

The impulse to monasticism is the pursuit of a mystical union with God—at least, the way it was practiced in ancient Ireland, and the way it was practiced in ancient Egypt. The evidence is strong that what began in Ireland—perhaps even the earliest form of Christianity in Ireland—was monasticism in the Egyptian style.

[123] *Contra collatorem*, Migne, *Patrologia Latina* 51, 215–76 at https://la.wikisource.org/wiki/Contra_collatorem.

[124] Harold Mytum, *The Origins of Early Christian Ireland* (London and New York, Routledge, 1992), 40.

[125] Chadwick, *The Age of the Saints*, 31–32.

The seventh-century *Antiphonary of Bangor* is quite explicit about the origins of its monastery in Number 95, "Versiculi Familiae Benchuir":

Domus deliciis plena
Super petram constructa
Necnon vinea vera
Ex Aegypto transducta.

House full of delight
Built on the rock
And indeed true vine
Transplanted from Egypt.[126]

The transplant of desert monasticism to Ireland was successful.

I believe what Bangor said about itself. First of all, why would they make it up? Furthermore, truth was valued so highly that monasteries were the most conservative institutions anywhere. They hung on tenaciously to what their founders had taught, fearing innovation lest it be heresy. The monks would have preserved the tradition of their own origins, as did St. Columba, who admonishes the monks in Adomnán's *Life of Columcille*: "Now, in three ways are men summoned to the knowledge of the Lord and to the membership of His family. This is the first way: the urging and kindling of men by the divine grace to serve the Lord after the example of Paul, and of Anthony, the monk, and of other faithful monks who used to serve God there in Egypt."[127]

[126] F. E., Warren *Antiphonary of Bangor*, part 2 (London: Harrison, 1895), 28, translation by W. H. Marshner.

[127] Whitley Stokes, ed. and trans., *Lives of Saints from the Book of Lismore*, Anecdota Oxoniensia (Oxford: Clarendon Press, 1890), 168–169.

In 1867, the *Irish Ecclesiastical Record* published the "Litany of Aengus Céile Dé." The litany, originally found in the Book of Leinster, included an intercession for "Seven Egyptian monks in Desert Uilaidh." Charles Plummer, a pioneer in the discovery of Irish and Hiberno-Latin literature, included that litany in his collection in 1925, *Litany of Irish Saints 2*, along with the *Litany of Irish Saints 1*, which references "Cerrui from Armenia."[128]

The Mystery of Irish Place-Names

Place-names are a back door to Irish history and literature. It often seems to visitors that every little spot in Ireland has a name. To this day, some places bear the names of events in history or legendary sagas.

Parish boundaries had been set in the twelfth century at the Synod of Kells. The English kept the same parish boundaries, which became the administrative areas used by government. After the Act of Union in 1800, London took over the administration of Ireland. An Ordnance Survey in the 1820s anglicized place-names as it worked its way around the country. That's why there are frequently words hidden in place-names: *kill*, for instance, is an English spelling of *cill*, the Old Irish for "church." *Bally* comes from *baile*, "town"; *carrig* means "rock"; *inis* means "island"; *dun* means "fort." *Donny* was originally *Domhnach*, "Sunday" — a clue that people went to Mass there.

[128] Charles Plummer, *Irish Litanies: Text and Translation* (London: Harrison and Sons, 1925), 57.

The townland, of which there are more than sixty thousand, is the basic unit of Irish rural addresses. Probably a similar system existed around Europe, but only in Ireland has it survived this long.

A historical dictionary of Irish place-names was produced in 1910 by Edmund Hogan, S.J., called the *Onomasticon Goedelicum*. Work is being done now on an updated edition of that. The place-names database of Ireland, Logainm.ie, is still collecting information.

Coptic historian Lucy Awad believes that the Seven were seven monks sent to Lérins in the fourth century, and that they are buried somewhere in Ulster.[129] Stanley Lane-Poole (1854–1931), professor of Arabic Studies at Dublin University, and the late Coptologist Otto Meinardus always shared the view that Irish Christianity was the child of the Egyptian Church.

In his 1910 *Onomasticon Goedelicum*, a dictionary of place-names around Ireland, Fr. Hogan found five hundred instances of the word *díseart* across Ireland.[130] A *díseart* was a place where one or more holy men (and possibly women, though there is less evidence of women hermits at this early stage) at one point in time would have lived: caves or simple wooden bothies in a forest. The presence of even a single holy man was enough for a place to be marked as a *díseart* down through the centuries.

[129] Lucy Awad, "Pray for Olan the Egyptian," Watani, September 7, 2012, https://en.wataninet.com/coptic-affairs-coptic-affairs/religious/pray-for-olan-theegyptian/10886/.

[130] Padraigín Clancy, *Celtic Threads: Exploring the Wisdom of Our Heritage* (Dublin: Veritas, 1999), 73.

The Role of Martin and Ninian

There is solid evidence that monasticism came to Ireland from Gaul, by way of Britain, through the work of St. Martin of Tours and St. Ninian. The monasticism in Gaul would already have been very Egyptian!

In the fourth century, a Roman cavalry soldier named Martin became a Christian, probably around the same time that he met a beggar and cut his cloak in half—the story for which he is best known. After his conversion he wouldn't have been riding a horse, nor probably wearing a cloak, because he became a monk. He settled in Milan, but he was run out of the city because the bishop became an Arian, and Martin did not agree with the Arian heresy. So he went by himself to an island off the coast of Italy. When he heard that the bishop of Poitiers—a man named Hilary—was orthodox, Martin headed to Gaul. For a few years, the two lived as solitary hermits in the same forest. But the inevitable happened, and others wanted to join them, so they became a community of hermits. Word of Martin's holiness spread, and in 372, he was made bishop of Tours. (In those days, bishops were chosen by their clergy for their holiness, not for their fundraising and management skills.) At Marmoutier, a mile or two out of town, he founded another community of hermits.

Some legends claim that Martin (†397) was the uncle of St. Patrick, but in any case, Martin traveled throughout Gaul on missionary journeys from his monastery at Marmoutier. His impact was considerable: he is remembered in carvings on some high crosses, and in the litany in the *Antiphonary of Bangor.*

The early—in legend, the first—British Christian Ninian visited Tours, apparently on his way home after receiving instruction in Rome. Much about Ninian is lost in legend, but the Venerable Bede records that, in 397, Ninian dedicated one of the first stone churches in Britain to Martin when he learned of his death. That was about the highest tribute a monk could offer. It was Ninian's monastery at Whithorn that trained St. Enda, who founded the monastic community on the Aran Islands[131] and is considered the father of Irish monasticism.

The monastery at Whithorn, just across from the northeastern tip of Ireland, has stones engraved with the *chi-rho*, which is definite proof of Eastern influence. Whithorn, then, lies along one of the routes by which Eastern monasticism may have come into Ireland, by way of Britain and Gaul. That entry path, then, would have been into the east of Ireland. By the middle of the fifth century, however, Anglo-Saxons were invading Britain, so further immigration of monks to Ireland would have had to come from the south or the west—more directly from Gaul.

The Influence of Lérins

The monastery at Lérins, an island off the coast of Marseilles, had been founded in 410 by Honoratus, a Gaul who visited St. Anthony's Egypt after his conversion to Christianity. Honoratus sought the desert when he returned home, so he retreated to the island. He was soon followed by hundreds of men similarly motivated, and so he established a monastery. This meant he had to write a rule. Honoratus's Rule followed the strict Pachomian framework of poverty, chastity, obedience, fasting, vigils, studying, and copying. When John Cassian visited Lérins, he was so impressed that he dedicated several of his *Conferences* to Honoratus.

[131] If you're wondering where you heard the name St. Enda before, it may be because you've heard of Scoil Éanna (St. Enda's School). That was the name of Padraic Pearse's famous school, which operated from 1910 to 1916. The girls' school was St. Ita's. Pearse was the leader of the Easter Uprising in 1916.

In the words of historian John Ryan, S.J. (1894–1973): "In the first half of the fifth century Lérins was the holy isle par excellence of the whole Occident."[132] For a long time a pious belief prevailed that monasticism came to Ireland by way of Lérins on the theory that Patrick spent time there after his conversion and escape from Ireland. That idea has been challenged because, among other things, Patrick himself says nothing about being in Gaul.[133] On the other hand, Patrick's prayer habits, as mentioned in his *Confession*, along with his Eastern fasting habits, his poverty and desire for martyrdom, and his creation of consecrated virgins, all suggest monastic influence. In any case, Lérins was a vital link in the transmission of monasticism from the Nile to the Shannon because Lérins is known to have sent missionaries to Llanilltud, the first Christian stronghold in southwest Wales.

Llanilltud had been founded by St. Illtud, who was the mentor of Gildas, who in turn influenced St. Finnian of Clonard, through whom the Lérins tradition was once again introduced into Ireland. Finnian's Rule, known as his *Penitential*, is largely based on Cassian. Gildas, a monk-historian of Britain after the departure of the Romans, died in 570, and Finnian in 549, so chronologically this line of transmission of Egyptian-style monasticism could not have preceded Patrick, no matter which Patrician theory one holds. It could, however, explain a continuing stream of Pachomian monasticism, that is, cenobitic monasticism in the tradition of St. Pachomius, the tradition of monastic community living, into Ireland. St. Anthony was the founder of the eremitic,

[132] John Ryan, S.J., *Irish Monasticism: Origins and Early Development* (Dublin: Four Courts Press, 1930/1992), 640.

[133] David N. Dumville et al., *Saint Patrick, A.D. 493–1993* (Woodbridge, UK: Boydell Press, 1993), 26.

or solitary, tradition: the solitary monk in his *díseart* would have been an Anthonian hermit.

Cassian's *Institutes* raised the standards for monastic life in Gaul. Cassian set high standards in the *Institutes* and the *Conferences*, urging his disciples to "follow the ways of the East, and especially, of Egypt." That especially included focusing on the amendment of faults and the attainment of perfection[134]—a point that resonated in the Irish heart.[135]

Cassian himself was known and read in Ireland, as were other Eastern Fathers. Durham University medievalist Clare Stancliffe finds textual confirmation that Columbanus's Rule, *Regula Monachorum*, is Egyptian in character and shows him to be deeply familiar with Cassian. In her estimation, most of Columbanus's own monastic offices seem to be modeled on Cassian's *Institutes*. Columbanus was familiar with other Fathers too: he quotes St. Basil in a sermon, and Basil's teaching on obedience is recognized as a major source for the first chapter of his Monks' Rule. He appeals to the authority of Jerome, Basil, and Gregory of Nazianzus in his letter to the Gallic bishops. In addition, knowledge of Cassian in Ireland and Iona is elsewhere attested, most explicitly in the *Amra Choluim Chille*, Elegy for Columcille, ascribed to Dallán Forgaill, where the nature of the reference shows that the author

[134] Columba Stewart, *Cassian the Monk*, Oxford Studies in Historical Theology (New York and Oxford: Oxford University Press, 1998), 17.

[135] Columbanus required daily confession of faults. See Clare Stancliffe, "Columbanus's Monasticism and the Sources of His Inspiration: From Basil to the Master?," in *Tome: Studies in Medieval Celtic History and Law in Honour of Thomas Charles-Edwards*, ed. Fiona Edmonds and Paul Russell (Woodbridge, UK: Boydell Press, 2011), 23, jstor.org/stable/10.7722/j.ctt81mmk.8.

was well-acquainted with Cassian's teaching.[136] Cassian is universally recognized by scholars as a major and pervasive influence on the texts of the *Antiphonary of Bangor*.[137] In the eighth century, Cassian was honored on November 25 in the *Martyrology of Óengus*: *Lasin nEoin Cassian assa érchain corann* (that's Old Irish, meaning approximately "with John Cassian whose crown is very fair"; interestingly, *corann* in Modern Irish also means tonsure).

Irish monasticism followed Eastern monastic practices: prayers and fasting on Saturdays and Sundays were different from the rest of the week. As in the East, Irish monastic rules forbid kneeling during the Paschal season or on Sundays. For the first five centuries or so, the universal Church practiced what today is called the seventh-day Sabbath on Saturday and the first-day "Lord's Day" on Sunday. Saturday was the day of rest, while Sunday was the day of worship. Interesting, isn't it, that worship was not considered rest? That may be a clue as to how actively the faithful were supposed to participate in it. It was a series of sixth-century councils in Gaul that "sabbatized" the Lord's Day and downgraded Saturday from a semi-holy day.The prohibition of labor on Sunday became a secular law in England late in the seventh century.[138]

At least in Columba's time, Ireland continued to separate the observance of the Sabbath and Sunday, as Adomnán causes Columba to remind us: "This day is called in the sacred books Sabbath which

[136] Stancliffe, "Columbanus's Monasticism," 27.

[137] Jane Stevenson, review of *The Antiphonary of Bangor*, by Michael Curran, *Peritia* 5 (2009): 435, www.brepolsonline-net.ucc.idm.oclc.org.

[138] *Dictionnaire d'archéologie chrétienne et de liturgie*, 4.938.43, 950–956, cited in Michael W. Herren and Shirley Ann Brown, *Christ in Celtic Christianity: Britain and Ireland from the Fifth to the Tenth Century* (Cambridge: Cambridge University Press, 2004), 109.

is interpreted rest. And truly this day is for me a Sabbath because it is my last day of this present laborious life. In it after my toilsome labours I kept Sabbath: and at midnight of this following venerated Lord's day, in the language of the Scriptures I shall go the way of the fathers. For now my Lord Jesus Christ deigns to invite me."[139]

Antiphonal singing (alternating verses sung by different groups) had been done by ancient Hebrews, and it was practiced throughout the East, especially in Egypt. It was not introduced into the Gallican liturgy until the seventh century—yet, along with other distinctive Eastern elements, it was practiced in Irish monasteries before then.[140] Also, the *Ratio de Cursus* (see chapter 7) confirmed that antiphonal singing was present in Ireland.

Daily private Mass is unknown in the East,[141] and it was unknown in antique Ireland. There is evidence that the early Irish Church, in accordance with the custom of the East, "rejected the celebration of Masses in honor of individual saints."[142]

Cassian was also the inspiration behind one of Ireland's first surviving works to express Christian ideas in Irish, the *Apgitir Chrábaid*,

[139] Adomnán of Iona, *Adomnán's Life of Columba*, ed. and trans. Alan Orr Anderson and Marjorie Ogilvie Anderson (London and New York: Thomas Nelson, 1961), 523.

[140] Peter Jeffery, "Eastern and Western Elements in the Irish Monastic Prayer of the Hours," in *The Divine Office in the Latin Middle Ages: Methodology and Source Studies, Regional Developments, Hagiography*, ed. Margot E. Fassler and Rebecca A. Baltzer, 99–143 (New York and Oxford: Oxford University Press, 2000), 111.

[141] Josef A. Jungmann, *The Early Liturgy, to the Time of Gregory the Great*, Liturgical Studies (Notre Dame: University of Notre Dame Press, 1959), 215.

[142] John Hennig, "The Feasts of the Blessed Virgin in the Ancient Irish Church," *Irish Ecclesiastical Record* 71, 5th series (March 1954): 162.

or "The Alphabet of Piety," which, in the opinion of literature scholars Clancy and Markus, "could actually be otherwise translated, as ... 'The Fundamentals of Monastic Life,'" since some early sections of the work so strongly echo Cassian's *Conferences*, 24:26, and book 4 of his *Institutes*.[143] "The title, which may well be original, sheds some light on the text's purpose: it describes the basics of living as a monk in a community."[144] The *Apgitir* refers not only to Cassian but also includes references to Old Testament wisdom literature, to the non-Roman form of renunciation at Baptism ("three waves pass over"), and to conversion (*athlaech*). Its employment of metrical rules from the oral tradition of the *filidh* marks it as coming from the very early period of Irish monasticism.[145]

Whether or not it was intended as a textbook for monastic life, however, the *Apgitir* is remarkable poetry: "In the lucid conciseness of its pregnant, interlocking teachings, the *Apgitir Chrábaid* often approaches the diction of poetry ... [with its] ... rhythmic cadences and chains of alliteration.... It was clearly intended to sink deep into the memories of those who heard it and, once absorbed, to guide them from within."[146] The ancient Druids were able to memorize vast amounts of text because they were in metrical form; the early Celtic Christians did the same.

Along with the *Apgitir*, the *Saltair na Rann*, the Psalms in poetry, is considered one of the oldest Irish religious poems. Particularly

[143] Thomas Owen Clancy and Gilbert Markus, *Iona: The Earliest Poetry of a Celtic Monastery* (Edinburgh: Edinburgh University Press, 1995), 197, jstor.org/stable/10.3366/j.ctvxcrp6p.14.

[144] Ibid., 196.

[145] Peter O'Dwyer, O. Carm., *Towards a History of Irish Spirituality* (Blackrock, Co. Dublin: Columba Press, 1995), 30.

[146] John Carey, *King of Mysteries: Early Irish Religious Writings* (Dublin: Four Courts Press, 2000), 232.

interesting about the *Saltair* is that it's partly Egyptian! In 1947, ecclesiastical historian Archdale King said that it was "simply an Irish eleventh or twelfth century edition of the Book of Adam and Eve, composed in the fifth or sixth century in Egypt, and known in no other European country save Ireland."[147]

In 1882, Dr. Whitely Stokes published *Anecdota Oxoniensia*, medieval series. Volume 1 includes 162 biblical poems attributed to Aengus the Culdee.[148] He wrote,

> The eleventh and twelfth are identical with the *Book of Adam and Eve*, translated by S. C. Malan, D.D. (London: 1882). This work was composed in Egypt about the sixth or seventh century, whence it was translated into Aethiopic. Some few years ago it was discovered in Aethiopia, and published in Germany by Dr. E. Trump, of the University of Munich. The identity of the tradition in both cases is fixed by one point. Both place Adam's skull or body in Golgotha, where it remained till Christ's cross was planted in it. Dr. Malan says the original work was unknown in the West, and presents no trace of Hellenic influence. If so, its presence in Ireland is very striking.[149]

The tradition that Adam was buried on what became Calvary survives in the Eastern Church and explains why Crucifixion icons

[147] King, *The Rites of Eastern Christendom*, vol. 1, 375.

[148] Aengus was a ninth-century bishop, a member of the interesting community known as Céli Dé that had been founded by Máel Ruain at Tallaght. The monastery at Tallaght produced a couple of significant devotional books that have survived.

[149] George T. Stokes, D.D., *Ireland and the Celtic Church*, 6th ed., rev. Hugh Jackson Lawlor, D.D. (London: Society for Promoting Christian Knowledge, 1907), 216n1.

often show a skull buried beneath the Cross—which, again, makes it entirely plausible that sixth-century Ethiopian devotional texts were being reproduced in ninth-century Ireland.

Further textual proof of connections with Egypt: word-for-word parallels between the *Antiphonary of Bangor* and the Coptic *Book of the Hours* were found by historian Fr. Joseph Crehan, S.J. In his dynamic article, "The Liturgical Trade Route: East to West," Crehan wrote that a Coptic Book of Hours published in 1970 includes a *Gloria in excelsis* that has an extension using versicles from psalms that match some of those in the *Antiphonary of Bangor.* Hans Quecke's edition of the *Antiphonary* numbers these as lines 31–43. The *Antiphonary of Bangor* contains nine out of thirteen versicles: lines 31–32, 39–40, 41–43, and 37 and 38. More surprising is that versicles 39 and 40 are not from Scripture but are found in the Te Deum. Since all the Coptic citations of psalms are worded according to the Greek and not the Coptic Psalter (where these differ), it is natural to suppose that Greek originals for the compilation existed and that this was prior to the copying of *Codex Alexandrinus.* "The versicles which got into the Latin *Te Deum* must then have travelled from the East to Ireland, and must also have become known somehow to the author of the *Te Deum*, whoever he was."[150]

This is new textual proof of ongoing exchange of ideas between Irish and Eastern monasteries that would not have been possible to find until 1970!

Psalms, Prostrations, and *Eulogia*

Columbanus absorbed the strictness of the East and wrote it into his own Rule. Like Cassian before him, he found Gaulish

[150] Crehan, "The Liturgical Trade Route," 89.

monasteries too lax. The Irish had adopted the Pachomian model, but Pachomius had put limits on the austerity in Egypt—whereas in Ireland "little effort at restraint can be discovered."[151] Food, sleep, clothes, furniture were all kept to the minimum necessary to survive—at least by Columbanus.

Some unique Irish monastic practices can be traced straight back to Egypt. For instance, to this day in Eastern Orthodox churches, kneeling and prostrations are forbidden between Easter and Pentecost. The same rule was included in number ten of the *Regula Coenobialis* of Columbanus.[152]

So, too, with the practice of genuflection. Or was it prostration? Sometimes the Latin language does not make a clear distinction, and Roman Catholic scholars in the post-Reformation era would be disposed to read what was familiar to them into their interpretation, namely genuflection.

Irish monasteries mandated a high number of genuflections performed by the monks. Dom Louis Gougaud, O.S.B. (1877–1942), was a pioneer in the field of Irish ecclesiastical history; among thousands of other articles, he wrote the "Liturgie Celtique" article in the definitive 1907 *Dictionnaire d'Archéologie et de Liturgie*. He was a skeptic of Eastern connections with Ireland, but on the subject of genuflection and prostration, confronting the record that St. Jarlath is said to have made three hundred prostrations a night and three hundred more in the day, and Aengus the Culdee the same, he had to admit, "This kind of mathematical mortification and adoration was not, however, peculiar to the Celtic saints. The Oriental monks practiced it before them."

[151] Ryan, *Irish Monasticism*, 643.

[152] Dom Louis Gougaud, *Christianity in Celtic Lands* (Dublin: Four Courts Press, 1932/1992), 559ff.

The Book of Lismore "mentions a sinner who, having retired to a solitary island, recited seven times during the day the *Beatus* and the Psalms, while he prostrated himself a hundred times." According to Gougaud, "Cassian further remarks that in his time the monks of Southern Gaul made it a rule to prostrate themselves at the end of each Psalm." He also notes that the custom passed into the rules of Sts. Isidore of Seville and Fructuosus of Braga: "Let us note, however, that in these texts it is a question of prostration and not of mere genuflection. In the writings of Cassian genuflection appears as the first stage, so to speak, of prostration."

The fifth rubric in the ninth-century Stowe Missal, *indablu tuair*, harks back to a much older Eastern usage, and refers to the bread that will be consecrated and consumed as the "Lamb."[153] This tradition requires explanation.

Originally, of course, the Eucharist was leavened bread offered by a member of the congregation. When the Eucharist is derived from a round loaf, or *prosphoron*, a circle is cut from the center. This circle is known as "the Lamb." Nowadays before baking, a special seal is impressed upon the center of the loaf, which when cut out becomes the Holy Eucharist. This is the practice in Eastern Catholic and Orthodox churches today. The rest of the loaf is not consecrated and is called *eulogia* in Greek.

A custom recorded in the Rule of Columbanus could be that of *Eulogia*. All the bread is part of the offertory, but only the Lamb is consecrated. In Eastern monasteries, after the Divine Liturgy, the Eulogia is carried from the church to the refectory accompanied by prayers and hymns. When the final blessing is given at the end of the common meal, the Eulogia is elevated, and the brethren partake of it.

[153] Rev. Charles Plummer, *Irish Litanies: Text and Translation* (London: Harrison and Sons, 1925), 444.

It seems that St. Columba kept this custom in his monastery. Adomnán mentions it in the *Vita Columbae*. In one story, Columba sent his monk Silnán to cure people and livestock by bringing "healing bread," which he dipped in water to create *aqua benedictionis*, which effected the cure. Another episode refers to *eulogia* by name. In book 2, 2.13, St. Cainnech at Aghaboe was "beginning to break the bread of blessing," the Eulogia, when he suddenly left the table and ran to the church, in such haste that he wore only one shoe. "We cannot have dinner at this time," he said, "for St. Columcille's boat is even now in peril on the sea." In 2.5 of the *Vita*, Columba sent a blessing to Mogain to cure her broken hip, and also a "pinewood box with a blessing inside it" along with instructions that the contents of the box should be dipped in water and then poured over the broken hip while all prayed for her full health. Since this text immediately follows the account of the blessed bread curing the plague, Fr. O'Donoghue considers it "at least possible that here also the *eulogia* was used."[154]

Further suggestion of the prevalence of this custom is that the *Regula Coenobialis* of Columbanus, part 4, stipulates a penance for "he who unwashed receives the Holy Bread, twelve strokes." Penance for unworthy reception of the Eucharist was far greater.

How the Irish Invented Penance (Sort Of)

A characteristic considered unique to Irish monasticism was the recitation of the Three Fifties, or the entire one hundred fifty psalms, at one time. It is often cited as an example of how demanding and stringent Irish monasticism was. Yet this was very much an Egyptian transplant that came to Ireland intact.

[154] O'Donoghue, "Insular Chrismals," 106–107.

Fundamental to all monasticism was the attempt to take literally the scriptural command to "pray constantly" (1 Thess. 5:17). In Egypt, praying constantly meant chanting the Psalms continuously, in numerical order and for extended periods of time, sometimes even the entire Psalter in a single night.[155] In the opinion of musicologist James W. McKinnon (1932–1999), Cassian's rule, *De institutis coenobiorum*, written sometime after 415, "is clearly an adaptation of Eastern practice to the circumstances of his own Gallican communities of monks and nuns."[156]

The practice came into Ireland as the "Three Fifties," and the monastic recitation of the Psalter became the ancestor of the medieval and monastic Office.[157] The Three Fifties were frequently recited while the monk held his arms outstretched in the posture of the cross—*cros-figell*, or, as it is called in art history, the *orans* posture. The *cros-figell* originated in the Rule of Pachomius, it must be noted.[158] Hennig reported in a footnote in 1942, referring to this custom as *le prier le bras en Croix*, that "this practice is still observed in Lough Derg."[159] As late as the ninth century in Ireland, the monastic rules of Céli Dé, a back-to-the-basics reform movement, stipulated that a monk was forbidden to eat until he had said all 150 psalms.[160] For penance, sometimes the Three Fifties had to be recited while the penitent stood in cold water up to his armpits.

[155] James W. McKinnon, "The Origins of the Western Office," in *The Divine Office in the Latin Middle Ages*, 63–73, 67.

[156] Ibid., 71.

[157] Ibid., 72.

[158] Telepneff, *The Egyptian Desert in the Irish Bogs*, 35.

[159] John Hennig, "The Historical Work of Louis Gougaud," *Irish Historical Studies* 3, no. 10 (September 1942): 183, jstor.org/stable/30006631.

[160] Jeffery, "Eastern and Western Elements in the Irish Monastic Prayer of the Hours," 102.

The practice of private Confession is also a legacy of Irish monasteries to the universal Church.

For the first thousand years of the Church, there was no sacrament of Reconciliation. Very, very early, there was public Confession during the celebration of the liturgy before the reception of Communion, but after that custom died away, there was only public Confession for public sins, like offering incense to the gods, or adultery—and it was followed by public penance, which sometimes lasted for the rest of one's life.

Within the small group of a monastic community, a different model could and did develop, one oriented toward an individual's spiritual growth.

Cassian had described how the wise men of Egypt delineated the eight principal vices and the antithetical virtues by which these vices were cured, with most of the formulas based on canons from synods of bishops of the East. Each sin was spoken of as an illness. The duty of a spiritual father was to search out and to apply the correct "medicine."

Based on Cassian's list, a penitential was written by Irish abbot Cummian around 650, to standardize which deeds merited which punishments. The notion of a book listing all the sins and the penances for each caught on throughout Europe and was used for centuries thereafter. The penitential system was strict by today's standard, but it brought consistency and predictability.

So the Irish invented penitentials.

Penances for monks were dramatic.[161] For instance, one old penitential demanded scourging: seven hundred properly administered lashes seven times, or two hundred genuflections properly

[161] D. A. Binchy, "The Old-Irish Table of Penitential Commutations," *Ériu* 19 (1962): 47–72, https://www.jstor.org/stable/30006859.

made, bending the body to the ground scrupulously.[162] Or that the sinner hold the cross-vigil posture through the chanting of fifty psalms, the arms not touching the sides until the chanting is over, even though there be nothing else to support him.[163] Or this: a black fast for three days without eating, drinking, or sleeping: one night spent in water, another naked on nettles, the third on nutshells.[164] Or to spend three days and three nights in a grave with a dead body without drinking, eating, or sleeping.[165]

Obviously, saying all one hundred fifty psalms was not something a farmer could do when the cows had to be milked. Yet the goal was that all Christians should move beyond sin and guilt. All needed a spiritual guide. To meet this need there arose the custom of the *anamchara* (soul friend), later *pater confessarius*. In the monastic context, the *anamchara* would be a fellow ascetic, but kings and princes, nobles and commoners all had *anamchairde*, and the relationship involved serious obligations. Maeldithruib, for instance, was received as a penitent by his *anamchara* only when he agreed to fast for forty days and nights on bread and water.

The most lasting Irish contribution was to make the process of Confession and penance accessible to the laity. Finnian of Clonard (470–549) was an abbot who had a heart for the lay faithful. He knew that people would not confess their secret sins if everybody in the community would know about them. So rule number ten in Finnian's *Penitential* includes this stunning innovation: "For, we say, sins are to be absolved in secret by penance and by very diligent devotion of heart and body."[166]

[162] Ibid., nos. 15–16, 63.
[163] Ibid., no. 18, 63.
[164] Ibid., no. 27, 67.
[165] Ibid., no. 26, 65.
[166] *Penitential of Finnian*, no. 10.

Private (secret) confession of failings can be traced back to the Syriac *Didascalia Apostolorum*, which claims to be written at the time of the Council of Jerusalem by the apostles, but which scholars date to the third century. The *Didascalia* urges a private hearing "between me and thee," and resort to public penance comes only after a visit by the bishop and deacons has failed. It should not be a surprise that "Irish monks should adopt for confession the spiritual practices of Eastern monks, about whom many tales are told in the *Apophthegmata Patrum* concerning their private penance, undertaken when they came from the world to start monastic life," comments Crehan.[167]

With the help of an *anamchara* a sin could be confessed, and the vice behind it could be identified and a spiritual cure pursued either inside or outside of a monastery. The duty of the spiritual guide was to draw on his wisdom to search out and apply the correct medicine appropriate to each failing. In Finnian's *Penitential*, the idea of "tariffed penance" was becoming visible.

Consider these items: if a cleric has started a quarrel, "he shall do penance for half a year with an allowance of bread and water and for a whole year abstain from wine and meats, and thus he will be reconciled to the altar"(number six). "But if he is a layman," it continues, "he shall do penance for a week, since he is a man of this world and his guilt is lighter in this world and his reward less in the world to come" (number seven). If a sin has been hidden for a long time, the punishment is worse: three years on bread and water and loss of clerical office, and for three more years abstention from meat and wine (number eleven).

In practice, penances were often moderated according to the penitent's station in life. Out of this developed the practice of

[167] Crehan, "The Liturgical Trade Route," 94.

"commutation," or "tariffed penance," through which a substantial reduction of the prescribed penance could be obtained upon the recommendation of the *anamchara*. By the seventh century, the system of "tariffed penance" developed. This meant making the punishment fit the crime: a penitent's heart and motive were to be considered, and could mitigate the guilt of the sin: "This is carefully to be considered in all penance: the length of time anyone remains in his faults; with what learning he is instructed; with what passion he is assailed; with what courage he stands; with what tearfulness he is seen to be afflicted."

Columbanus was famous for his sternness: his *Regula Coenobialis* and *Penitential* imposed strict penalties on monks for infractions as small as coughing at the wrong time. But Columbanus is also credited with taking to Europe the very humane tradition of personal penance,[168] which became the foundation of the sacrament of Penance as it is known in the Western Church.

Confession, forgiveness, and amendment of life were done for spiritual reasons—but making repentance and forgiveness accessible to the laity had public benefits too: historian Richard Fletcher notes that it was shortly after Columbanus introduced the practice of private Confession and penance to the violent Franks that the nature of the Frankish aristocracy changed, between 575 and 625, and became more cohesive and less inclined to wage war.

[168] Brendan Bradshaw, "The Wild and Woolly West: Early Irish Christianity and Latin Orthodoxy," in W.J. Sheils and Diana Wood, *The Churches, Ireland and the Irish: Papers Read at the 1987 Summer Meeting and the 1988 Winter Meeting of the Ecclesiastical History Society*, 1–23 (Oxford: Blackwell, 1989), 13.

The Twelve Apostles of Irish Monasticism

St. Finnian of Clonard first founded the monastery at Skellig Michael before he moved to the banks of the Boyne River to found the monastery at Clonard. Clonard was famous for the training it gave to monks: it grew to have three thousand students! Among them were twelve particularly famous ones, who founded other monasteries, of course. They are affectionately called the Twelve Apostles of Irish Monasticism, and they all died toward the end of the sixth century.

Anybody looking for boys' names would do well to review the list: St. Ciarán of Saighir, St. Ciarán of Clonmacnoise, St. Brendan of Birr, St. Brendan of Clonfert (the Navigator), St. Columba of Terryglass, St. Columba, St. Mobhí of Glasnevin, St. Ruadhán of Lorrha, St. Seanán of Iniscathay, St. Ninnidh of Lough Erne, St. Laisrén, and St. Canice.

The innovation of "tariffed penance" was challenged in due time, after Irish monks had carried the practice to England. When questioned on the matter, Archbishop Theodore of Canterbury balanced St. Basil's teaching and Eastern monastic customs and did not resist the Irish system, which had become common in Britain.

Theodore, the bishop of Canterbury (602–690), protected it, perhaps tolerating what he remembered from his own sojourn in the East. He had studied at Antioch, then fled to Constantinople for a time before joining a community of Eastern monks in Rome, where his learning attracted attention. He was unexpectedly nominated as archbishop of Canterbury in "Great Britain"—"by which the East Romans meant 'Outer, Faraway' Britain," says antique historian Peter Brown, much as we today might regard an appointment to be bishop of Outer Mongolia. It meant that Rome really wasn't paying much attention to Britain or to Ireland. However, Brown maintains, "The success of his 'school' at Canterbury shows that Ireland and Britain were joined in a single 'sound-chamber' where every word spoken in one island resonated in the other."[169]

The Divine Office, Baptism, and Communion

The Divine Office was modeled after the Palestinian monastic liturgy, which itself grew out of Egyptian monastic practice blended with urban and cathedral traditions in Palestine. The goal was to achieve the biblical admonition to "pray constantly." "This method of prayer became known in Gaul through the writings of Cassian and indeed it was established at Marseilles and Lérins,"[170] whence (presumably) it made its way to Ireland.

The so-called "unique" Irish adaptation that the longer the night, the more psalms were said—twenty-four on an ordinary summer night, but up to seventy-five on a longer winter night[171]—is in fact similar to what is found in Cassian's *Institutes.*[172]

Evidence also supports that these sacraments were administered in the Irish Church in the same way as in the East. There is a variety of independent evidence that the method of receiving Communion in Ireland followed the original Eastern customs.

[169] Peter Brown, *The Rise of Western Christendom: Triumph and Diversity A.D. 200–1000* (Malden, MA, Oxford, England, and Victoria, Australia: Blackwell, 2003), 369–370.

[170] Michael Curran, *The Antiphonary of Bangor* (Dublin: Irish Academic Press, 1984), 181.

[171] Ibid., 183.

[172] Telepneff, *The Egyptian Desert in the Irish Bogs*, 52.

Ryan noted that monks made three prostrations on their way to the altar to receive Communion, an Eastern monastic custom. Communion was administered under both species. As late as the sixteenth century, Ryan noted that infants received Communion by the priest placing a drop on their tongue.[173]

Archaeological "mysteries" from Tallaght, an eighth-century site of a major monastery, are probably baptismal fonts. They are granite boulders carved into the shape of giant bowls. Both measure more than three feet by three feet across, and are about one and a half feet deep. Comments archaeologist Chris Corlett, who wrote about them in *Archaeology Ireland* in 2012:[174] "If it was really designed for infant baptism, however, it is worth considering whether it was designed for partial submersion or even full immersion. It is certainly hard to believe that this font was designed for conventional baptism with a palmful or ladleful of water."

Mr. Corlett is on the right track. In those days, Baptism was by full immersion, as it is to this day in the Eastern Church.

Before I leave the topic of monasticism, let me leave you with one final thought. In modern Ireland, people more and more say "Haigh" (hi) to one another. But the traditional greeting, which fortunately is still taught in Gaeilge textbooks, is "Dia duit," or "God to you." Where does that traditional greeting come from? Here's my own idea.

Archdale King's study of the liturgy of the Western Church reveals that "peace be to all" is the customary greeting in the East, except for—guess where?—in Egypt![175] In Egypt, the customary

[173] John Ryan, "The Sacraments in the Early Irish Church," *Studies: An Irish Quarterly Review* 51, no. 204 (Winter 1962): 511–513.

[174] Chris Corlett, "A Font of Majuscule Proportions at Tallaght," *Archaeology Ireland* 26, no. 3 (Autumn 2012): 6.

[175] King, *Liturgy of the Roman Church*, 242.

greeting is "The Lord be with you." In other words, "Dominus vobiscum" shows, in King's words, "Alexandrine parentage."

With its Alexandrine parentage, "Dia duit," or "God be with you," moved beyond the monastery into the common parlance!

Another reminder of the Eastern Christian nature of Irish Christianity is the names of the days of the week. Monday and Tuesday are *Luan* and *Márta*, cognate with modern French and Spanish in revealing Latin origins. But now watch this: Wednesday is *Céadaoin*, Friday is *Aoine*. *Céad* means first. What does *Aoine* mean? Fasting! So, Wednesday was the first day of fasting, and Friday was the other day of fasting. In the early Church, and to this day in Eastern monasteries, Wednesday and Friday were both days of fasting. Gaeilge remembers!

For Further Reference

Adomnán of Iona. *Adomnán's Life of Columba.* Edited and translated by Alan Orr Anderson and Marjorie Ogilvie Anderson. London and New York: Thomas Nelson, 1961.

——. *Life of St. Columba.* Translated by Richard Sharpe. London: Penguin Books, 1995.

Awad, Lucy. "Pray for Olan the Egyptian." Watani. September 7, 2012. https://en.wataninet.com/coptic-affairs-coptic-affairs/religious/pray-for-olan-theegyptian/10886/.

Bieler, Ludwig. *The Irish Penitentials.* Dublin: Dublin Institute for Advanced Studies, 1975.

Binchy, D. A. "The Old-Irish Table of Penitential Commutations." *Ériu* 19 (1962): 47–72, https://www.jstor.org/stable/30006859.

Bowersock, G. W., Peter Brown, and Oleg Grabar. *Late Antiquity: A Guide to the Postclassical World.* Cambridge: Belknap Press, 1999.

Brown, Peter. *The Rise of Western Christendom: Triumph and Diversity A.D. 200–1000.* Malden, MA, Oxford, England, and Victoria, Australia: Blackwell, 2003.

Chadwick, Nora K. *The Age of the Saints in the Early Celtic Church.* London: Oxford University Press, 1963.

——. *Poetry and Letters in Early Christian Gaul.* London: Bowes, 1955.

Chitty, Derwas J. *The Desert a City: An Introduction to the Study of Egyptian and Palestinian Monasticism under the Christian Empire.* Crestwood, NY: St. Vladimir's Seminary Press, 1966.

Clancy, Thomas Owen, and Gilbert Markus. *Iona: The Earliest Poetry of a Celtic Monastery.* Edinburgh: Edinburgh University Press, 1995. jstor.org/stable/10.3366/j.ctvxcrp6p.14.

Corlett, Chris. "A Font of Majuscule Proportions at Tallaght." *Archaeology Ireland* 26, no. 3 (Autumn 2012): 6.

Dumville, David N., et al. *Saint Patrick, A.D. 493–1993.* Woodbridge, UK: Boydell Press, 1993.

Finnian, St. *Penitential of Finnian.* https://medievalbruno.weebly.com/uploads/2/7/5/2/2752477/the_penitential_of_finnian.pdf.

Gougaud, Dom Louis. *Christianity in Celtic Lands.* Dublin: Four Courts Press, 1932/1992.

Hennig, John. "The Historical Work of Louis Gougaud." *Irish Historical Studies* 3, no. 10 (September 1942): 180–186. jstor.org/stable/30006631.

——. "The Feasts of the Blessed Virgin in the Ancient Irish Church." *Irish Ecclesiastical Record*, 5th series (March 1954): 161–167.

Herren, Michael W., and Shirley Ann Brown. *Christ in Celtic Christianity: Britain and Ireland from the Fifth to the Tenth Century.* Cambridge: Cambridge University Press, 2004.

Jeffery, Peter. "Eastern and Western Elements in the Irish Monastic Prayer of the Hours." In *The Divine Office in the Latin Middle Ages: Methodology and Source Studies, Regional Developments, Hagiography*, edited by Margot E. Fassler and Rebecca A. Baltzer, 99–143. New York and Oxford: Oxford University Press, 2000.

McKinnon, James W. "The Origins of the Western Office." In *The Divine Office in the Latin Middle Ages: Methodology and Source Studies, Regional Developments, Hagiography*, edited by Margot E. Fassler and Rebecca A. Baltzer, 63–73. New York and Oxford: Oxford University Press, 2000.

O'Dwyer, Peter, O. Carm. *Towards a History of Irish Spirituality.* Blackrock, Co. Dublin: Columba Press, 1995.

Plummer, Rev. Charles. *Irish Litanies: Text and Translation.* London: Harrison and Sons, 1925.

Ryan, John, S.J. *Irish Monasticism: Origins and Early Development.* Dublin: Four Courts Press, 1930/1992.

——. "The Sacraments in the Early Irish Church." *Studies: An Irish Quarterly Review* 51, no. 204 (Winter 1962): 508–520.

Smyth, Marina. "Monastic Culture in Seventh-Century Ireland." *Eolas* 12 (2019): 64–101. jstor.org/stable/10.2307/26763328.

Stancliffe, Clare. "Columbanus's Monasticism and the Sources of His Inspiration: From Basil to the Master?" In *Tome: Studies in Medieval Celtic History and Law in Honour of Thomas Charles-Edwards*, edited by Fiona Edmonds and Paul Russell. Woodbridge, UK: Boydell Press, 2011. jstor.org/stable/10.7722/j.ctt81mmk.8.

Stevenson, Jane. Review of *The Antiphonary of Bangor*, by Michael Curran. *Peritia* 5 (2009): 430–437. www.brepolsonline-net.ucc.idm.oclc.org.

Stewart, Columba. *Cassian the Monk.* Oxford Studies in Historical Theology. New York and Oxford: Oxford University Press, 1998.

Stokes, George T., D.D. *Ireland and the Celtic Church.* 6th ed. Revised by Hugh Jackson Lawlor, D.D. London: Society for Promoting Christian Knowledge, 1907.

Stokes, Whitley, ed. and trans. *Lives of Saints from the Book of Lismore.* Anecdota Oxoniensia. Oxford: Clarendon Press, 1890.

Telepneff, Gregory. *The Egyptian Desert in the Irish Bogs*. Etna, CA: Center for Traditionalist Orthodox Studies, 1998.

Warren, F. E. *Antiphonary of Bangor*. Part 2. London: Harrison, 1895.

Chapter 6

Marian Devotion in Ancient Ireland

Prior to the tenth century, there simply was no devotional (i.e., non-liturgical) literature in praise of the Virgin Mary anywhere in Europe in the vernacular—*except in Ireland.*[176]

In Ireland, there was abundant Marian devotion, manifested particularly in hymnody, by the seventh century. The presence of this devotion is further evidence of Eastern influence in pre-Norman Christianity in Ireland. That this devotion would appear earlier in Ireland than elsewhere in Europe should come as no surprise, as Ireland had continuous contact with the Church in the East, but more tenuous connections to Rome in the early monastic days. And the first Marian prayer known had been composed in Egypt in the third century.[177]

The late Jaroslav Pelikan, one of the world's experts in Christian and medieval intellectual history, stated it succinctly: devotion to Mary, as well as the development of Marian doctrine, came "first

[176] Hennig, "The Feasts of the Blessed Virgin in the Ancient Irish Church," 162.

[177] Luigi Gambero, *Mary in the Middle Ages: The Blessed Virgin Mary in the Thought of Medieval Latin Theologians*, trans. Thomas Buffer (San Francisco: Ignatius Press, 2005), 69.

and most fully in the Greek-speaking East, where the ascetical and devotional precursors of the doctrine of Mary were present long before they appeared in the West."[178]

Devotion to Mary was originally a popular (almost *populist*) movement. The lay faithful loved her before it was officially approved —hence the non-liturgical nature of the earliest devotions to her. Soon after 313, when Christianity became legal, pilgrimages are recorded in Palestine, and Ephesus, where Mary was said to have lived; by the eighth century St. Willibald, the first English pilgrim to leave a written record, told how he had gone to the place in Galilee where Gabriel had first come to Our Lady.[179] It would seem that the earliest pilgrims in Palestine visited the spots where living memory recorded she had been present, and folk memory kept the tradition alive. In Ireland, Marian devotion took on tangible form: a portion of a garment she had made for Christ and a lock of her hair were treasured as relics.[180]

At a University College Cork seminar on *De Finibus* in 2011, Fr. Martin McNamara of the Irish Biblical Society wove together many threads linking the early appearance in Ireland of Marian devotion with very early writings in the East. Apocryphal literature was available in Ireland at the Irish Church's beginnings, its *initia*, he emphasized; in his presentation he appealed for more study of the beginnings of Christianity in Ireland.

[178] Jaroslav Pelikan, *Mary through the Centuries: Her Place in the History of Culture* (New Haven, CT: Yale University Press, 1996), 65.

[179] Donald Attwater, *A Dictionary of Mary* (New York: P.J. Kenedy and Sons, 1955), 220.

[180] James Carney, "Old Ireland and Her Poetry," in *Old Ireland*, ed. Robert McNally, S.J., 147–172 (New York: Fordham University Press, 1965), 165.

McNamara demonstrated that early Irish scholars had access to the commentary of Theodore of Mopsuestia in Julian of Eclanum's translation, and to works based on it, which were based on an Antiochene understanding of the text. Antioch and Alexandria had very different approaches to understanding Scripture, which was the source of theological arguments back in the day, and Theodore of Mopsuestia was eventually condemned for some of his ideas.

Apocrypha in Ireland

Biblical apocrypha are texts, often called "Gospels," that were for one reason or another not accepted into the official canon of Scripture. One set of heretical New Testament apocrypha was the Gnostic Gospels, but they never reached Ireland. There were other apocryphal New Testament gospels all around the East in the early days of the Church, written in Latin, Greek, Syriac, Georgian, Ethiopian, and Coptic. Ireland had many of them. They were not necessarily all dangerous to the Faith. For instance, the apocryphal *Protoevangelium of James* is the only source the Church has for the name of the Blessed Virgin's mother, and also the earliest witness for the Marian feasts of today.[181]

Two others were the *Acts of Thomas* and the *Transitus Mariae*. There are versions of both of those in Old Irish in eighth-century manuscripts. The *Childhood Deeds of Jesus*, also known as the Infancy Narrative, goes back to the second century, and can be found in manuscripts in Greek, Arabic, Ethiopic, Syriac, and Slavonic, as well as Irish. It was formerly known as the *Gospel of Thomas*, though

[181] Thomas O'Loughlin, "The Many Feasts of Mary in the Contemporary Catholic Liturgy: A Study of the Persistence of the Protoevangelium of James within Liturgical Memory," *Maria* 1, no. 1 (July 2021): 1–20.

there's no reason to think that Doubting Thomas or any other contemporary of Christ had any hand in writing it. It includes a section known as the *Childhood Deeds of Jesus*, which had worldwide readership in its day.

The *Transitus* belongs to a genre known as "apocryphal romance" and is an account of the last hours, death, burial, and Assumption into Heaven of the Virgin Mary—all of which was referred to as the Dormition, or falling asleep. There are only a few copies of the *Transitus* in existence, one in Oxford, one in Paris, and one at Trinity College Dublin. Dating back to the second century, it is the first record of the belief in Mary's bodily Assumption into Heaven. In 1997, Pope John Paul II asked, "How can we not see that the Assumption of the Blessed Virgin has always been part of the faith of the Christian people?" and cited the *Transitus* as evidence, calling it an "intuition of faith on the part of God's people."[182]

These apocryphal works appear in different surviving Irish manuscripts. Confusion alert: old manuscripts have interesting names. Sometimes these names are based on their history, such as the *Antiphonary of Bangor*. Sometimes they are based on where they were found, such as the Book of Lismore. Sometimes they are named after their one-time owners, such as the *Liber Flavus Fergusiorum* or the Stowe Missal.

Typically, the manuscripts of yore were anthologies, compilations of various other material.

In the days before printing, a man of substance could commission the copying of a book to order, to collect random things he wanted to be able to read and reread, and could have included items from centuries earlier if he wanted to have them available. One such is the *Leabhar Breac*, so-called because of the appearance of its cover. It

[182] John Paul II, General Audience (July 2, 1997), no. 2.

is sometimes called the Speckled Book (*breac* is the Gaeilge word for "trout" as well as for "speckled"). It was copied on vellum by a single scribe between 1408 and 1411, and it includes numerous religious and secular items, literature and poetry, history and biography, and things written far earlier, including the ninth-century *Féilire Óengussu* ("Calendar of Aengus")—which, by the way, invokes Mary.

It also includes a lengthy narrative of the *Childhood Deeds of Jesus*. Another contemporary manuscript, the *Liber Flavus Fergusiorum* (Yellow Book of the Ó Fearghuis, or Fergus), also includes the *Childhood Deeds* along with a rare version of the *Transitus*.

Of particular interest is that the story of the Magi contained in the Old Irish verse rendering of the *Childhood Deeds* "probably originated in the east (Greek or Syriac) in the second century,"[183] according to McNamara's studies. "The section on the Magi is particularly interesting, representing a very old form of the tradition found in an abbreviated form in the Latin *Opus imperfectum in Matthaeum* (mid-sixth century), and in Syriac in the *Zuqnin Chronicle*. It probably originated in the east (Greek or Syriac) in the second century." The Zuquin Chronicle was written in a Syrian monastery around 775 and is now in the Vatican Library.

Also amazing is the similarity between the Irish version and the Ethiopic versions of the Infancy Narrative. Only the Irish version among all versions keeps the story of the journey into Egypt.

Furthermore, it seems that we don't know what we don't know. For example, the traditions around the end of Mary's earthly life, the *Transitus*, can be found in multiple texts in Irish and Latin.

The *Leabhar Breac* version includes the Infancy Narrative, the Flight into Egypt, and the miracle of the palm tree—all passages that were later lost in Latin versions.

[183] McNamara, "De Initiis," 31.

The Irish *Transitus* version, "in spite of its considerable geographic distance, is a key witness to the earliest traditions from the eastern Mediterranean," says scholar Stephen Shoemaker.[184]

Victor Arras, a specialist in the Ethiopic version of the *Transitus* (known as *Liber Requiei*) said about the Irish version: "The fact that it alone retains the narration of the journey into Egypt, that it alone reports the account of the testing of Paul, and has retained the account of the otherworld journey, is sufficient to indicate that at the time the Irish vernacular author was composing his work Greek or Latin manuscripts existed which were much more complete than those known to us today."[185] It goes without saying that the Irish vernacular author was able to read the Greek and Latin manuscripts that have since disappeared. And perhaps some Ethiopic manuscripts too.

Also interesting is the connection McNamara found between Irish versions of the Apocalypse and Tyconius, an important fourth-century North African theologian who influenced Augustine of Hippo: "What is worthy of note with regard to the presumed lost Hiberno-Latin commentary of the Apocalypse, standing behind three known texts, is the use of the African commentator Tyconius. Thus, for early commentary material, the early Irish Church had access to writers not used, or widely used, elsewhere, in particular Julian and Pelagius.... I have examined the evidence for only three apocryphal texts, but undoubtedly there were very many more."[186]

[184] Stephen J. Shoemaker, "The Virgin Mary in the Ministry of Jesus and the Early Church according to the Earliest Life of the Virgin," *Harvard Theological Review* 98, no. 4 (October 2005): 441–467, https://www.jstor.org/stable/4125276.

[185] Translation of M. Herbert, in M. Herbert and M. McNamara, eds., *Irish Biblical Apocrypha: Selected Texts in Translation* (Edinburgh: T. and T. Clark, 1989), 119–120.

[186] McNamara, "De Initiis," 35.

The extent of Tyconius's possible influence in Ireland is one of many topics that deserve more exploration by scholars. McNamara calls for further study into the Gaelic/Eastern connection.

Blathmac's Poems: Motherhood and Maidenhood

Those apocryphal gospels had a silver lining: the Acts of Thomas inspired a remarkable early poem to Mary. Blathmac (pronounced "Blah-muc") mac Con Brettan maic Conguso do Feraib Rois, "Blathmac, Son of Cú Brettan, son of Congus of the Fir Rois," was an eighth-century poet who wrote in Old Irish. That's the name he gave himself in the manuscript, identifying his ancestors and thus positioning himself in the educated universe. Some accounts are that he was a king before he became a monk.

In any case, he wrote a 259-stanza poem to the Virgin Mary that tells the legend of five-year-old Jesus making twelve birds of clay. This tale comes directly from the apocryphal second-century Gospel of Thomas.[187] The poem was well-known and loved enough that it was included in the fifteenth-century *Leabhar Breac*.

Another long poem, usually titled "A Devoted Offering to Mary and Her Son," anticipates the "Stabat Mater" by about five hundred years. It begins "Come to me, loving Mary, that I may keen with you your very dear one" as Blathmac weeps with Mary at the death of her Son, and begs her intercession for his salvation.[188] Some of its 149 stanzas are addressed directly to the Virgin by way of a description of events in the life of Christ—a technique reminiscent

[187] James Carney, "Two Old Irish Poems," *Éiru* 18 (1958): 4–5; https://www.ria.ie/publications/books/irish-language/irish-texts-society-volume-47-poems-blathmac-son-cu-brettan.

[188] The entire poem may be found here: "To Mary and Her Son," Encyclopedia.com, https://www.encyclopedia.com/international/encyclopedias-almanacs-transcripts-and-maps/mary-and-her-son.

of hymns in the Eastern tradition that reiterate doctrine while infusing emotion into the acceptance of it.

All of Blathmac's surviving poems are in a manuscript known as MS G 50 in the National Library of Ireland. The manuscript was acquired by the National Library in 1931—but the poems were not discovered until 1953, by Nessa Ní Shéaghadha (1916–1993), an Irish language scholar. They were first published by James Carney (1914–1989) when he was a young scholar, and the publication of them helped establish him as a leading Celtic scholar. Carney dated the poems to the years 750–770.

Blathmac's poetry offers yet another proof that Ireland was not a remote island on the fringe of civilization, and at the same time proof of Ireland's early and deep devotion to the Mother of God. On the one hand, it is the work of a monk; on the other hand, it is the work of a man who loves his subject. Blathmac's personal, intimate tone is not a mere exercise in syllables and stresses but an act of devotion of the heart.

Art historian Peter Harbison notes an overlap between some of the images in Blathmac's poem and images in the mosaics on the walls of Santa Maria Maggiore and Santa Maria Antiqua (now called Santa Francesca Romana). Maggiore was built in 432, and Santa Maria Antiqua is the oldest Christian structure in the Roman Forum. Harbison finds an interesting correspondence between the scenes Blathmac writes about and physical images on the walls of fifth-century churches and basilicas in Rome.[189] He speculates that Blathmac must have visited Rome—which is possible, of course. Equally possible is that those same Old Testament and New Testament

[189] Peter Harbison, "Early Christian Texts: Blathmac—an Eighth-Century Irish Poet in Rome," *Gaelic Ireland* 24, no. 4 (July/August 2016): 18–20.

events were the stuff of the devotionals Blathmac might have read, or passages he would have heard repeatedly in the recitation of the Office, or that he heard about them from visitors or immigrants.

Particularly interesting are the similarities of Blathmac's poetic images with images from the East. In stanza 57 of *Poems to Mary and Her Son*, Blathmac employs the image of the blood from the body of Christ baptizing the head of Adam. This is an allusion to the ancient tradition that Golgotha was the burial place of Adam; Blathmac may have seen an icon depicting that.

His poem on the Harrowing of Hell depends quite explicitly in part on the apocryphal Gospel of Nicodemus, which dates from around the fourth century. It is believed to have originally been in Greek but was copied into Latin, Syriac, Coptic, Georgian, Slavonic, and other languages.[190]

He blends emotional intimacy with doctrine:

> Come to me, loving Mary,
> That I may keen with you your very dear one....
>
> Your womb has conceived Jesus—
> It has not marred your virginity.
>
> Come to me, loving Mary ...
> That we may have talk together
> With the compassion of unblemished heart.[191]

The idea of motherhood combined with maidenhood—a virgin conceiving a child—is so far removed from ordinary experience that it creates a poetry of amazement that lingers in the mind. The

[190] Johannes Irmscher and Anthony Cutler, "Gospel of Nicodemus," in *The Oxford Dictionary of Byzantium*, ed. Alexander Kazhdan (Oxford and New York: Oxford University Press, 1991), 1472.

[191] "To Mary and Her Son."

concept appears most famously as the climax of different stases of the Akathistos hymn to the Theotókos from Constantinople: "Rejoice, O Bride Unwedded."[192]

The Akathistos hymn is so named because since the eighth century, the congregation has stood while it is sung, a custom that began when patriarch St. Germanus of Constantinople prayed it in all-night vigils of thanksgiving to the Mother of God for saving the city from barbarians.

Like much Irish poetry, the Akathist is a complicated structure; in Greek, it is an alphabetical acrostic with twenty-four stanzas that begin with the twenty-four letters of the Greek alphabet. It is divided into two parts of twelve stanzas each: the first part is primarily narrative, the second part more doctrinal. Every stanza ends with a refrain: praise with Alleluia for the even-numbered stanzas, or strophes, and doctrinal teaching, "Hail Virgin Bride" or "Hail, O Bride Unwedded," for the odd-numbered ones. That phrase alone contains multiple theological concepts, reminding the listener of Mary's extraordinary relationship with her Son and Creator, and her unique, indispensable role in our salvation.

Could Blathmac have heard this hymn? The dates work. Sixth-century Romanos the Melodist is most often cited as the author of the Akathistos hymn; seventh-century George of Pisidia is another candidate. Recent studies, however, point to Romanos because they agree that the date of composition was either in the second half of the fifth century or in the first years of the sixth century.[193] If Blath-

[192] "Office of Praise of the Mother of God or Acathist Hymn," in *Byzantine Daily Worship*, ed. Most Rev. Joseph Raya (Allendale, NJ: Alleluia Press, 1969), 959–979.

[193] Luigi Gambero, *Mary and the Fathers of the Church: The Blessed Virgin Mary in Patristic Thought*, trans. Thomas Buffer (San Francisco: Ignatius Press, 1999), 338.

mac did indeed visit Rome, and see those images on the church walls, as Carney theorized, he might have visited Constantinople too and heard that hymn.

The Protoevangelium

One of the sources of devotion was the Protoevangelium of James. As the Church worked her way through the careful, slow process of making definitive decisions about which books were to become part of Sacred Scripture, the love of the Christian people for Mary took hold at the grassroots level, fed in part by this work.

Some argue that traditions from the Protoevangelium are earlier than the second century. This Gospel, which ultimately was ruled uncanonical, was ascribed to James the Less, who is also referred to as James son of Alphaeus. It was copied into Greek, Latin, Syriac, Coptic, and Armenian—all the languages of Christianity, all at the same time. It was taken very seriously by the Church for centuries because of its putative authorship, its great antiquity, and because it was referred to so frequently in the writings of early Church Fathers.

The Protoevangelium is the foundation of iconographic and other traditions around Mary. The first reference to the perpetual virginity of Mary originally comes from this text as well. St. Luke's Gospel mentions only that baby Jesus was laid in a manger; it is tradition based on the Protoevangelium that has shown Joseph and Mary in a cave. Traditional icons of the Nativity show Joseph as an old man; the tradition that Joseph was an aged widower comes from the Protoevangelium.

How do we know that the Virgin Mary's parents were named Joachim and Anna? The only source of those names, whose feasts the Church celebrates on July 26, is the Protoevangelium. This is also the source of three other great feasts of Mary: the Presentation of Mary in the Temple (November 21), the Nativity of the Blessed Virgin Mary (September 8), and the Immaculate Conception (December 8), variously called "Conception of the Virgin Mary" or "Conception of St. Anne" or "Maternity of Holy Anna" in the East.

The feasts of the Annunciation, Nativity, Conception of Jesus, and Assumption (called the Dormition or "falling asleep" of the Virgin) all began in Constantinople. The feast known since 1854 as the Immaculate Conception was originally celebrated in Antioch on December 9. Torchlight processions on Marian feasts seem to have originated there, too, and were brought by St. John Chrysostom to Constantinople. Three centuries after Chrysostom, Pope Sergius I finally introduced them in Rome. The Annunciation was introduced as a feast at Rome by Pope Leo II (681–683), a Sicilian of Greek cultural background. The Assumption owes its existence as a feast to Pope Theodore I (642–649), who was originally from Jerusalem, where the Dormition had long been observed.

The proclamation of the doctrine of the divine maternity of the Blessed Virgin at the Council of Ephesus in 431 is sometimes credited with creating an impetus to Marian devotion. But more likely, that Council was responding to what was already the devotion of the faithful. The council was not merely settling a theological dispute: it was affirming the piety of the people of God. "The Council itself reads much better as a reaction to (certain aspects of) Marian piety than as a catalyst for the same," wrote Thomas Arentzen, a scholar of Byzantine Christianity in Late Antiquity who teaches at Lund University in Sweden.[194]

[194] Thomas Arentzen, review of *Mary in Early Christian Faith and Devotion*, by Stephen J. Shoemaker, *Journal of Early Christian Studies* 26, no. 2 (Summer 2018): 344–346, https://muse.jhu.edu/article/698497/pdf.

The Oldest Hymn to Mary

Alexandria was the birthplace of devotion to Mary. The first church built in Alexandria was dedicated to the Virgin under the name of *Theometer*, which means "Mother of God" in Greek.[195] When the Third Ecumenical Council (Ephesus in 431) condemned Nestorius for teaching that Christ and God the Word were not the same Person, it also officially gave the title *Theotókos*, or "God-bearer." This was distinct from *Christotókos*, for that would have been Christ-bearer.

Neither the proclamation nor the title were innovations—they merely confirmed what was already widespread popular devotion. It is documented that the title was used in liturgical services by the year 250.

The use of the term *Theotókos* is one way of dating ancient texts. Since the Council of Ephesus in 431 made the term official, for a long while it was assumed that documents that used the term had to be more recent than that. However, Alexander, the patron and immediate predecessor of Athanasius as bishop of Alexandria, referred to Mary as *Theotókos* in an encyclical written around 319 about the heresy of Arius[196]—more than a hundred years before the Council of Ephesus. The discovery of formerly unknown documents tells that the term was in use in the Church, and in hymns, before the Council of Ephesus.

The first completely authenticated instances of the use of the title *Theotókos* come from Alexandria, Egypt,[197] where it was

[195] Aziz S. Atiya, *Coptic Encyclopedia* (New York: Macmillan, 1991), 2255.

[196] Epistle to Alexander of Constantinople, 12, *PG* 18:568, in Pelikan, *Mary through the Centuries*, 57n16.

[197] Pelikan, *Mary through the Centuries*, 65.

found in the very oldest hymn to Mary, which is reliably dated to a third-century papyrus from Alexandria. That hymn is known by its eleventh-century Latin title, "Sub Tuum Praesidium," and is a plea to the Mother of God for protection.

The hymn was used in a Coptic Christmas liturgy. Arguably the oldest version of it in a museum is in the John Rylands Library in Manchester, England. I say "arguably" because scholars argue about such things as the dating of ancient papyri. It was first published in 1938, having been recently discovered in a pile of other papyri that had been acquired in 1917. What intrigued scholars was that it seemed to have been written between the years 250 and 280, during a time of persecution of Christians, and yet it used the word *Theotókos*.

This seems like a side trip, but I mention this tale to show how scholarship evolves: at the time when the 1930 *Catholic Encyclopedia*, which many regard as definitive, was written, this information about this papyrus probably was not available to the authors! New information brings new insights. Since new information about ancient Irish manuscripts, prayers, and practices keeps getting discovered, new insights keep getting acquired.

The concept and images of Mary in the ancient East were quite different from what they evolved into in the West—and they are reminiscent of early Irish poetry. In Cú Chuimne's "Cantemus in Omni Die," for instance, Mary is celebrated as the "Mother of the Most High Lord."

The focus of early devotion is also different from what became familiar in the West. The primary focus of Mary's achievement was her participation in the exercise of divine power to bring about the redemption of mankind through the wonder of the Incarnation —not her suffering, the sinfulness of man, and the suffering of Christ, which became the major themes and representations in later medieval Europe. For example, in the Irish/Egyptian Adam and Eve story in *Saltair na Rann*, the emphasis is on divine grace and redemption, rather than Eve's sinfulness and humanity's suffering.[198]

Hymn of Cú Chuimne

Iona was a large active monastery that had a remarkable literary output and was also a center of Marian devotion. Adomnán, the ninth abbot, was active in both traditions. He wrote the biography of Columba, the founder of Iona, and he wrote the first law code to explicitly protect women and children. He explained that he wrote the law "for the sake of Mary the mother of Christ." He wrote *De Locis Sanctis*, a detailed description accompanied by a map of Jerusalem, which was narrated to him by Gaulish bishop Arculf whose ship went astray in a storm. He tells a story about an icon of the Virgin in *De Locis Sanctis*.

Two of the high crosses at Iona have images of Mary, making them perhaps the oldest icons in the Celtic Mediterranean. The images themselves resemble the Virgin and Child page in the Book of Kells.

Also out of Iona came what for a long time was considered the first hymn in honor of Mary. In fact, "Sub Tuum Praesidium" is older, as mentioned earlier—but it was a compliment to the Irish that Cú Chuimne's "Cantemus in Omni Die" was given the honor until "Sub Tuum Praesidium" became known throughout the scholarly world.

The hymn of Cú Chuimne, "Cantemus in Omni Die," dated to between 693 and 704, is a major piece of work, one that influenced

[198] Elizabeth A. Lerner, "Virgins and Mothers: Feminine Ideals and Female Roles in the Early Irish Church," *Proceedings of the Harvard Celtic Colloquium* 14 (1994): 169, jstor.org/stable/20557281.

Christian hymnody for centuries. Its images and conceits can still be heard in Marian piety. The poem was included in the *Collectio Canonum Hibernensis*, a compilation of biblical and patristic teaching and ecclesiastical governance compiled by Cú Chuimne (†747) and Rubin Dair-Inis (†725) that appeared in Gaul in the eighth century.

Cú Chuimne must have been a remarkable man. Maybe he should be named as the patron saint of failed marriages, for as such he described his own: in his youth, he said, he "had a wife and lived badly with her." What became of his wife is unknown, but as a monk-poet on Iona he made amends to all womankind with his hymns to Mary, and as a compiler of Church laws of Ireland he laid the groundwork for the entire Church's canon law.

How the Irish Invented Canon Law (or at Least Helped)

Here's an example of how different the Church of even centuries ago was from today. There was not one comprehensive *Corpus Juris Canonici* (body of canon law) until the thirteenth century!

Rome's first official organization and compilation of canon law was made by Gratian in 1234 — but Ireland had long been following its own *Collectio Canonum Hibernensis,* which served the same purpose. The *Collectio* had been compiled by Cú Chuimne of Iona and Reuben of Dair-Inis, who died in 747 and 725 respectively. The *Hibernensis* was used throughout Europe for four centuries, and was actually a model for Gratian's *Decretum Gratiani* of 1234. Gratian's work, by the way, stayed in force until the 1917 Code of Canon Law — for about seven hundred years, in other words.

One of the excuses King Henry II of England made to invade Ireland in 1171 was that some Irish practices were different from Rome's practices, and he was going to bring Ireland into compliance with Rome. That was the spin he put on it — but when Henry invaded, with the permission of the (only ever) English pope, Adrian IV, there was no universal Code of Canon Law, so Ireland was not really in dire variance from Rome, and there was no doctrinal difference.

"Cantemus in Omni Die" consists of thirteen quatrains, and was written in *aicill*, a system by which rhymes and assonances bind the end of the third line of a stanza to the beginning or interior of the fourth line, a technique requiring considerable skill.

The approach to Mary in "Cantemus" reflects the theology of the Eastern Fathers. It emphasizes Mary's place in the story of salvation not primarily at the Crucifixion, but in the Incarnation when divine nature and human nature are conjoined in one Person through her agency. "The hymn tells of Gabriel's role in her conception of Jesus, and some of the extraordinarily fertile imagery of early medieval mariology is employed."[199] The Akathist hymn follows the same exact conceit, with Gabriel speaking certain stanzas.

A Virgin, a Tree, and Archangel Gabriel

The images and interplay of Mary's *fiat* and the Cross are drawn out and explored in Cú Chuimne's poem.

Stanza 7 of "Cantemus" reads: "By a woman and a tree / the world first perished; by the power of a woman it has returned to

[199] Clancy and Markus, *Iona*, 188.

salvation." There are two ideas here: the Virgin and the Cross, and the New Eve. Both come from the East, from the very beginning of the Church.

The ruination of the world by a virgin and a tree first appears in *Adversus Haereses*, by St. Irenaeus of Lyon (ca. 130–ca. 202). As I mentioned earlier, Irenaeus had known St. Polycarp of Smyrna, a disciple of St. John the Evangelist, who was the guardian of the Virgin Mary in her last years on earth.[200] The links of Irenaeus with Mary, thus, were almost living memory. Remember that St. Irenaeus was known for his role in expanding monasticism in southern Gaul, that key source of insular Christianity.

St. Irenaeus wrote, "If he has summed up, by his obedience on the tree, the disobedience perpetrated by means of the tree; if that deception of which Eve (a virgin espoused to a man) has been a miserable victim, has been dispelled by the good news of truth magnificently announced by the angel to Mary, also a virgin espoused to a man, then the bonds fastening mankind to death are now unloosed."[201] Andrew Breeze, a Celtic scholar who is now professor of philology at the University of Navarre, suggests that the motif was known in Irish circles at the time the Ruthwell Cross, an Anglo-Saxon high cross in Northumbria, was carved, and may have influenced one of its designs.[202]

The theme of the virgin and the cross was also articulated in St. John Chrysostom's sermon *De coemeterio et de cruce*: "A virgin, a beam, and a death were the symbols of our defeat. The virgin was Eve; the beam, the Tree of Knowledge; the death, the

[200] Andrew Breeze, *The Mary of the Celts* (Leominster, Herefordshire: Gracewing, 2008), 92.

[201] Ibid., 92–93.

[202] Ibid., 94–96.

punishment of Adam. But wait: a Virgin, a beam, and a death are also the symbols of victory. In the place of Eve is Mary; for the Tree of Knowledge of Good and Evil, the beam of the Cross; and for the death of Adam, the death of Christ. Do you see now how the Devil has been defeated by the very things with which before he triumphed?"[203]

The same motif is found elsewhere in Eastern Christianity. Eusebius of Emesa employed it in a sermon before 359, which survived only in Armenian translation: "For the Tree in Paradise, lo, the Tree of the Cross. There is the woman, who brought sin into the world; here is the Virgin, who heard the words 'behold your mother.' Adam on that evil day stretched forth his hand; Jesus stretched out his fair and holy arms."[204] Gregory of Nyssa (ca. 330–ca. 395) used the image in a Christmas homily in 386: "That woman by means of a tree brought about sin; this woman by means of a tree restored good."[205]

Would Cú Chuimne have had access to *Adversus Haereses*? Certainly. To Chrysostom's sermon? Certainly—Chrysostom's works were known in Anglo-Saxon England; Alcuin mentions his writings in the library at York. So they probably were at Iona. Would he have had access to homilies by Eusebius and Gregory of Nyssa? Very possibly.

Cú Chuimne's opening allusion to Gabriel in line 7 ("Gabriel aduexit Verbum sinu prius Paterno"; "From the everlasting Father, Gabriel brought the glad decree") immediately brings to mind the First Chant of the Akathist hymn: "An archangel was sent from Heaven to greet the Mother of God. And as he saw you taking a

[203] Ibid., 95.
[204] Ibid., 94.
[205] Ibid., 93.

body, O Lord, at the sound of his bodiless voice, he stood rapt in amazement and cried out to her in these words: Hail, O you through whom joy will shine forth; hail, O you through whom the curse will disappear! Hail, O Restoration of the fallen Adam; hail, O Redemption of the tears of Eve!... Hail, O star who manifest the Sun.... Hail, O you through whom creation is renewed."

The New Eve

The second image hidden in Cú Chuimne's stanza 7 is that of the New Eve: through a disobedient woman, Eve, sin and death came into the world; by an obedient woman, Mary, the New Eve, salvation came into the world.

Mary as the Second Eve, sometimes called the Eva-Ave parallel, occurred frequently in the writings of Justin Martyr and Irenaeus and is one of the constantly recurring themes in early Irish Mariology.[206] Cyril of Jerusalem (†386) also used it: "Since through the virgin Eve came death, it is fitting that through a Virgin, or rather from a Virgin, should life appear. That as a serpent has deceived the one, so Gabriel might bring good tidings to the other."[207] (The virginity of Eve, though married, and the virginity of Mary, though married, is another parallel.)

Eve and Mary are sometimes called the "Two Eyes" of the world: Ephrem the Syrian (ca. 306–373) wrote, "Behold the world! To it were given two eyes: Eve was the left eye, the blind eye; the right eye, the luminous eye is Mary."[208] Ephrem describes Eve and Mary as the two spiritual eyes of the world, and the second

[206] James Good, D.D., "The Mariology of the Early Irish Church," *Irish Ecclesiastical Record* 100, 5th series (August 1963): 73–79, 79.

[207] Clancy and Markus, *Iona*, 188.

[208] Ephrem, *Hymns on the Church* 37, 5–7, quoted in Gambero, *Mary and the Fathers of the Church*, 116.

Person of the Trinity is the light by which these eyes can function. Eve's eye has become darkened and no longer receives into itself the light, thus losing its power of vision; as a result, when the world relies on her eye, it gropes around after error. Mary's eye, on the other hand, has been preserved luminous, and so "she is the eye which receives the source of light: through her it has illumined the whole world with its inhabitants, which had grown dark through Eve."[209]

Likewise, the eighth stanza of Cú Chuimne's hymn includes the following: "Mary, amazing mother, gave birth to her Father!" This image, too, is older than Cú Chuimne; it goes back to Augustine, who wrote of Christ: "He is created of her, whom He created."[210] It could also be an allusion to the Troparia of the Fourth Ode of the Akathist: "Hail, O ladder who through grace have lifted us from the earth! . . . Hail, for without pain you have borne within your womb the Foundation of the earth!"[211] Or to Hirmos of the Fifth Ode of the Akathist: "You are a virgin and have not known man, and yet in your womb you have borne God, the Master of all . . . a Son who grants salvation to those who sing your praise."[212]

In stanza 9, Cú Chuimne views Mary as an oyster and praises her for conceiving the pearl for which "sensible Christians have sold all they have." In the Troparia of the Fourth Ode hiermos of Ode 4 of the Akathist, she is a "murex shell, who with your blood have dyed a robe of purple for the King of Hosts."[213] And in the

[209] Sebastian Brock, trans., *The Syriac Fathers on Prayer and the Spiritual Life* (Kalamazoo, MI: Cistercian, 1987), xxix.
[210] Clancy and Markus, *Iona*, 190.
[211] Raya, "Office of Praise," 962.
[212] Ibid.
[213] Ibid.

Fifth Ode, she is a "wondrous shell from whom came forth the Pearl divine!"[214]

Stanza 10 includes a frank borrowing from a tale in another apocryphal Gospel, that of Nicodemus: "The mother of Christ had made / a tunic of a seamless weave." It is not the only time that conceit appears in early Irish texts.

The Protoevangelium tells that at the moment of the Annunciation, Mary was spinning purple wool to weave a veil for the Temple. But this image is richer than just the Protoevangelium: the image of Mary as the weaver of Christ's seamless robe is an "echo of one of the images of the Incarnation in the writing of third-century theologian Hippolytus," states Peter Weeda.[215]

Peter Weeda teaches at the University of Melbourne School of Historical and Philosophical Studies. He has analyzed five attributes of the Virgin Mary from four Old Irish texts, all written before the end of the eighth century.[216] In the Old Irish tract on the Mass in the Stowe Missal, Mary's womb is expressed as a linen sheet; in the *Cáin Adomnáin*, Mary is described as "clothing everyone." In the hymn of Cú Chuimne she is described as the "Tree of Life" and Blathmac calls her *grian ar clainde* (the sun of our children) and *grian na mban* (the sun of women). Weeda notes that "these references are nowhere to be found in the West up to and including the eighth century"[217]—yet they can all be found in homilies delivered by Bishop Proclus of Constantinople between 429 and 431.

[214] Ibid., 963.

[215] Peter Weeda, "The Irish, the Virgin Mary and Proclus of Constantinople," *Peritia* 22–23 (2011–2012): 86, doi.org/10.1484/J.PERIT.1.103281.

[216] Ibid., 83–106.

[217] Ibid., 85.

In 428, Proclus delivered a homily that was immediately picked up by Cyril of Alexandria (ca. 376–444) and reused in other works. In it, he claimed that the Holy Spirit used threads from Mary's "undefiled flesh" in the "workshop" of her womb. The womb-loom image appears in the Stowe Mass at the moment when the paten holding the bread is given by the celebrant to the subdeacon, covered with the white linen cloth, and placed on the altar to await consecration. The host represents Christ's body in the womb, and the linen cloth symbolizes Mary's womb, as Weeda sees it. Understanding the preparation of the gifts in this manner places the Virgin Mary at the center of the Mass, and tells "a very different salvation narrative" than that developed and promulgated in subsequent centuries, Weeda acknowledges.[218] Proclus did not invent the image—he had encountered it in the words of third-century theologian Hippolytus, who had suggested that Christ's flesh came from the Virgin's womb, but that the loom was the Passion.

Bishop Proclus may be an important link between the East and Iona—but more study is needed.

Nicholas Constas, a professor of patristics and Orthodox spirituality at Holy Cross School of Theology in Brookline, Massachusetts, has done pioneering research on the imagery of Proclus's homilies. "The nearly exhaustive profusion of Old Testament Marian typologies in the writings of Proclus is without precedent in the whole of early Christian literature, and would later determine the basic features of all subsequent Byzantine Mariology," he writes.[219] She is a spiritual garden of Eden, a new Eve, the ladder of

[218] Ibid., 86.

[219] Nicholas P. Constas, "Weaving the Body of God: Proclus of Constantinople, the Theotokos, and the Loom of the Flesh," *Journal of Early Christian Studies* 3, no. 2 (Summer 1995): 177, https://doi.org/10.1353/earl.0.0063.

Jacob, the fleece of Gideon drenched with the dew of Heaven, the burning bush ablaze but not consumed, a jar filled with manna. In addition to biblical images, Proclus portrays her as a harbor, a ship, a bridge, a city, a throne, a bridal chamber, virgin earth, a fertile field yet unplowed, a shelter, a dwelling, a temple, and a container of the uncontainable.

A few of these images are evident in the Akathist and in Cú Chuimne. There may well be many more to be found in the poetry of Iona and elsewhere from Ireland's golden age.

Proclus delved into deeper symbolism in his Fourth Homily. He claimed that Mary was the enrober of humankind in the garments of salvation. From the beginning of Christianity, baptizands had been robed in white when they came out of the water—but the understanding was that the Church was renewing them. Proclus suggested that they "were imitating Christ's entry into Mary's womb"[220]—a new concept, but one entertained by Adomnán.

Proclus's idea is repeated in Adomnán's claim that an angel commanded him to establish his *Cáin* for the sake of the Virgin, "who labours in carrying the distaff and clothing everyone."[221] Until now, it was the Church who clothed everyone—but for Proclus, and for Adomnán, it was Mary who clothed Christ, and therefore she was the one "who clothes everyone." This is a notion that "stands very much alone in early Christian liturgical history," Weeda admits.[222]

Weeda notes that "the Irish had a deeper knowledge of Proclus's homilies on Mary than anything expressed elsewhere in Western

[220] Weeda, "The Irish," 90–91.
[221] Ibid., 92.
[222] Ibid.

writings." He concludes by noting that "analogues with the East in Irish sources are constantly being found."[223]

The findings of Weeda's study are tantalizing. What else might be discovered through further research? Textual comparison and analysis have yet to be done comparing the foundational hymns of Gaelic Marian devotion with those of the time and place of the origins of Christianity.

There are no doubt more to be found—but to find them must be the work of scholars with experience in Greek, Latin, Old and Middle Irish, and probably Arabic and theology too. Your humble author cannot aspire to such heights. I can only hope that this book will inspire someone in the future to make the discoveries that I am confident are waiting to be found.

For Further Reference

Arentzen, Thomas. Review of *Mary in Early Christian Faith and Devotion*, by Stephen J. Shoemaker. *Journal of Early Christian Studies* 26, no. 2 (Summer 2018): 344–346. https://muse.jhu.edu/article/698497/pdf.

Attwater, Donald. *A Dictionary of Mary*. New York: P.J. Kenedy and Sons, 1955.

Breeze, Andrew. *The Mary of the Celts*. Leominster, Herefordshire: Gracewing, 2008.

Brock, Sebastian, trans. *The Syriac Fathers on Prayer and the Spiritual Life*. Kalamazoo, MI: Cistercian, 1987.

Carney, James. "Two Old Irish Poems." *Éiru* 18 (1958): 1–43.

——. "Old Ireland and Her Poetry." In *Old Ireland*, edited by Robert McNally, S.J., 147–172. New York: Fordham University Press, 1965.

[223] Ibid., 103.

Constas, Nicholas P. "Weaving the Body of God: Proclus of Constantinople, the Theotokos, and the Loom of the Flesh." *Journal of Early Christian Studies* 3, no. 2 (Summer 1995): 169–194. https://doi.org/10.1353/earl.0.0063.

Gambero, Luigi. *Mary and the Fathers of the Church: The Blessed Virgin Mary in Patristic Thought*. Translated by Thomas Buffer. San Francisco: Ignatius Press, 1999.

——. *Mary in the Middle Ages: The Blessed Virgin Mary in the Thought of Medieval Latin Theologians*. Translated by Thomas Buffer. San Francisco: Ignatius Press, 2005.

Good, James, D.D. "The Mariology of the Early Irish Church." *Irish Ecclesiastical Record* 100, 5th series (August 1963): 73–79.

Harbison, Peter. "Early Christian Texts: Blathmac—an Eighth-Century Irish Poet in Rome." *Gaelic Ireland* 24, no. 4 (July/August 2016): 18–20.

Herbert, Máire, and Rev. Martin J. McNamara, eds. *Irish Biblical Apocrypha: Selected Texts in Translation*. Edinburgh: T and T Clark/Bloomsbury Academic, 1989/2004.

Irmscher, Johannes, and Anthony Cutler. "Gospel of Nicodemus." In *The Oxford Dictionary of Byzantium*, edited by Alexander Kazhdan. Oxford and New York: Oxford University Press, 1991.

Lerner, Elizabeth A. "Virgins and Mothers: Feminine Ideals and Female Roles in the Early Irish Church." *Proceedings of the Harvard Celtic Colloquium* 14 (1994): 162–174. jstor.org/stable/20557281.

O'Loughlin, Thomas. "The Many Feasts of Mary in the Contemporary Catholic Liturgy: A Study of the Persistence of the Protoevangelium of James within Liturgical Memory." *Maria: A Journal of Marian Studies* 1, no. 1 (July 2021): 1–20.

Pelikan, Jaroslav. *Mary through the Centuries: Her Place in the History of Culture*. New Haven, CT: Yale University Press, 1996.

Raya, Most Rev. Joseph, ed. *Byzantine Daily Worship*. Allendale, NJ: Alleluia Press, 1969.

Shoemaker, Stephen J. "The Virgin Mary in the Ministry of Jesus and the Early Church according to the Earliest *Life of the Virgin*." *Harvard Theological Review* 98, no. 4 (October 2005): 441–467. jstor.org/stable/4125276.

Weeda, Peter. "The Irish, the Virgin Mary and Proclus of Constantinople." *Peritia* 22–23 (2011–2012): 83–106. doi.org/10.1484/J.PERIT.1.103281.

Chapter 7

Echoes of the East in the Liturgy of Old Ireland

Connections can be traced between the architecture, art, decoration, and illuminated manuscripts of late antique Ireland and Ethiopia, Armenia, and Egypt. Themes and images of poetry in late antique and early medieval Ireland are rich with imagery from Eastern Christianity. The practice of monasticism in pre-Norman Ireland has deep connections with Egypt. But what about liturgy?

Liturgy in Ireland before the ninth century had characteristics quite distinct from the Roman Rite of the day; Warren attributed the differences to the influence of the Gallican liturgy, which developed in the sixth century and thrived for the first millennium. However, there are elements of the liturgy that do not trace back to Gaul but are in fact rooted in older, more Eastern traditions, specifically from Jerusalem and Egypt, the two most influential liturgical centers in the early Christian period. Traditions from both these places found their way into the Irish Office through Cassian and other Western sources.[224]

[224] Jeffery, "Eastern and Western Elements in the Irish Monastic Prayer of the Hours," 128.

As more research is done in this area, it may emerge that, far from being on the fringe of innovation, Ireland may have been in the mainstream of it. Recent historical-critical work on the Roman *Canon Missae* has a high degree of consensus regarding similarities between it and the Alexandrian liturgies, especially that of Mark and the Coptic liturgy of Cyril.[225]

However, there is no reason to believe that the liturgy in early Ireland was in the vernacular, that is, Old or Middle Irish, even though the vernacular was and still is the practice of the Eastern Churches. It may have been that Egyptian monks celebrated their liturgy in the Coptic manner—but we have no way of knowing, so speculation like that must be left to the imagination.

Nonetheless, the liturgy of late antique Ireland did include a number of elements derived from the East—not necessarily by an Irish initiative but by the organic process of the development of the liturgy itself. The story of the liturgy of ancient Ireland is a fascinating glimpse into the vitality of the early Church.

Where Does the Mass Come From?

By way of background, a long view is helpful: first, the Mass did not always look or sound like the Mass that we know. It was the Council of Trent in the sixteenth century that first successfully "froze" the Mass at that particular point in time and for the following four centuries, right up until the last half century. Prior to Trent, efforts had been made in different places at different times to standardize the practice of the Mass, but with varying degrees of success. But then, the starting points were different.

[225] Matthew S. C. Olver, "Connections between the Roman Canon Missae and the East Syrian Anaphora of Mar Theodore," *Questions Liturgique* 101, no. 3–4 (January 2021): 276–304, doi.org/10.2143/QL.101.3.3290090, 276.

It all begins with Greek. For the first three centuries, Greek was the (more or less) universal language of the Church. Greek was the international language that linked Rome with Asia, Africa, and Gaul at the time of Christ. St. Paul wrote the Letter to the Romans in Greek, St. Mark wrote his Gospel in Greek, and so on. The oldest inscriptions in the catacombs are in Greek. As Dom Gregory Dix notes:

> Right down to the eighth century, even in some measure down to the eleventh, Rome is not, properly speaking, a truly "Western" church.... There were Greek and Syrian and Egyptian monasteries in Rome. Some of these orientals were from time to time elected to the throne of S. Peter.... Rome is not only the heart of Western Christendom, but the meeting point of East and West. And its liturgy reflects the fact.[226]

Christianity became legal in 313. From then through the pontificate of Pope Gregory the Great (590–604), Christianity under the Roman and the Byzantine Empires spread from Mesopotamia to western China, and from Georgia to Ethiopia, and had liturgical rites not only in Coptic and Greek and Syriac, but also in Armenian, Georgian, and Ethiopian.

To put liturgy in general into the broadest perspective: in the beginning, there were four Eastern liturgical families: Syrian, Alexandrian/Egyptian, Persian/Nestorian/East Syrian, and Byzantine/Constantinopolitan. There were also five Western liturgies: the Mozarabic, Ambrosian, Hispano-Gallican, Gallican, and Roman.[227] The Roman was chronologically the last to develop.

[226] Dix, *The Shape of the Liturgy*, 543.

[227] John Ryan, S.J., "The Mass in the Early Irish Church," *Studies: An Irish Quarterly Review* 50, no. 200 (Winter 1961): 371.

In each "family," the liturgy was fairly unified and standard. The churches in Egypt, for instance, would all celebrate more or less the same way—that is, the Alexandrian way. The Alexandrian way was different from the Constantinopolitan way, which was different from the Roman way, and so on. They were all valid, they all were descended from the apostles. They were living things, however, and as time went on, they became more and more different from each other.

The Liturgy of St. James, named after Jerusalem's first bishop, was the original eucharistic liturgy of Jerusalem, though it was replaced by the Divine Liturgy of St. John Chrysostom (i.e., the contemporary "Byzantine Rite"). The Liturgy of St. James was overtaken by events, you might say, but it didn't disappear: it is still celebrated at least twice a year in Eastern Churches, including Eastern Catholic ones. According to tradition, St. Mark the Evangelist was the first bishop of Alexandria, and the liturgy of Alexandria bore his name. What is believed to be the oldest written fragment of that liturgy is called the Strasbourg Papyrus, now in a museum in France, and has been dated to the middle of the fourth century, though the words themselves are believed to be of first-century origin. The Coptic liturgy of today does not resemble it very much.

Pope St. Gregory the Great, who reigned from 590 to 603, is regarded as the man who defined the Roman liturgy—though, in fact, he incorporated Eastern elements into it. Andrew Ekonomou, the Byzantinist, writes: "If the East had begun to influence the ritual practices of the Roman church, Gregory himself was at least in part responsible for it."[228] In brief, some changes in the Roman liturgy incorporated Eastern attributes: "The introduction of Eastern liturgical customs and practices into the Roman

[228] Ekonomou, *Byzantine Rome and the Greek Popes*, 17.

church is symptomatic of a growing oriental presence in Rome even before the sixth century came to a close."[229] It should be remembered that eleven Greeks and six Syrians occupied the Chair of Peter before 741.[230]

Some of those Eastern attributes were included in what was known as the Gallo-Roman liturgy, and then more were added in the Gallican liturgy, which was the oldest known liturgy of Ireland.

When Did Latin Come In?

At the beginning, Latin was the official language of Roman Empire bureaucrats, and the vernacular language among the Christian people of Rome; Greek remained the "liturgical language." All public worship and all official Church documents were conducted or written in Greek. Then, in the middle of the third century, the bishops and clergy officially adopted Latin for use in their documents and correspondence. Around the middle of the fourth century, it became the official liturgical language for the Roman Church (and only the Roman Church). The official adoption of Latin for the liturgy has been ascribed to St. Damasus, who was pope from 366 to 384. It is speculated that Damasus wanted to make the liturgy simpler and briefer: Greek phraseology was more ornate than Latin.

Latin went where the Roman Empire went. After the Romans withdrew, however, Latin in Gaul began to evolve into French, and in Italy it began to evolve into Italian, and so forth, developing into new vernacular languages now called "Romance languages."

After Damasus, the liturgy remained in Latin in the West, but it continued to be celebrated in the vernacular, the language the

[229] Ibid., 18.

[230] King, *Liturgy of the Roman Church*, 445.

people spoke, in the East. In his 1945 masterpiece *The Shape of the Liturgy*, Dom Gregory Dix reported that the Roman Mass has been found in Georgian and Armenian translations in the eleventh century, having been put into Greek along the way. He also confirmed that the first appearance in the West of Greek litanies of the saints appeared in the monasteries of Anglo-Saxon England.[231]

St. Patrick had studied Latin because his father was a Roman official, but he was the first to tell the world that his Latin was poor. Still, it was the language he wrote in and it was the language he celebrated liturgy in.

Yet the best scholarship maintains that most of the West would have celebrated the Eucharist in some form of the Gallican Rite from the very beginning until the eighth century, though there are no records before the fifth century. France, Germany, the Low Countries, Britain—and, most likely, Ireland—were in that group until the eighth century.

Where did the liturgy come from? The short answer is that nobody really knows.

A hundred years ago, some scholars thought that it originated in Rome, but there were so many differences that that idea was superseded by the opinion that it came from Milan. From 355 to 374, the bishop of Milan was Auxentius of Cappadocia, who is credited with including some similarities to Eastern usage, such as the position of the Kiss of Peace and the appearance of an epiclesis in the Canon.[232]

Then it was noticed that the Gallican was actually older than the Milanese, and had important similarities with African

[231] Dix, *The Shape of the Liturgy*, 544–545.

[232] Bard Thompson, *Liturgies of the Western Church* (Cleveland and New York: Collins World, 1961/1974), 29.

liturgy, and also incorporated liturgical material from Ephesus and Jerusalem. Then scholars noticed similarities with the Rite of Spain, which was fairly widely used from the fifth century to the eleventh (and that still lingers on in certain chapels in Toledo and Salamanca), so the term *Hispano-Gallican* was invented. (Note: this is distinct from the Mozarabic Rite.) Then another scholar noticed that some of its formularies are to be found word for word in the Greek texts that were in use in the churches of the Syro-Byzantine Rite either in the fourth century or somewhat later.

Possibly the best concise explanation of the ancient Gallican liturgy is found in an issue of the Irish scholarly Catholic review *Studies* from 1931.[233] Originally, the liturgy of Gaul resembled the liturgy of Rome and Africa; then certain Chaldean usages, which themselves had been adopted from the churches of Ephesus and Jerusalem were incorporated into it. How did that come about? The author explains:

> The celebrated protagonist of cenobitic life in the Occident and founder of the monastery of St Victor at Marseilles, John Cassian, is indicated as the person responsible for the introduction of the modifications into the old Gallo-Roman liturgy. Pope St. Innocent I, writing in 416, refers with displeasure to the innovations; but the movement made headway in South Gaul, especially at Lérins. Two great archbishops of Arles, Honoratus in the fifth century

[233] J. R., review of *L'ancienne liturgie gallicane: Son origins et sa Formation en Provence au V et VI siècles*, by P. J.-B. Thibaut; review of *Der Entail des Volkes an der Messliturgie im Frankeneiche von Chlodwig bis auf Karl den Grossen*, by Georg Nickl, *Studies: An Irish Quarterly Review* 20, no. 78 (June 1931): 346–347, jstor.org/stable/30094779.

and Caesarius early in the sixth, had both been trained in the island monastery.

These bishops used their influence to get it across the English Channel. "British churchmen of the sixth century carried it to Ireland, where it took its place beside the old Gallo-Roman liturgy introduced by St Patrick."

In short, the Gallican liturgy, with its origins known and unknown, its mystery, its history, its uniqueness, and its numerous variations, was a living, breathing personification of the universality of the living, breathing, growing Catholic Church.

The Gallican Rite did not survive in the long run, because there was no single bishop or group of bishops using it who could command enough influence. The Court of Charlemagne might have been able to pull it off had it been so inclined, but Amalarius (ca. 775–850), the theologian of influence there, made liturgical changes in a different direction. It was his idea to deny the chalice to the laity, which led to less and less frequent reception of Communion by the same. The liturgical preferences of Charlemagne's court influenced Roman liturgical practice—and the rest is history.

Celtic Christianity? Celtic Liturgy?

But I digress. Back to the sixth century, when Ireland used the Gallican liturgy—albeit with an Irish flavor.

The most notable characteristic of the Gallican Rite, in all its versions, was its flexibility. Roman prayers tended to be of a very simple structure, whereas Gallican prayers were more complex and wordy—what the loquacious *filidh* would have liked!—perhaps hearkening back to Greek liturgy. The celebration of the Eucharist would probably have required between one and two hours. It contained three scriptural readings, chants and prayers, at least one litany, a homily, dismissal of catechumens and penitents, a lengthy eucharistic synaxis, blessings before Communion, Communion, post-Communion prayers, and a dismissal—roughly in that order.

The Church in Ireland was different from the Church anywhere else. Of course it would be!

It was isolated by geography; it was surrounded by pagans for several centuries. It is only to be expected that the early generations of the Faith in Ireland would have celebrated the liturgy and brought the customs of the first generations—whether they were Egyptian or Gallican.

Dom Jean Mabillon, who is known as the founder of the discipline of paleography, the study of historical writing, is credited with first using the term *Celtic liturgy* in 1685.[234] Subsequent generations have disputed what the term means, whether a "Celtic liturgy" ever existed, and, if so, when. When the phrase is found, it generally refers to liturgy in the Celtic countries between 500 and 1100. Was there really a "Celtic liturgy"?

There is no evidence of a liturgy that originated in a Celtic country. There were different ways of celebrating the Eucharist in Ireland, different ways of making the Offering to God on Sunday. (*Aifrinn* is the modern Irish word for "Mass." It comes from the older Irish word *offrenda*, which is cognate with the Latin "Offering.")

In Ireland there were different texts that had come from different places in the world, and existed for a moment in the liturgy of Ireland, and then were absorbed into other ways of celebrating the Eucharist. None of it was heterodox in faith, however. And, when looked at closely, it is a fascinating case study of how liturgy evolves.

[234] John Hennig, "Old Ireland and Her Liturgy," in Robert McNally, *Old Ireland* (Dublin: M. H. Gill and Son, 1965), 60.

The phrase *Celtic liturgy* is a linguistic misnomer in the first place "because Celtic linguistic unity was already a thing of the past when Christ was born," said Próinséas Ní Chatháin, the late professor of early and medieval Irish at University College Dublin, who suggested " 'insular Christianity' or the like" as a less misleading alternative.[235] Liturgist Neil Xavier O'Donoghue prefers the term *pre-Norman*.

Whatever we call it, the liturgy in Celtic lands cannot be considered as an independent liturgy, because it consisted of elements borrowed from the rest of the world, as mentioned above.

Was there Eastern influence on insular Christianity? Of course there was. There was Eastern influence on all of Christianity! And Egyptian influence too. Is it discernible? It is; liturgiologists have found some. Has it been much looked for? Perhaps not as much as it deserves.

Frederick Edward Warren, whom I have discussed already, noticed that the "Celtic liturgy" was not the Roman Mass of his day and concluded that the faith in Ireland had been independent of Rome. In 1895, in the *Irish Ecclesiastical Review*, Bartholomew MacCarthy characterized the position of Warren and his colleagues thus: "Full willingly would they admit that the early Britons and Irish, down to the ninth or tenth century, were Christian, nay Catholic and Apostolic, without, however, being in communion with Rome."[236]

To give credit where it is due, however: Warren was a serious scholar, and a pioneer in what today is known as Celtic studies.

[235] Próinséas Ní Chatháin, "The Liturgical Background of the Derrynavlan Altar Service," *Journal of the Royal Society of Antiquaries of Ireland* 110 (1980): 128, www.jstor.org/stable/25508780.

[236] Bartholomew MacCarthy, "Hibernia Christiana," *Irish Ecclesiastical Record* 16 (May 1895): 442–452, 446.

He prepared the earliest critical editions of some of the oldest liturgical works of the British Isles. His 1881 *Liturgy and Ritual of the Celtic Church* still frames the conversation.

His observations were keen, and he enumerated numerous "Points of Difference between Roman and Celtic Church" including the calculation of the date of Easter and the style of tonsure; triple immersion Baptism with Chrismation immediately thereafter; pedilavium, or ceremonial washing of feet, after Baptism; the consecration of a bishop by a single other bishop; anointing of hands of deacons and priests at ordination; the giving of a stole to deacons at their ordination; different lections, or readings, of Scripture; and the rite of investing priests with a stole at ordination. Warren also was of the opinion that Celtic priests wore cuffs (*epimanikia*) as part of their vestments;[237] these have always been liturgical vestments of the East.

Warren considered these evidences of "Oriental influence" in the Celtic liturgy, and he speculated that "the most probable hypothesis is that Christianity reached the British isles through Gaul, and that whatever traces of Eastern influence may be found in the earliest Liturgy and Ritual of Great Britain and Ireland are not due to a direct introduction of Christianity from the East, but to the Eastern character and origin of that Church through which Christianity first reached these shores."[238]

Liturgical Diversity

We already mentioned how, according to the Venerable Bede, Pope Gregory the Great made a virtue out of necessity and tolerated liturgical diversity in Britain.

[237] Warren, *The Liturgy and Ritual of the Celtic Church*, 117.
[238] Ibid., 57.

When St. Augustine came to Kent in 597—a missionary sent by Pope Gregory—he not surprisingly found a multiplicity of liturgies among British Christians, since some of them had been evangelized by Irish monks, others by Gaul. He asked the pope how he should handle the situation. Gregory's answer accepted diversity followed by consistency, as recorded in Bede's *Ecclesiastical History of the English People*, book 1, chapter 27: "If you have found anything either in the Roman or the Gaulish church or any other Church, which may be more pleasing to Almighty God, you should make a careful selection of them and sedulously teach the Church of the English, which is still new in the faith, what you have been able to gather from other churches.... Therefore choose from every individual Church whatever things are devout, religious, and right. And when you have collected these as it were into one bundle, see that the minds of the English grow accustomed to it."[239]

Later, at the Synod of Bangor, Augustine met with bishops of England and Wales and offered them a path to unity, which Warren's version of Bede renders: "In many respects you act in a manner contrary to our customs, and indeed to those of the Universal Church; and yet if you will obey me in these three things: to celebrate Easter at the proper time; to perform the office of baptism, in which we are born again to God, according to the custom of the Holy Roman and Apostolic Church; and to join us in preaching the word of God to the English people (*Anglorum genti*) we will tolerate *all your other customs, though contrary to our own.*"[240]

Despite these assurances to Augustine, Gregory nevertheless began the process of supplanting the local rites with those of Rome.

[239] Bede, *Ecclesiastical History*, 1, 27.

[240] Warren, *The Liturgy and Ritual of the Celtic Church*, 76, emphasis Warren's.

This was a lengthy process, however. The Council of Whitby in 644 signaled the official beginning of the end of the liturgical diversity as Rome began to consolidate its ecclesiastical and liturgical authority in Ireland and Britain, when all the abbots and bishops were asked to use the Roman date of Easter. A hundred years later, the final agreement among Anglo-Saxons to follow Roman liturgical conformity was the synod of bishops known as the Council of Cloveshoe in 747—but that was Britain, not Ireland.

Despite Whitby, diverse customs continued to be practiced enough in Ireland that when King Henry II of England wanted to invade Ireland in 1179, his talking point to obtain a papal grant of Ireland was that he was doing it for the pope—so as to unite the Irish Church with Rome.

Other points of difference between Ireland and the Roman Church were the tonsure and the dating of Easter. The Roman tonsure is the one with which we are familiar today: the "halo" of hair on the top of a bald head. The Irish tonsure shaved the front part of the hair from ear to ear—a pattern that perhaps originated with the Druids.

The Controversy over the Dating of Easter

This toleration of diversity in general eventually had grave consequences for the Irish Church: the debate over Easter lasted so long in Ireland because of the toleration there of diversity of practice. Divergent dates for Easter presented serious diplomatic problems if an Irish king wanted to celebrate Easter while his Anglo-Saxon wife was still fasting for Lent. It's important to understand the roots of the controversy — so here is a brief summary.

Bede explains it all in book 3 of his *Ecclesiastical History*, chapter 5. The Irish calculated Easter in a perfectly orthodox manner — but they were given inaccurate information. Initially, they were using lunar tables from Rome that were made in A.D. 457, by Victorius of Aquitaine on a ninety-five-year cycle. Those were replaced by calculations of Dionysius the Small sometime in the sixth century (isn't it amazing how widely competent these abbots were back in the day?). Then, in 525, Bede produced a table for calculating Easter based on a lunar cycle of 532 years, that is, twenty-eight periods of nineteen years each, reckoned from the year of the birth of Christ — which Dionysius had had wrong, apparently. These minor differences caused the dates sometimes to coincide, sometimes to be a week apart, sometimes four weeks apart. To Anglo-Saxon Christians such differences were intolerable, and so the Council of Whitby was called in 664, after which most of the Irish agreed to observe the new Roman Easter. By 731, even the conservative Iona had followed suit.

Echoes of the East

Four documents in particular reveal some influence of the East on insular, that is, Irish, Christian liturgy: first, the Palimpsest Sacramentary of 650; second, the *Antiphonary of Bangor* of 680–691; third, *Ratio de Cursus* or *Explanation about the Liturgies*, written in the mid-eighth century as liturgical conformity was being imposed and liturgical diversity was disappearing, to defend the apostolic authority of the Irish and the Gallican liturgies; and fourth, the Stowe Missal of 842.

The Irish Palimpsest Sacramentary[241] in Munich is one of the best examples of early Gallican liturgy, and the Stowe Missal is a perfect example of later Gallican liturgy that had accepted many Roman elements including the Roman Canon. There are other surviving manuscripts such as the Book of Mulling, the Book of Dimma, and the Book of Deer, and various fragments around the Continent that reflect different stages of liturgical evolution, but these are the main ones. The Bobbio Missal, in earlier times ascribed to insular Christianity because of its association with Columbanus's monastery in Italy, is now considered thoroughly Gallican.

Chances are you have never heard the word *palimpsest*. It refers to a reused vellum manuscript. A calfskin would be used one time for the first book; then, when that book was no longer needed, or had to be changed, the ink would be scraped off, and new writing put on. Sometimes the new layer of ink would let some of the old ink show through, and that's why palimpsests are so important to historians.

The Palimpsest Sacramentary was first published in 1964 in Germany—so it had been lost and forgotten for thirteen hundred years. This is yet another example of why Celtic studies is such an exciting field. New discoveries are being made all the time.

Based on the script itself and the artwork, the date of 650–675 was given to it, and it was attributed to an Irish scribe working in Ireland or possibly at an Irish monastery in Northumbria. Two centuries afterwards, much of the seventh-century work was scraped off, and different writing was done on the same vellum.

Altogether, the sacramentary consists of 158 fragments from thirty-one different Masses—all very Gallican, with a few traces of

[241] A sacramentary is a book that contains the rites and prayers to be used in administering different sacraments.

Gnostic texts, none of which are in the eucharistic liturgy. It gives evidence of liturgical importations. The Mass in Latin for January 1 includes a phrase in the epiclesis from the Acts of Thomas, a Gnostic work that existed in Syriac and Greek from before the year 250—and yet here it is in Latin. "Nowhere else, save in Syria and Ireland, is there any trace of this epiclesis,"[242] writes Crehan. There are a few Roman sections, "but the Roman Canon is not presupposed as the norm, as it is in the Stowe Missal."[243]

If only the vellum could speak! Second-century Syriac or Greek prayers, but in Latin, a Syrian epiclesis, and no Roman Canon. Who put it together and what were they doing?

The Palimpsest only became widely available for study when it was published in 1964, so it is not factored into older research. O'Donoghue refers to it as the "unwanted child" of scholars of ancient Ireland, reflecting their uncertainty because it doesn't exactly fit into any preconceived patterns. The first use of the vellum in the Palimpsest was in the third quarter of the seventh century; in the second half of the ninth century, the vellum was reused by an Irish hand, and the original writing scraped off. When the original text was partly reconstructed, some text was lost before it was published by Dold and Eizenhofer. It is now not only a treasure as a surviving Irish manuscript (though it resides in Munich) but, in the view of liturgist O'Donoghue, "the oldest surviving liturgical manuscript with strong Irish connections pointing to Ireland as being one with most of Western Europe in using a form of the Gallican rite."[244]

[242] Crehan, "The Liturgical Trade Route," 91.

[243] O'Donoghue, "Insular Chrismals," footnote to Dold and Eizenhofer, *Das Irische Palimpsestakramentar,* 78.

[244] Ibid., 77ff.

The *Antiphonary of Bangor*

I've mentioned the *Antiphonary of Bangor* in passing, but I've barely scratched the surface of its vast significance.

An antiphonary contains the chants for all the canonical hours for every day of the year. The *Antiphonary of Bangor* is not a real antiphonary, but it got that name when it was discovered, and the name has stuck. The *Antiphonary* (which is more a hymn book for the Liturgy of the Hours than an actual antiphonary) is a codex of thirty-six leaves written at the monastery of Bangor, County Down, between 680 and 691, and brought to the Ambrosian Library in 1609 from Columbanus's Library at Bobbio, which is northeast of Genoa, Italy. This is another manuscript that could tell a fascinating tale of how it traveled: from Ireland to Bobbio to Milan!

It was found in the Ambrosian Library in Milan by Ludovico Muratori (1672–1750), a priest and leading scholar of the early Italian Enlightenment, as he was organizing ancient manuscripts collected there. It includes: six canticles and twelve hymns; sixty-nine Collects for use at the canonical hours and four others, seventy anthem hymns, antiphons, and Collects in no particular order, a Creed, and a Pater Noster. No fewer than fifteen different people seem to have written the manuscript, with the items in no special sequence, and without any close connection—that is, according to Warren, who included it in his *Liturgy and Ritual of the Keltic Church* of 1881, and later published the first facsimile in collotype in London in 1893. A *collotype* is a photographic-based reproduction, a very early copying technology. The *Antiphonary* has been often reprinted since.

The *Antiphonarium Benchorense*, for that is its name in Latin, has been studied by one of the world's premier scholars of the ancient liturgical music, Peter Jeffery, a man after my own heart, because he sued a rock band for causing him hearing loss. Jeffery notes that the second section is a collection of Collects or prayers to be said at the different liturgical hours, or after the psalms and canticles of the Office, according to widespread Eastern and Western practice. It is Jeffrey's opinion that the *Antiphonary* is a version of St. Columbanus's Office, as it had developed after a time on the Continent, under influence of Gallican and northern Italian traditions. But he has his doubts: it has enough of a relationship to the Mozarabic liturgical traditions of Spain that maybe it had an Irish rather than a Continental origin. Other scholars have traced a line of liturgical transmission running from Syria and Egypt in the sixth and seventh centuries to Visigothic Spain and thence to Brittany, to Cornwall, to South Wales, and to Ireland.[245]

Liturgical Back to the Future?

The idea that there was, and should be again, a "Celtic Church," an Irish-Scottish-Welsh unique form of Christianity, out of the reach of Rome, has attracted a following among some Anglicans, who, confronted with the theological and liturgical disarray in their church, are understandably looking for something authentic. As if by some curse of race-memory, they cannot find their way to Rome, even through the Personal Ordinariate of the Chair of St. Peter, which was established in 2012 to welcome Episcopal and Anglican clergy and congregations into union with Rome while using the Sarum Rite of 1549 in England.

[245] See Crehan, "The Liturgical Trade Route," 87–99.

Some branches of Eastern Orthodoxy also have gone back to the future liturgically. The ancient Gallican liturgy, recast as the "Divine Liturgy according to St. Germanus of Paris," was put into use in 1946 by the Orthodox Catholic Church of France (ECOF) and has since spread to other European nations and to North and South America. A similar impetus has created a "Western Rite" in a branch of the Russian Orthodox Church Outside Russia (ROCOR) — with a liturgy that relies on no less than the seventh-century Stowe Missal and *Antiphonary of Bangor* as its service book.

Some poems in the *Antiphonary* are treasures of Gaelic literature, the earliest written verse. Much of its content is in verse or rhythmical form, evidence that "Irish poets discovered the rich possibilities of rhyme and stanzaic division soon after the introduction of Latin literature, and they exploited these possibilities in quite an original and masterly way.... In both hymns and collects we will find echoes of the old rhythmical, alliterative type of verse, which continued to be used along with the new syllabic metres until the end of the Old Irish period."[246]

What is probably the first eucharistic hymn in the entire West is "Sancti Venite" in the *Antiphonary*. O'Donoghue considers it seventh-century;[247] Curran thinks it was composed in the sixth.[248] Seven Communion antiphons appear in the *Antiphonary*, the first of which occurs as a Mozarabic *ad accedentes*. Carl Baumstark (1872–1948), a German orientalist, philologist, and liturgist,

[246] Curran, *The Antiphonary of Bangor*, 20–21.
[247] O'Donoghue, "Insular Chrismals," 88.
[248] Curran, *The Antiphonary of Bangor*, 47.

considered the first part of that text "to be an almost verbatim translation of a Greek original of the sixth century, and of Palestinian origin."[249]

Another item, "Hymnum Dicat," has attracted some scholarly discussion about its origins. Traditionally attributed to St. Hilary of Poitiers, that idea has been challenged, though "the hymn is certainly not Irish—there is nothing like it in metre or language in the whole extent of Irish hymnody," says one critic.[250] On textual examination, it does not conform to known writings of Hilary. Italian patristics scholar Manilo Simonetti (1926–2017) regarded one aspect of the final stanza to be "a clear sign of Oriental influence on the Irish, since Oriental hymnody alone furnishes adequate models for it."[251]

The two most influential liturgical centers in the early Christian period were Jerusalem and Egypt, and traditions from these places found their way into the Irish Office through Cassian and other Western sources. The hymn "Precamur Patrem," unlike all the other hymns in the *Antiphonary*, does not appear in other Irish documents of the time.[252] It has a poetic form distinct from other Late Latin forms, since it is based not on syllable length but on syllable counting and stress.[253] Stancliffe points out that "this hymn contains verbal echoes of Cassian's *Institutes*, of Jerome's famous letter Twenty-Two to Eustochium on virginity, of an oration of

[249] Carl Baumstark, *Liturgie Comparée* (Editions de Chevetogne, 1953), 108, quoted in King, *Liturgies of the Past*, 272.

[250] Curran, *The Antiphonary of Bangor*, 22.

[251] Ibid., 23n18.

[252] Ibid., 56.

[253] Michael Lapidge, "Columbanus and the Antiphonary of Bangor," *Peritia* 4 (1985): 104–116, https://codecs.vanhamel.nl/Lapidge_1985a, 114.

Gregory of Nazianzus, and Basil's Rule."[254] This is further evidence that Columbanus, to whom it has been attributed, was steeped in the Eastern Fathers.

Some historians considered the hymn in honor of Bangor itself, "Benchuir bona regular," to be a "problem" because in it the monastery calls itself "a true vine brought over from Egypt," attesting to the Irish monks' sense of continuing with the Egyptian founders of monasticism, and the scholarship of previous generations deemed that impossible (see page 126 for the complete verse).

Ratio de Cursus

Liturgy and Church practice in Ireland varied considerably—which meant that the liturgy taken by Irish monks and missionaries across the sea also varied considerably. From the beginning, the free rein given to liturgical adaptation from sources was noticeable: "Even in their liturgy the Irish differed from other early churches by celebrating the Eucharist with great variation and a multiplication of collects and prayers," Warren noted.[255]

This diversity shocked Bede, who was a staunch advocate of everything Roman. The late Fr. Brendan Bradshaw, a Catholic priest who was a professor at Cambridge University and longtime editor of the *Journal of Ecclesiastical History*, recognized that Ireland's ties to Rome were "tenuous and tension-ridden" and said discreetly that Bede's account of Ireland "registers the shock of an orthodox Latin churchman on encountering the institutional

[254] Stancliffe, "Columbanus's Monasticism," 27.

[255] F. E. Warren, *The Liturgy and Ritual of the Celtic Church*, 3rd ed, ed. Neil Xavier O'Donoghue (Piscataway, NJ: Gorgias Press, 2010), 96. Further references to *The Liturgy and Ritual of the Celtic Church* will be distinguished by year.

form of the Celtic Church."[256] "Those wild Irish!" I can imagine Bede saying to himself.

Gallican or otherwise, by the eighth century, the Irish Office and liturgy was called the *Cursus Scottorum* (remember that *Scotti* was the old Latin name for the Irish), and it was becoming clear that it was on the road to extinction. The *Ratio de Cursus* was written in about the mid-eighth century by an anonymous monk, in order to present and defend both the Irish and Gallican liturgies in the face of the innovation and standardization that were coming with the new directives from Rome.

The *Ratio*, along with another recently rediscovered work called the *Life of Samson*, makes a clear case for the apostolic authority for those older liturgies.

Today the *Ratio* is a single manuscript, known as Cotton Nero A.II, fos. 37–42, in the British Museum. It was first edited in the seventeenth century and was translated by Moran in 1864. It reads like one side of an eighth-century liturgy war, as it responds to unidentified claims that Irish and Gallican liturgy were not as authentic as the liturgy in use at Rome. The author defends both the *Cursus Scottorum* and the Gallican liturgy from charges they lacked apostolic authority by arguing that true liturgy derives not just from the Church of St. Peter but also from the other apostles, particularly St. Mark (†68), who founded the See of Alexandria, and St. John, who are the sources of the *Cursus Scottorum*.

The *Ratio* claims the Gallican liturgy was inherited from the earliest bishops of Gaul (Trophimus, Pothinus, and Irenaeus of Lyons), who took their practice from Peter in Rome and John in Ephesus. Irenaeus, the second bishop of Lyon in Gaul, was from

[256] Bradshaw, "The Wild and Woolly West," 3.

Polycarp's hometown in Smyrna, modern-day Turkey. Columbanus also had a particular awareness of Polycarp, the mentor of Irenaeus.[257]

How the Office was recited was one of the points of controversy. The author of the *Ratio* insists on the apostolic authority of Gallican bishops to create reciprocating antiphons and responsories, culled from the Old and New Testaments, as from the writings of various authorities and first sung by St. John the Evangelist, and passed down to his disciple Polycarp, from whom it was brought to Gaul by St. Irenaeus. Insistence by the *Ratio*'s author that his liturgy had not been composed by "any Gallican or British cleric given to singing, as many think" suggests that he was defending the Eastern practice of chanting the Hours or the liturgy, a part of Gallican tradition, against those who promoted the quieter Roman liturgical model.[258] If Warren had not dismissed the *Ratio* and had taken it more seriously, he might have found therein some grist for his mill: like the *Vita Samsonis*, it does not celebrate Roman authority.

The *Ratio*'s author demonstrates that the Office and liturgy were sung, beginning with the *Cursus Romanus*. He emphasizes that in the liturgy of St. Mark, which was followed by the Irish, the entire community, "male and female used to sing together the Gloria, the Sanctus, the Lord's Prayer and the Great Amen," implying that this was an ancient apostolic practice. By the eighth century in Roman practice, all these prayers were recited by the priest alone or by the

[257] Constant J. Mews, "Apostolic Authority and Celtic Liturgies: From the Vita Samsonis to the Ratio de Cursus," in *St. Samson of Dol and the Earliest History of Brittany, Cornwall and Wales*, ed. Lynette Olson, 115–136 (Woodbridge, UK: Boydell Press, 2017), doi.org/10.1017/9781787440319.008, 115.
[258] Ibid., 126–127.

priest with only other clergy. Gregory the Great confirms that the Lord's Prayer was recited by the priest alone, even though he notes that it had been sung by all the people in the Greek Church.[259] The *Cursus Scottorum*, thus, followed this Greek custom.

Peter Jeffery has analyzed the argument of the *Ratio.* There was first the *Cursus Orientalis*, the author of the *Ratio* wrote, citing Eusebius and Josephus, that was prayed by St. Mark the Evangelist in the days when all Egypt and Italy were as one church, when "all, both men and women, sang *Sanctus* or *Gloria in excelsis deo* or the Lord's Prayer and *Amen.*"[260] It was edited by St. Athanasius, but not used in Gaul. It had an office for each of the twelve hours and was sung by St. Macarius, probably the Desert Father, though the name was also identified with Lérins.

After writing down the Gospel dictated to him by St. Peter, St. Mark brought this *cursus* from Rome to Egypt, where it spread both through the Egyptian monasticism of Anthony, Paul, and Macarius, and through the Cappadocian monasticism of Gregory of Nazianzus and Basil the Great. From Egypt Cassian brought it to Lérins, whence Caesarius brought it to Arles and it spread throughout Gaul. Germanus of Auxerre and Lupus of Troyes used it in their monasteries and brought it to Britain, where they taught it to St. Patrick ... and after him it passed to St. Comgall the founder of Bangor, where it was used by three thousand monks. It was Comgall who sent Columbanus into Gaul, and he established the Irish *cursus* at Luxeuil.[261]

All this was known as the Ephesine theory of the origin of the Celtic liturgy.

[259] Ibid., 128.

[260] Jeffery, "Eastern and Western Elements in the Irish Monastic Prayer of the Hours," 133.

[261] Ibid.

The *Ratio* was anonymous and very politically incorrect for its day, and since it was on the losing side it remained ignored for centuries afterwards, dismissed and largely forgotten. Only recently has it been reconsidered.

"Of course we do not believe this fantastic story," writes Jeffrey. "Yet the writer was not completely wrong, for the Irish monks did make use of varying combinations of elements and traditions from most of these places, and the number of religious men and women who had once followed Irish usages may indeed have been as great as he claimed it was."[262] Then Jeffrey adds a poignant comment:

> But we who have lived through another era of liturgical upheaval, with its own excesses of competing and fanciful historical claims, can look back with sympathy on the anonymous writer who, in solitary defiance of the spirit of his age, sat down to pen, against an irresistible wave of Romanizing uniformity, a final protest on behalf of the tradition of Cassian and Columban and all those saintly monks—the last desperate defense of the Irish monastic office.

Warren dismissed the whole account as "outlandish." Nineteenth-century Roman Catholic scholar Louis Duchesne (1843–1922) also sought to disprove the Ephesine theory on the basis of then-current knowledge. Duchesne, however, left open the possibility that Eastern (or what he called "Oriental") inclusions in the rite of Milan may have been allowed by Bishop Ambrose. He believed that the Gallican liturgy had roots in Milan, as a channel from the East—but that St. Ambrose had had the prudence not to declare a liturgy war. He "thought it inopportune to introduce

[262] Ibid., 134.

useless changes in the domain of ritual," as Duchesne phrased it in this passage:

> It is well known that the Gallican Liturgy, in the features distinguishing it from the Roman use, betrays all the characteristics of the Eastern liturgies.... Some of its formularies are to be found word for word in the Greek texts in use in the Churches of the Syro-Byzantine rite either in the fourth century or somewhat later. This close resemblance implies an importation. The Gallican Liturgy is an Oriental liturgy, introduced into the West towards the middle of the fourth century. Now, apart from the presence of the Court at Milan, and the numerous assemblies of Oriental bishops held there, we have to take into account the important fact that the Church of Milan had at its head for nearly twenty years (355–374) a Cappadocian, Auxentius, who had been designated by the Emperor Constantius to occupy the see of St. Dionysius, when the latter was exiled for the Catholic faith. Auxentius belonged to the clergy of the Court, who were out of sympathy with St. Athanasius and the defenders of "consubstantial" orthodoxy.... After the defeat of the Arianising party which, in the east, followed closely upon the breaking up of this council [of Ariminum, 359], Auxentius maintained his position, and remained fifteen years in his see, notwithstanding the efforts made to dislodge him. This would seem to indicate that he had a strength of mind beyond the common. We can readily believe, therefore, that during his long episcopate he made some impression upon his clergy and upon the internal organisation of his Church. St. Ambrose, his

> successor, found many customs established which did not all seem to require correction. His broad-mindedness ... is shown by his retention of the whole of the clerical staff left or organised by his predecessor. *Possibly, doctrine being safeguarded by the very fact of his elevation to the see of Milan, Ambrose thought it inopportune to introduce useless changes in the domain of ritual* [emphasis added]. Certainly many of the most important Milanese peculiarities in discipline and worship go back to his episcopate, and, seeing that these peculiarities have a distinctly Oriental character, they could not have been introduced by him. It is more natural to believe that they existed before him, and that he had only sanctioned customs previously imported.
>
> ... Milan was in easy communication with Constantinople.... Auxentius was not the only Greek who in the fourth century may have exercised episcopal functions in a Latin country. His action in the liturgical domain may have been but an episode in a larger movement.

"It must be considered certain that St Ambrose would have left nothing in them which could possibly have fostered heresy."[263]

Later scholars followed Duchesne's lead: "The Celtic liturgy ... consisted for the greater part of foreign elements: of texts taken from the old Spanish, or the Gallican, sometimes also from the Roman and even the Oriental liturgies," wrote Josef Jungmann, one of the eminent liturgists of the twentieth century.[264] Mozarabic elements in the Irish liturgy had been noted by Warren[265] and were

[263] Duchesne, *Christian Worship: Its Origin and Evolution*, 93–94; last paragraph from n. 2.

[264] Jungmann, *The Early Liturgy*, 232.

[265] Warren, *The Liturgy and Ritual of the Celtic Church* (1881), 63.

confirmed as far back as 1907. In 1961, Hillgarth explained how the "Spanish symptoms" could have come about.[266]

Vita Samsonis

Constant Mews, professor of medieval thought at Monash University, is a pioneer in research on an almost forgotten and yet hugely consequential bishop named Samson of Dol. Mews has examined Samson's little-known biography from the seventh century, the *Vita Samsonis*, in conjunction with the *Ratio de Cursus* from the eighth century.

St. Samson of Dol was a fifth-century bishop from Wales who had an interest in liturgy. He went to Ireland and Cornwall, then ended up a bishop in Brittany, where a biography of him was written around the year 620. The *Vita* records the beginning of a British/Irish mission to the Continent; the *Ratio* celebrates and defends the expansion of an Irish-inspired monastic network.

Samson's key mentor was Illtud, who had been ordained by Germanus of Auxerre—in other words, at the very beginning of insular Christianity, circa 435–447. *Vita Samsonis* was written by an unidentified nephew of Samson's cousin Enoch, who enumerates the library available to Samson in fifth-century Gaul: the *Dialogues* and *Life of St. Martin* by Sulpicius Severus, the writings of Cassian, Evagrius, Jerome, Pomerius of Arles, and Rufinus's history of the monks of Egypt—in other words, the Desert Fathers. Like them, Samson understood his liturgical duties to be in a tradition that went back to the apostles. The Irish and British celebration of Easter followed the practice of Sulpicius Severus (†425). It focused more on Christ's Resurrection than on His Passion, as in

[266] Hillgarth, "Visigothic Spain and Early Christian Ireland," 193–194.

the African and Roman churches[267]—a joyous focus echoed in monastic poetry, and continued in the Eastern liturgy yet. Says Mews: "It seems more likely that in the sixth century Samson simply continued British liturgical custom."[268]

Mews compared the *Ratio de Cursus* and the *Vita Samsonis* and concluded: "Comparing these two texts allows us to see how both British and Irish monks understood their traditions prior to the imposition of Roman liturgical practice in the mid-eighth century and consolidation during the age of Charlemagne,"[269] noting that they also recorded the historic origins of the other rites: *Cursus Romanus*, *Gallorum*, *Ambrosii*, *Benedicti*, and *alius orientalis*. The author repeated the same argument that Colmán had used at the Synod of Whitby to defend the Irish date of Easter.

As Mews sees it, "After the anointing of Pepin by the pope in 754, the Roman liturgy became the vehicle by which a new dynasty could assert its power."[270] Leaving politics aside, suffice it to say that the *Ratio de Cursus* connects the dots between the Gallican liturgy and the Desert Fathers.

The "Ephesine" theory of the *Ratio* attracted new scholarly attention with the 2013 volume *L'Enluminure et le Sacré Irlande et Grande-Bretagne*, by Dominique Barbet-Massin, a French scholar of Irish manuscripts. Barbet-Massin found the debt to Irenaeus significant because the only place where knowledge of the writings of Irenaeus was preserved in the Latin West in the early medieval period was in a so-called "Irish" group of manuscripts at Corbie, a monastery in Picardy founded in the seventh century by Bathild from Luxeuil.[271]

[267] Mews, "Apostolic Authority and Celtic Liturgies," 120.
[268] Ibid., 120.
[269] Ibid., 115.
[270] Ibid., 133.
[271] Ibid., 126.

Peter Jeffery sums it up nicely. He is primarily referring to the Divine Office, but his words apply equally to liturgy: "By the eighth century a new center was emerging in the West, and the liturgical situation in Europe was beginning to change radically, as the various local traditions of the Gallican churches were beginning to be suppressed in favor of the rite of the city of Rome. . . . What really happened, in short, was the creation of a new liturgical tradition —an amalgam of Roman and non-Roman texts and customs, forged by Frankish smiths in a Gallican workshop. It was this new creation that, after being reintroduced into Rome itself, passed into history as the medieval Roman rite we know."[272]

The *Cursus Scottorum*, whatever it may have been, was melted into and became part of the precious metal used in the forge, despite the defense of it by the author of the *Ratio*.

The Stowe Missal

Likewise, I have hardly begun to discuss the Stowe Missal.

Until the Palimpsest was discovered, the missal[273] had been considered the oldest existing manuscript from the ancient Irish Church. First (re)published by the Henry Bradshaw Society in 1893, it was the primary source used by Warren to develop the concept of "Celtic liturgy." George Frederic Warner, who brought it to publication, was keeper of manuscripts at the British Museum. His opinion that the missal seems to have been originally written around the year 800 is accepted as a conservative estimate today,

[272] Jeffery, "Eastern and Western Elements in the Irish Monastic Prayer of the Hours," 128.

[273] Royal Irish Academy MS D II 3, cat. 138, fol. 67 v5=Thes. ii 250. Also available at: https://archive.org/details/publications32henruoft/page/n1/mode/2up. Sir George F. Warner, *The Stowe Missal* (London: Henry Bradshaw Society, 1915).

which means that it could be even older. One indication of an earlier date is that the litany in the missal includes petitions for the emperor and for the Roman Army, and for catechumens and penitents—but it makes no mention of the pope.

Some consider the missal to be a sacramentary, technically speaking, because it contains only the words spoken by the priest, and not rubrics or instructions about actions to perform. Marion Hatchett (1927–2009), an Anglican liturgical scholar, however, considered it "the earliest book that can properly be called a missal rather than a sacramentary for it apparently contains in one volume all of the texts necessary for a celebration of the eucharist."[274] For O'Donoghue it is "perhaps the first book anywhere in the west to which the title 'missal' can be attributed, since it contains an order of the eucharistic liturgy and three 'common' Masses: one for saints, one for penitents, and one for the dead."[275]

It is a small manuscript of sixty-seven leaves or folios, 5⅝ inches long by 4½ inches broad, located in the Royal Irish Academy library. That small size suggests that it was a "pocket missal," perhaps meant to be carried by a traveling priest. It is written in Latin in five different hands, and the last three folios are in Old Irish. Between 1026 and 1033, it was honored with a magnificent *cumhdach* of oak clad with copper and silver, decorated with angels, animals, and other art.[276] This book shrine is a treasure itself: it is one of only five to have survived to modern times. The missal disappeared

[274] Marion J. Hatchett, "The Eucharistic Rite of the Stowe Missal," chap. 10 in *Time and Community: In Honor of Thomas Julian Talley*, ed. J. Neil Alexander, 153–170 (Washington, D.C.: Pastoral Press, 1990), 154.

[275] O'Donoghue, "Insular Chrismals," 63.

[276] "Stowe Missal," Irish Script on Screen, https://www.isos.dias.ie/search.html?q=Stowe+Missal&f=%7B%7D.

sometime after the *cumhdach* was made, until it was discovered in the eighteenth century hidden inside a wall of twelfth-century Lackeen Castle near Lorrha, County Tipperary, during some reconstruction; hence, it is sometimes called the Lorrha Missal.

Whoever hid it did a great service to history, because being inside that wall allowed it to survive the Reformation's destruction. George Nugent, the first marquess of Buckingham, lived at Stowe House in Buckinghamshire, England, at the time of those wall-moving renovations on his castle in Ireland, and he sold it to the nation (which would have been the United Kingdom). From thence it eventually passed to the Royal Irish Academy in Dublin, where today it is catalogued as MS D II 3.

To be sure, the missal is a puzzle in itself. Two editions exist within the same manuscript, the first by Maelruain (†792), which contains no rubrics, the second by Móelcaích, approximately fifty years later. Moélcaích erased, rearranged, and added material. One of the things he apparently added was a "Treatise on the Mass," called the Tract, which is an instruction in Old Irish on a then-new canon from Rome. There is nothing like that Tract in any other manuscript. The presence of the two editions is a great resource for the study of the late stage of the different liturgical practices.

Overall, the missal seems to have been written about the turn of the eighth century, was probably copied from an earlier manuscript, and is "eighty percent Roman liturgy."[277] Crehan made the case that, based on the use of the word *dominicum* for "Mass," the date should more probably be the fifth or sixth century.[278] Forty years before Crehan, McCarthy had thought that it may have been

[277] Dix, *The Shape of the Liturgy*, 468.

[278] J. H. Crehan, "Canon Dominicus Papa Gelasi," *Vigilar Christianae* 12, no. 1 (May 1958): 47, jstor.org/stable/1582114.

compiled as early as 500.[279] The missal has been studied continuously since 1819, when Dr. Charles O'Connor first included it in the catalogue of manuscripts in the Stowe Library. In Hatchett's view, Móelcaích's version of the Stowe Missal has "all the elements of a complete Gallican eucharistic prayer surrounding or included as an insertion in the now obligatory Roman canon."[280]

The first version of the liturgy in the Stowe Missal is earlier than the manuscript itself. The *Hanc Igitur* text, which is not found in any other known manuscript, indicates that there were still pagans around: "*Hanc igitur oblationem servitutis nostrae sed et cunctae familiae tuae*—This is the offering of our service to you and your entire family. . . . *Quessumus domine ut placatus suscipias eumque adque omnem populum ab idulorum cultura eripias et ad te deum verum patrem convertas*—We beseech thee, Lord, that thou mayest receive with mercy and deliver him and all the people from the worship of the idols, and turn to thee the true God the father."

Some maintain that the Stowe Missal evidences a liturgy in which the liturgical building housed only the celebrant bishop and priests, while the congregation and perhaps the deacon stayed outside unless they entered to receive Communion. This conclusion is reached because deacons' parts are separate from the celebrant's part.

Hatchett's analysis indicates that the first liturgy in the missal is very Romanized, though it lacks some Roman Rite features such as the Introit, the Kyrie, and the Agnus Dei. Most of the prayers are in the concise Roman form; the Old Testament reading is gone; the Eucharistic Prayer is the Roman Canon; and the *Pax* (Kiss of

[279] E. J. Gwynn, "The Stowe Missal," *Irish Church Quarterly* 9, no. 34 (April 1916): 123, www.jstor.org/stable/30026443.

[280] Hatchett, "The Eucharistic Rite of the Stowe Missal," 162.

Peace) has been moved to the Roman position, after the Fraction Rite but before Communion. Yet a number of Gallican features remain, including a canticle in the entrance rite, the Creed, a chant after the Gospel, and the location of the Pater Noster. It has several unusual, if not unique, features: inclusion of prayers after the Epistle and Alleluia; the placement of a litany between the Epistle and the Gospel; and a commemoration of Old Testament saints within the Eucharistic Prayer. It contains relatively early forms of the Gloria, the Nicene Creed, and the Roman Canon.[281]

Despite the lateness of its provenance, Stowe shows some interesting Eastern traits. The Treatise on the Mass, for instance, "shows that the chalice was prepared before the mass."[282] "It may be inferred that the offerings were prepared before mass,"[283] as continues to be the custom in the East.

The missal includes a vesting prayer, which closely resembles the types of formula that, according to Dom Gregory Dix, "are found in the Alexandrian Liturgy of S. Mark, and that reached the Gallican churches about the tenth century."[284] Yet here the formula is in Ireland in the eighth century—or earlier! The Alexandrian Liturgy of St. Mark could, of course, have come to Ireland earlier with those hypothetical Egyptian monks.

The Creed in the Stowe Missal is different from the Creed in the *Antiphonary of Bangor*. Recent research indicates that it was directly translated from the Greek of the Council of Chalcedon!

Aidan Breen, of the School of Celtic Studies of the Dublin Institute for Advanced Studies, drew this stunning conclusion in

[281] Ibid.

[282] Ryan, "The Mass in the Early Irish Church," 379.

[283] Ní Chatháin, "The Liturgical Background of the Derrynavlan Altar Service," 131.

[284] Hunwicke, "Kerry and Stowe Revisited," 6.

1990. "The Stowe Creed," he says, "shows clear evidence of direct derivation from a Greek or Eastern liturgical source, of certainly a pre-seventh century date.... Its closest affinities throughout are ... its adherence to the authoritative Greek text of Actio II of Chalcedon." He concluded that it is an "independent translation of an early Greek version of the Creed, and ... in all probability both Greek text and usage were imported directly into the early Irish church from the same source."[285]

In other words, he says that the Creed in the Stowe Missal was directly translated from the Greek Constantinopolitan Creed! From a Greek source that gave both the text and instructions on where to place it in the liturgy, no less! He explicitly rejects the theory that the Stowe Creed is from a bilingual Roman baptismal liturgy of the late sixth and seventh centuries, because the same exact Stowe version is in an Egyptian papyrus fragment of a possibly earlier date than two Roman documents that might be considered its source.

Here we have further evidence that Ireland may have had direct contacts with the Eastern Church, even at this late date.

The very use of any Creed in the Mass hearkens to the East, since the Creed did not come into the Roman Rite until the eleventh century. The Creed began as a confession of faith at the time of Baptism in the Eastern Churches from the time of the Council of Constantinople (381). It was inserted into the liturgy by Peter the Fuller, patriarch of Constantinople from 471 to 478, and its use quickly became established throughout the Eastern Churches,[286] where it has always been chanted by the congregation

[285] Aidan Breen, "The Text of the Constantinopolitan Creed in the Stowe Missal," *Proceedings of the Royal Irish Academy: Archaeology, Culture, History, Literature* 90C (1990): 107–109, www.jstor.org/stable/25516064.

[286] Ibid., 108.

(Peter the Fuller had been a clothmaker before he became a priest, hence his odd name).

In imitation of the East, Reccared, a Visigothic king of Spain, introduced the Creed into the Mozarabic liturgy at the Third Council of Toledo (in 589, can. 2). Alcuin, the Northumbrian monk who had been trained by Irish monks, was at the court of Charlemagne, and he put it into the Gallican liturgy during the time of the Carolingian reforms. Here is more evidence of Fr. Crehan's "liturgical trade route" from Spain to Ireland to France.

The Creed made its way into the Roman Mass only in the year 1014, when King Henry II of Germany († 1024) insisted on having it as part of the Mass in which he was crowned Holy Roman Emperor by Pope Benedict VII. From there it passed into more common use.

It is not clear in Stowe how the Creed was recited. Alcuin repeatedly affirmed that it had been the custom at York to sing the Creed, in a text-form similar to that of Stowe.[287] Interestingly, under Alcuin's influence, Charlemagne had begun using the *Filioque* long before Rome did. That suggests that the Irish monks who evangelized the Anglo-Saxons followed Eastern practice. However, the list in the *Ratio* of what was chanted by the congregation does not include the Creed. Some scholars think that the practice of saying the Creed in the Mass came from the East to Spain, and from there to Ireland;[288] others think it came from the East to Ireland but not by way of Spain.[289]

In any event, the Nicene Creed is in the Mass of the Stowe Missal. It is in the first person singular and is located in the same

[287] Ibid., 119.

[288] Chadwick, *The Age of the Saints*, 57.

[289] Hillgarth, "Visigothic Spain and Early Christian Ireland," 194.

place as in later Western liturgies (not in the same position as in the Eastern or Mozarabic Rites).[290] The Stowe Creed suggests early influence from the East because there is no *Filioque* clause in it, and it hopes for (*spero*) rather than looks for (*expecto*) the resurrection of the dead.[291] Breen is of the opinion that "it is very likely that the additions to the creed, far from being added in the ninth or tenth centuries, were made but a few years after it had been copied into Stowe."[292] The *Filioque* clause is in Moélcaích's emendations to the second part, the Tract that is written in Old Irish, and it is the exact words of the text from the Councils of Friuli and Aachen (796/7 and 798). That it was added accurately within six years of those councils is an indication that the Irish liturgists "were literate and subtle members of mainstream Latinophone western society," notes Breen.[293]

One of the intriguing unique things in the Stowe Missal is the *oratio periculosa*, a kind of warning that appears in the text just prior to what today would be called the Consecration. It was already ancient when the missal was compiled: the Penitential of Gildas, who lived from about 500 to 570, imposes three days' penance if anyone has changed anything in the words where "Danger" is noted.[294] The Penitential of Cummian has the same penance.

This is a stunning indication of how seriously transubstantiation was regarded, and how profoundly the Real Presence was

[290] Hatchett, "The Eucharistic Rite of the Stowe Missal," 157.

[291] Ibid.

[292] Breen, "The Text of the Constantinopolitan Creed in the Stowe Missal," 121.

[293] Ibid., 11.

[294] Joseph H. Crehan, "The Theology of Eucharistic Consecration: Role of the Priest in Celtic Liturgy," *Theological Studies* 40, no. 2, (June 1979): 335, https://doi.org/10.1177/004056397904000206.

respected: if the priest's attention wavered, it could cost him his soul.

The Stowe Treatise on the Mass in Warner's 1915 translation, page 40, reads thus: "At the words *Accepit Iesus Panem* the priest bows himself down thrice to repent of his sins. He offers it [the chalice] to God and the people kneel, and here no voice cometh, lest it disturb the priest, for this is the right of it, that his mind separate not from God while he chants this lesson. Hence its *nomen* is *periculosa oratio*."[295] The congregation, according to verse 11 of the Tract, was already prostrate on the floor. "It would not be surprising if this detail of the liturgy came to South Wales and Ireland from Syria by what I have described as the liturgical trade route via Spain and Brittany," comments Fr. Crehan.

The giving of Communion to infants is part of the rite of Baptism in the Stowe Missal. It occurs immediately after the *Pedilavium*, or washing of the feet, another baptismal custom that has since disappeared.

The administration of Communion to infants was normal in the early Church. It is testified to by Pope Paschal II in a letter to Bishop Turgot of St. Andrews, Scotland, in answer to questions from King Alexander, circa 1112–1114. Originally in a cover letter accompanying a book, Pope Paschal says: "From ancient times the Roman church has given the Body and Blood to those capable of receiving them. To those not capable an infusion of the Blood alone is given to revive and conserve them. Therefore what the Lord said in the Gospel, 'unless you eat my flesh and drink my blood you do not have life within you,' applies only to those who are capable of receiving them." Pascal seems to advocate that infants be given Communion in the form of a drop from the chalice, as

[295] Ibid., 336.

they were "not capable" of receiving in the normal way (that is, the eucharistic bread).[296] The ancient custom continues to this day in Eastern Churches both Catholic and Orthodox, where baptized infants and children of all ages receive Communion by intinction or spoon.

Another interesting echo of the East is in the fifth Old Irish rubric in Stowe, which refers to the *ablu tuáir*. That would seem to be the celebrant's host, and it might refer to the large piece of bread in the middle of the paten at the time of the very complicated fraction laid out in the missal. One scholar, Plummer, suggested that it might correspond to the large host in the middle of the paten styled *Agnus*, or "Lamb," in a ninth-century Spanish liturgy. In the Byzantine Liturgy of John Chrysostom, the first portion detached from the round leavened loaf is called *ho aminos* "the lamb." The further confraction, the separation of the Eucharist into numerous pieces on the paten, is described in detail in the Stowe Missal and is unique in Christendom.

An interesting passage immediately after the words of Consecration is written in Moélcaích's hand in 842: "*Adventum meum sperabitis donec iterum veniam ad vos de caelis*" (You all must wait until I come to you again from Heaven). The same passage occurs in the Palimpsest Sacramentary of 650. Noteworthy is that the same words are in the common form of the Jerusalem Liturgy of St. James.[297]

Another point illustrating the combination of Eastern and Western elements in the Irish Church is the memento of the dead in the litany of the names of the blessed. This lengthy list invokes the memory of patriarchs, prophets, John the Baptist, the Virgin Mary, apostles, martyrs, the earliest monks of Egypt, Paul the

[296] O'Donoghue, *The Eucharist in Pre-Norman Ireland*, 145.

[297] Crehan, "The Liturgical Trade Route," 93.

Hermit, Anthony of the Desert, the rest of the Fathers of the desert of Scete, bishops, and priests. This litany is not modified in Móel Caích's Tract. Clearly, these were the people the Irish considered the forefathers—and foremothers!—of their faith.

The bidding prayer, or second litany, in the first Mass in Stowe includes "*pro piissimis imperatoribus et pro omni exercitu Romano*" (for our most devout emperors and all the Roman Army). Certainly this a "reminder of the Byzantine origin of the prayer." Hatchett concurs that it is "related in placement and content to some eastern litanies."[298] He considers it to have been written quite early because it includes petitions for the emperor and the Roman Army—but not for the pope. In the opinion of Edmund Bishop (1846–1917), this litany was originally Greek, but he does not speculate how it may have come to be in Stowe or in the Book of Cerne, an early ninth-century prayer book in Latin with Old English glosses and Hiberno-Saxon decoration, or in the Cotton MS Galba, another Anglo-Saxon manuscript, where the identical text appears.[299]

The Tract on the Mass that is bound with the Stowe Missal refers to an Alleluia after the Gospel, then a prayer, then another prayer, which have all been erased by a later editor. This is considered to be an indication that at one time, the *Pax* would have come at this point in the Gallican liturgy.

The Stowe Missal is devoid of rubrics. This seems odd by contemporary standards, but liturgist Robert Taft notes that "the early Constantinopolitan-type euchologies, almost totally rubric-free, were little more than a list of prayers, sometimes numbered. Where

[298] Hatchett, "The Eucharistic Rite of the Stowe Missal," 155–159.

[299] Edmund Bishop, "The Litany of Saints in the Stowe Missal," *Journal of Theological Studies* 7, no. 25 (October 1905): 122–136, jstor.org/stable/23947173.

they were to be inserted into the course of the service was indicated at most by a rudimentary title. Whatever else the presbyter or bishop was supposed to do during the celebration, and the diakonika of the deacon, were left to oral tradition and praxis."[300]

Liturgy in Ireland before the ninth century had characteristics quite distinct from the Roman Rite of the day; Warren attributed the differences to the influence of the Gallican liturgy, which developed in the sixth century and thrived for the first millennium. However, there are elements of the liturgy that do not trace back to Gaul but are in fact rooted in older, more Eastern traditions, specifically Jerusalem and Egypt, the two most influential liturgical centers in the early Christian period. Traditions from both these places found their way into the Irish Office through Cassian and other Western sources.[301]

As more research is done in this area, it may emerge that, far from being on the fringe of liturgical development, late antique Ireland may have been in the mainstream of it. Recent historical-critical work on the Roman *Canon Missae* has a high degree of consensus regarding similarities between it and the Alexandrian liturgies, especially that of Mark and the Coptic liturgy of Cyril.[302]

A Closing Thought

And why does all this matter? Why should we care that there were Christians in Ireland before St. Patrick and that they may have

[300] Robert Taft, S.J., "Mount Athos: A Late Chapter in the History of the Byzantine Rite," *Dumbarton Oaks Papers* 42 (1988): 179–194, jstor.org/stable/1291596, 192.

[301] Jeffery, "Eastern and Western Elements in the Irish Monastic Prayer of the Hours," 128.

[302] Olver, "Connections," 276.

come from Egypt? Or that seventh-century liturgy in Ireland may have adverted more to Alexandria than to Rome?

If you have Irish blood, of course, hopefully you want to know your own history. I hope this book has helped you to realize that Gaelic culture was the equal of any in the world in its time. And that there's much more to celebrate on St. Patrick's Day than green beer and shamrocks.

But even if you're not fortunate enough to be Irish, it matters.

It matters because as Catholic Christians we all need to have a long view of our own history. Tracing the fascinating forgotten history of the linkages between that (formerly) most post-Reformation Roman Catholic of countries, Ireland Mother Ireland, and Egypt, a place that most people would never even associate with the Faith, has been an exciting investigative journey. It has also helped me to better realize that in different centuries and different cultures and different languages faithful people have worshipped Our Lord and Savior Jesus Christ and received His true Body and Blood in different but equally reverential ways.

Angst over pious customs and liturgy has occupied the minds and conversations, and hindered relationships between many faithful Catholics, for three generations now. Angst can sometimes be relieved by knowledge: the Mass was not always in Latin, for instance, yet it was still valid; there was no Rosary in the fifth century, but devotion to the Mother of God was abundant and its expression magnificent.

How many times, and in how many contexts, have I written "more research needs to be done" or words to that effect?

In saying that, I was unconsciously repeating the plea of one of the first scholars to recognize the connections that I have just written about, though I did not realize it until I was doing my final revisions.

English philologist and Celticist Nora Chadwick (1891–1972) said it in 1960 in her groundbreaking Riddell Memorial Lecture series at King's College in University of Durham. Those lectures became *The Age of Saints in the Early Celtic Church.* Sixty years later her closing plea bears repeating: "Closer evidence is to be looked for from a comparative study of the earliest literary texts of the Irish and the Eastern Churches—a task which as yet few are qualified to undertake."[303]

Few are yet qualified to undertake it—but hopefully this volume will plant some seeds in the minds of future scholars who may yet qualify to undertake it.

[303] Chadwick, *The Age of Saints*, 117.

Appendix 1

Beware Modern-Day Druids

Before departing from the delights of exploring the past, a word of caution is in order. Pagan Druidism—or what is popularly believed to be Druidism—may be making a comeback in the twenty-first century.

Druidism has managed to slip easily into today's New Age miasma. If you visit a New Age store you will see Celtic knot designs all over the place, often along with fantastic explanations. At Renaissance festivals you may find a blending of Celtic influence with Wicca, a modern religion that sometimes claims descent from pre-Christian Irish and British paganism. It is replete with flowers, rocks, lakes, wild animals, horses, pigs, bulls, trees, sacred groves, and—oh, yes, the "little people" who live under the ground but are actually our ancestors in a different form, all of more or less equivalent value and sources of good magic and spiritual energy.

Yet, because the ancient Celts did not have a written language, modern reconstructions of Druid paganism are as much fantasy as fact. Some of it is half fantasy, some of it is evil, and some of it is sheer nonsense. Some of it is frankly anti-Christian, even though some modern "Druids" claim to be carrying on the original Christianity of Ireland, or Scotland, or Wales.

This siren song can be heard in varying degrees on some "Celtic spirituality" websites. One of the most extreme, in Britain, says that Celtic spirituality is "rooted in a Native Gaelic Spirituality, it has a deep reverence for our Mother Earth and all Her children" (note the capitals in the original!) and strives to develop the "imaginal faculties, the language of soul, through observing the Celtic Holy Days" that mark the "Wheel of the Year" and through creative study of Celtic mythology, the "Old Testament of the Gael." It encourages its adherents to "meet in groups, seeking together for the only Heaven there is; the one that must first be found hidden within, so that they may learn to live from there and call it home."[304]

"Observing the Celtic Holy Days" through "the creative study of ancient legends"? The Druidic festivals were the same as those of most primitive religions: they marked the changing of the seasons, as the moon traveled around the earth and the earth around the sun. Imbolc (February 1) was the end of winter; Samhain (November) was the beginning of winter. Today, February 1 is St. Brigid's Day, and November 1 is All Saints' Day. The evangelists of Ireland did not try to eliminate the preexisting festivals. Instead, they converted them to feasts.

To call Celtic mythology the "Old Testament of the Gael" is not only contrary to fact but an insult to Gaelic Christians: they certainly would not have seen it that way! One indisputable fact about Christians in Ireland from the earliest records was their devotion to the Scripture, and especially to the Old Testament—the real, written canonical one.

A less extreme form of Celtic spirituality begins with the premise that "because Ireland was out of the reach of Rome, the Celtic

[304] Céile Dé, https://www.ceilede.co.uk/company/welcome.

Church was not influenced by the rigid patriarchy and rules of Rome, and evolved into a more pure form of Christianity, more along gospel intentions." Therefore, "Celtic spirituality" manifests a wonderful connectedness and equality and friendship between men and women, and between humans and nature, that has otherwise been lost. This iteration of "Celtic spirituality" is eco-friendly and woman-empowering. Words you will not hear are *sin* or *right* or *wrong*. And you will not find the name of Jesus Christ or His Mother either!

However, there is a silver lining to this cloud of apocryphal "Celtic spirituality." The rediscovery of ancient Irish Christian writings has put into popular circulation some prayers and hymns that sadly had been lost for centuries. Originally in Old or Middle Irish, and translated anew recently, some of them are striking in their imagery. The Irish monks did live close to nature and they wrote beautifully about it. That shines through and in the intensity of their authors' attachment to the High King of Heaven, Jesus Christ.

The bottom line is this: take self-styled "Celtic spirituality" with a large grain of salt if you are a Catholic.

For Further Reference

Collections of Ancient Prayers and Poetry

Breeze, Andrew. *The Mary of the Celts*. Leominster, Herefordshire: Gracewing, 2008.

Carey, John. *King of Mysteries: Early Irish Religious Writings*. Dublin: Four Courts Press, 2000.

Clancy, Padraigín. *Celtic Threads: Exploring the Wisdom of Our Heritage*. Dublin: Veritas, 1999.

O'Loughlin, Thomas. *Celtic Theology*. London and New York: Continuum, 2000.

Other References

Bishop, Edmund. "The Litany of Saints in the Stowe Missal." *Journal of Theological Studies* 7, no. 25 (October 1905): 122–136. jstor.org/stable/23947173.

Breen, Aidan. "The Text of the Constantinopolitan Creed in the Stowe Missal." *Proceedings of the Royal Irish Academy: Archaeology, Culture, History, Literature* 90C (1990): 107–121. www.jstor.org/stable/25516064.

Crehan, J. H. "Canon Dominicus Papa Gelasi." *Vigilar Christianae* 12, no. 1 (May, 1958): 45–48. jstor.org /stable/1582114.

Crehan, Joseph Hugh. "The Theology of Eucharistic Consecration: Role of the Priest in Celtic Liturgy." *Theological Studies* 40, no. 2 (June 1979): 334–343.

Curran, Michael. *The Antiphonary of Bangor*. Dublin: Irish Academic Press, 1984.

Gwynn, E. J. "The Stowe Missal," *Irish Church Quarterly* 9, no. 34 (April 1916): 119–133. www.jstor.org/stable/30026443.

Hatchett, Marion J. "The Eucharistic Rite of the Stowe Missal." Chapter 10 in *Time and Community: In Honor of Thomas Julian Talley*, edited by J. Neil Alexander, 153–170. Washington: Pastoral Press, 1990.

Hennig, John. "Old Ireland and Her Liturgy." In *Old Ireland*, edited by Robert McNally. Dublin: M. H. Gill and Son, 1965.

J. R. Review of *L'ancienne liturgie gallicane: Son origins et sa Formation en Provence au V et VI siècles*, by P. J.-B. Thibaut; review of *Der Entail des Volkes an der Messliturgie im Frankeneiche von Chlodwig bis auf Karl den Grossen*, by Georg Nickl. *Studies: An Irish Quarterly Review* 20, no. 78 (June 1931): 346–347. jstor.org/stable/30094779.

Jungmann, Josef A. *The Early Liturgy, to the Time of Gregory the Great*. Liturgical Studies. Notre Dame: University of Notre Dame Press, 1959.

Lapidge, Michael. "Columbanus and the Antiphonary of Bangor." *Peritia* 4 (1985): 104–116. https://codecs.vanhamel.nl/Lapidge_1985a.

MacCarthy, Bartholomew. "Hibernia Christiana." *Irish Ecclesiastical Record* 16 (May 1895): 442–452.

Mews, Constant J. "Apostolic Authority and Celtic Liturgies: From the Vita Samsonis to the Ratio de Cursus." In *St. Samson of Dol and the Earliest History of Brittany, Cornwall and Wales*, edited by Lynette Olson, 115–136. Woodbridge, UK: Boydell Press, 2017. doi.org/10.1017/9781787440319.008.

Ní Chatháin, Próinséas. "The Liturgical Background of the Derrynavlan Altar Service." *Journal of the Royal Society of Antiquaries of Ireland* 110 (1980): 127–148. www.jstor.org/stable/25508780

Olver, Matthew S. C. "Connections between the Roman Canon Missae and the East Syrian Anaphora of Mar Theodore." *Questions Liturgique* 101, no. 3–4 (January 2021): 276–304. doi.org/10.2143/QL.101.3.3290090.

Ryan, John. "The Mass in the Early Irish Church." *Studies: An Irish Quarterly Review* 50, no. 200 (Winter 1961): 371–384.

Smith, Allyne L., Jr. Review of *St. Andrew Service Book: The Administration of the Sacraments and Other Rites and Ceremonies according to the Western Rite Usage of the Antiochian Orthodox Christian Archdiocese of North America*, 2nd ed., edited by Michael E. Trigg, John Dowling, and Karl Steinhoff. *St. Vladimir's Theological Quarterly* 41, no. 23 (1997): 249–268.

Taft, Robert, S.J. "Mount Athos: A Late Chapter in the History of the Byzantine Rite." *Dumbarton Oaks Papers* 42 (1988): 179–194. jstor.org/stable/1291596.

Thompson, Bard. *Liturgies of the Western Church.* Cleveland and New York: Collins World, 1961/1974.

Other Sources

The Stowe Missal is located in the Royal Irish Academy in Dublin; its identification number is: MS D II 3, cat. 138, fol. 67 v5=Thes. ii 250.

The *Ratio de Cursus* is located in the British Museum, where it is known as the manuscript Cotton Nero A.II, fos. 37–42.

The *Antiphonary of Bangor* is located in the Ambrosian Library in Milan, where it is catalogued as Gamber 150, Manus Digit., Ambrosiana C 005 inf.

Appendix 2

Pangur Bán

A famous gloss is in the *Codex Sanctii Paulii,* now at the Monastery of St. Paul in Carinthia, Austria. This was probably the private notebook of a student monk, used to jot down his thoughts and record his own observations, including an astronomical chart. Monks studied astronomy, by the way. In his notebook he also doodled a famous poem that begins in Old Irish: "Messe ocus Pangur Bán ..." The poem was first translated by Robin Flower and is known to every student of Irish literature.

I and Pangur Bán, my cat,
'Tis a like task we are at;
Hunting mice is his delight,
Hunting words I sit all night.

Better far than praise of men
'Tis to sit with book and pen;
Pangur bears me no ill-will,
He too plies his simple skill.

'Tis a merry thing to see
At our tasks how glad are we,

When at home we sit and find
Entertainment to our mind.

Oftentimes a mouse will stray
In the hero Pangur's way;
Oftentimes my keen thought set
Takes a meaning in its net.

'Gainst the wall he sets his eye
Full and fierce and sharp and sly;
'Gainst the wall of knowledge I
All my little wisdom try.

When a mouse darts from its den,
O how glad is Pangur then!
O what gladness do I prove
When I solve the doubts I love!

So in peace our tasks we ply,
Pangur Bán, my cat, and I;
In our arts we find our bliss,
I have mine and he has his.

Practice every day has made
Pangur perfect in his trade;
I get wisdom day and night
Turning darkness into light.

Appendix 3

Be Thou My Vision

You've probably sung it at Mass sometime and were struck by the freshness of its conceit. One of the most popular hymns of the twentieth century has been attributed to Dallán Forgaill, who wrote in Old Irish in the sixth century. Dallán was the chief *ollamh* (top professor) in sixth-century Ireland, and it's quite likely that he wrote the *Amra Choluim Chille*, the Elegy for Columba. It's not so certain that Dallán wrote "Be Thou My Vision," which might actually have been written a century or two later because the earliest versions of it are in Middle Irish, but he is given the credit for it.

The journey of this poem from sixth to twenty-first century demonstrates the difficulties of translation.

The poem, "Rop tú mo baile" in its original Old Irish, wasn't translated into English until 1905. Here are a few of those verses:

Rop tú mo baile, a Choimdiu cride:
ní ní nech aile acht Rí secht nime.

Rop tú mo scrútain i l-ló 's i n-aidche;
rop tú ad-chëar im chotlud caidche.

Rop tú mo labra, rop tú mo thuicsiu;

rop tussu dam-sa, rob misse duit-siu.

Rop tussu m'athair, rob mé do mac-su;
rop tussu lem-sa, rob misse lat-su.

Here are the first two verses in Elizabeth Byrne's 1905 translation, which appeared in the second volume of *Éiru*, the journal of the Royal Irish Academy—which was merely the School of Irish Learning at the time, the early days of the Gaelic Revival.

Be thou my vision O Lord of my heart.
None other is aught but the King of the seven heavens.

Be thou my meditation by day and night.
May it be thou that I behold ever in my sleep.

Be thou my speech, be thou my understanding.
Be thou with me, be I with thee.

Be thou my father, be I thy son.
Mayst thou be mine, may I be thine.

Eleanor Hull was an Anglo-Irish scholar of the Gaelic Revival. She versified Byrne's translation in 1912 for popular use, and she had a winner:

Be Thou my Vision, O Lord of my heart;
Naught be all else to me, save that Thou art.
Thou my best Thought, by day or by night.
Waking or sleeping, Thy presence my light.

Be Thou my Wisdom, and Thou my true Word;
I ever with Thee and Thou with me, Lord;
Thou my great Father, I Thy true son;
Thou in me dwelling, and I with Thee one.

And here are the same verses in Modern Irish, by Máire Ní Bhraonáin (Moya Brennan), translated from Hull's 1912 translation of Byrne's 1905 translation of the monk's sixth-century original. You may have heard of Máire's family's band, Clannad, or of her sister, who goes by the stage name of Enya.

Bí Thusa 'mo shúile a Rí mhór na ndúil
Líon thusa mo bheatha mo chéadfaí 's mo stuaim
Bí thusa i m'aigne gach oíche 's gach lá
Im chodladh nó im dhúiseacht, líon mé le do ghrá.

Bí thusa 'mo threorú i mbriathar 's i mbeart
Fan thusa go deo liom is coinnigh mé ceart
Glac cúram mar Athair, is éist le mo ghuí
Is tabhair domsa áit cónaí istigh i do chroí.

Taken as a whole, it bears but a nodding resemblance to "Rop tú mo baile," but it is a grand hymn in its own right, and it testifies that the Irish language still lives, as does the Faith that is so deeply rooted in Ireland.

Appendix 4

Old Irish Hymn to the Blessed Virgin

"Cantemus in Omni Die": The Hymn of Cú Chuimne[305]

In alternate measure chanting, daily sing we Mary's praise,
And, in strains of glad rejoicing, to the Lord our voices raise,

With a two-fold choir repeating Mary's never-dying fame,
Let each ear the praises gather, which our grateful tongues proclaim.

Judah's ever-glorious daughter—chosen mother of the Lord—
Who, to weak and fallen manhood, all its ancient worth restor'd.

From the everlasting Father, Gabriel brought the glad decree,
That, the Word divine conceiving, she should set poor sinners free.

[305] Patrick Francis Moran, *The Catholic Prayer Book and Manual of Meditations* (Dublin: Browne and Nolan, 1883), 627–628, https://archive.org/details/TheCatholicPrayerBook/mode/2up.

Of all virgins pure, the purest—ever stainless, ever bright—
Still from grace to grace advancing, fairest daughter of the
light.

Wondrous title—who shall tell it—whilst the Word divine
she bore,
Though in mother's name rejoicing, virgin purer than before!

By a women's disobedience, eating the forbidden tree,
Was the world betray'd and ruin'd—was by woman's aid set free.

In mysterious mode a mother, Mary did her God conceive,
By whose grace, through saving waters, men did heav'nly
truth receive.

By no empty dreams deluded, for the pearl which Mary bore,
Men, all earthly wealth resigning still are rich for evermore.

For her Son a seamless tunic Mary's careful hand did weave;
O'er that tunic fiercely gambling, sinners Mary's heart did
grieve.

Clad in helmet of salvation—clad in breast-plate shining
bright—
May the hand of Mary guide us to the realms of endless light.

Amen, amen, loudly cry we—may she when the fight is won,
O'er avenging fires triumphing, lead us safely to her Son.

Holy angels gathering round us, lo, His saving name we greet,
Writ in books of life eternal, may we still that name repeat!

Sources and Further Reading

Adomnán of Iona. *Adomnán's Life of Columba*. Edited and translated by Alan Orr Anderson and Marjorie Ogilvie Anderson. London and New York: Thomas Nelson, 1961.

——. *Life of St. Columba*. Translated by Richard Sharpe. London: Penguin Books, 1995.

Arentzen, Thomas. Review of *Mary in Early Christian Faith and Devotion*, by Stephen J. Shoemaker. *Journal of Early Christian Studies* 26, no. 2 (Summer 2018): 344–346. https://muse.jhu.edu/article/698497/pdf.

Atiya, Aziz S. *Coptic Encyclopedia*. New York: Macmillan, 1991.

——. *History of Eastern Christianity*. Notre Dame: University of Notre Dame Press, 1968.

Attwater, Donald. *A Dictionary of Mary*. New York: P. J. Kenedy and Sons, 1955.

Augustine. *Sermo 13 de Tempore*. Quoted in "St. Augustine: God Became Man So That Man Might Become God." *Te Deum Laudamus!* (blog). January 3, 2009. *PL* 39, 1097–1098. https://te-deum.blogspot.com/2009/01/st-augustine-god-became-man-so-that-man.html.

Auslander, Diane Peters. "Gendering the 'Vita Prima': An Examination of St. Brigid's Role as 'Mary of the Gael.'" *Proceedings of the Harvard Celtic Colloquium* 20, no. 21 (2000/2001): 187–200.

Awad, Lucy. "Pray for Olan the Egyptian." Watani. September 7, 2012. https://en.wataninet.com/coptic-affairs-coptic-affairs/religious/pray-for-olan-theegyptian/10886/.

Bede. *The Ecclesiastical History of the English People*. Edited by Judith McClure and Roger Collins. Oxford: Oxford University Press, 1969.

Bieler, Ludwig. *The Irish Penitentials*. Dublin: Dublin Institute for Advanced Studies, 1975.

Binchy, D. A. "The Old-Irish Table of Penitential Commutations." *Ériu* (1962): 47–72. https://www.jstor.org/stable/30006859.

Bishop, Edmund. "The Litany of Saints in the Stowe Missal." *Journal of Theological Studies* 7, no. 25 (October 1905): 122–136. jstor.org/stable/23947173.

Bowersock, G. W., Peter Brown, and Oleg Grabar. *Late Antiquity: A Guide to the Postclassical World*. Cambridge: Belknap Press, 1999.

Bradshaw, Brendan. "The Wild and Woolly West: Early Irish Christianity and Latin Orthodoxy." In W. J. Sheils and Diana Wood, *The Churches, Ireland and the Irish: Papers Read at the 1987 Summer Meeting and the 1988 Winter Meeting of the Ecclesiastical History Society*, 1–23. Oxford: Blackwell, 1989.

Breen, Aidan. "The Text of the Constantinopolitan Creed in the Stowe Missal." *Proceedings of the Royal Irish Academy: Archaeology, Culture, History, Literature* 90C (1990): 107–121. www.jstor.org/stable/25516064.

Brock, Sebastian, trans. *The Syriac Fathers on Prayer and the Spiritual Life*. Kalamazoo, MI: Cistercian, 1987.

Brown, Michelle P. "Strategies of Visual Literacy in Insular and Anglo-Saxon Book Culture." Chapter 4 in *Transformation in*

Anglo-Saxon Culture: Toller Lectures on Art, Archaeology and Text, edited by Charles Insley and Gale R. Owen-Crocker, 71–104. Barnsley, UK: Oxbow Books, 2017. www.jstor.org/stable/j.ctvh1dhhq.9.

Brown, Peter. *The Cult of the Saints: Its Rise and Function in Latin Christianity*. Chicago: University of Chicago Press, 1981.

——. *The Rise of Western Christendom: Triumph and Diversity A.D. 200–1000*. Malden, MA, Oxford, England, and Victoria, Australia: Blackwell, 2003.

Carney, James. "Old Ireland and Her Poetry." In *Old Ireland*, edited by Robert McNally, S.J., 147–172. New York: Fordham University Press, 1965.

Carey, John. *King of Mysteries: Early Irish Religious Writings*. Dublin: Four Courts Press, 2000.

——. "Saint Patrick, the Druids, and the End of the World." *History of Religions* 36, no. 1 (August 1996): 42–53.

Chadwick, Nora K. *The Age of the Saints in the Early Celtic Church*. London: Oxford University Press, 1963.

——. *Poetry and Letters in Early Christian Gaul*. London: Bowes, 1955.

Chitty, Derwas J. *The Desert a City: An Introduction to the Study of Egyptian and Palestinian Monasticism under the Christian Empire*. Crestwood, NY: St. Vladimir's Seminary Press, 1966.

Churchill, Winston. "A History of the English-Speaking Peoples, Part 1: The Birth of Britain." *Life*, March 19, 1956.

Clancy, Padraigín. *Celtic Threads: Exploring the Wisdom of Our Heritage*. Dublin: Veritas, 1999.

Clancy, Thomas Owen, and Gilbert Markus. *Iona: The Earliest Poetry of a Celtic Monastery*. Edinburgh: Edinburgh University Press, 1995. jstor.org/stable/10.3366/j.ctvxcrp6p.14.

Cone, Polly, ed. *Treasures of Early Irish Art: 1500 B.C. to 1500 A.D.* Dublin: Royal Irish Academy, 1977.

Constas, Nicholas P. "Weaving the Body of God: Proclus of Constantinople, the Theotokos, and the Loom of the Flesh." *Journal of Early Christian Studies* 3, no. 2 (Summer 1995): 169–194. https://doi.org/10.1353/earl.0.0063.

Corish, Patrick J. "The Christian Mission" in *A History of Irish Catholicism*. Vol. 1. Dublin: Gill and Macmillan, 1972.

Corlett, Chris. "A Font of Majuscule Proportions at Tallaght." *Archaeology Ireland* 26, no. 3 (Autumn 2012): 6.

Crehan, J. H. "Canon Dominicus Papa Gelasi," *Vigilar Christianae* 12, no. 1 (May 1958): 45–48. jstor.org /stable/1582114.

Crehan, Joseph H. "The Liturgical Trade Route: East to West." *Studies: An Irish Quarterly Review* 65, no. 258 (Summer 1976): 87–99. jstor.org/stable/30090005.

——. "The Theology of Eucharistic Consecration: Role of the Priest in Celtic Liturgy." *Theological Studies* 40, no. 2 (June 1979): 334–343. https://doi.org/10.1177/004056397904 000206.

Curran, Michael. *The Antiphonary of Bangor*. Dublin: Irish Academic Press, 1984.

Darcy, R., and William Flynn. "Ptolemy's Map of Ireland: A Modern Decoding." *Irish Geography* 41, no. 1 (2008): 49–69, DOI: 10.1080/00750770801909375.

Dix, Dom Gregory. *The Shape of the Liturgy*. London: Dacre Press, 1945.

Doan, James E. "Mediterranean Influences on Insular Manuscript Illumination." *Proceedings of the Harvard Celtic Colloquium* 2 (1982): 31–38. jstor.org/stable/20557117.

Doherty, Charles. "The Basilica in Early Ireland." *Peritia* 3 (1984): 303–315.

Duchesne, Msgr. L. *Christian Worship: Its Origin and Evolution: A Study of the Latin Liturgy up to the Time of Charlemagne*. 5th ed.

Translated by M. L. McClure. London: Society for Promoting Christian Knowledge, 1927.

Dumville, David N., et al. *Saint Patrick, A.D. 493–1993*. Woodbridge, UK: Boydell Press, 1993.

Ekonomou, Andrew J. *Byzantine Rome and the Greek Popes*. Lanham, MD: Lexington Books, 2007.

Eluére, Christiane. *The Celts: Conquerors of Ancient Europe*. New York: Harry Abrams, 1993.

Finnian, St. *Penitential of Finnian*. UHC: Medieval Europe. https://medievalbruno.weebly.com/uploads/2/7/5/2/2752477/the_penitential_of_finnian.pdf.

Fletcher, Richard. *The Barbarian Conversion: From Paganism to Christianity*. Berkeley, CA: University of California Press, 1999.

Flower, Robin. "Irish High Crosses." *Journal of the Warburg and Courtauld Institutes* 17, no. 1/2 (1954): 87–97. www.jstor.or/stable/750133.

Freeman, Philip. *Ireland and the Classical World*. Austin: University of Texas Press, 2001.

Gambero, Luigi. *Mary and the Fathers of the Church: The Blessed Virgin Mary in Patristic Thought*. Translated by Thomas Buffer. San Francisco: Ignatius Press, 1999.

———. *Mary in the Middle Ages: The Blessed Virgin Mary in the Thought of Medieval Latin Theologians*. Translated by Thomas Buffer. San Francisco: Ignatius Press, 2005.

Gillis, John. *The Faddan More Psalter: The Discovery and Conservation of a Medieval Treasure*. Dublin: National Museum of Ireland, 2021.

Gingras, George E., translator and annotator. *Egeria: Diary of a Pilgrimage*. Ancient Christian Writers: The Works of the Fathers in Translation, no. 38. New York: Newman Press, 1970.

Good, James, D.D. "The Mariology of the Early Irish Church." *Irish Ecclesiastical Record* 100, 5th series (August 1963): 73–79.

Gougaud, Dom Louis. *Christianity in Celtic Lands*. Dublin: Four Courts Press, 1932/1992.

Gwynn, E. J. "The Stowe Missal." *The Irish Church Quarterly* 9, no. 34 (April 1916): 119–133. www.jstor.org/stable/30026443.

Hamlin, A. "A Chi-Rho-Carved Stone at Drumaqueran, Co. Antrim." *Ulster Journal of Archaeology* 35 (1972): 22-28. http://www.jstor.org/stable/20567707.

Hamlin, Ann. "The Archaeology of the Irish Church in the Eighth Century." *Peritia* 4 (1985): 279–299.

Harbison, Peter. "Early Christian Texts: Blathmac—an Eighth-Century Irish Poet in Rome." *Gaelic Ireland* 24, no. 4 (July/August 2016): 18–20.

Harbison, Peter, Homan Potterton, and Jeanne Sheehy. *Irish Art and Architecture*. London: Thames and Hudson, 1978.

Hatchett, Marion J. "The Eucharistic Rite of the Stowe Missal." Chapter 10 in *Time and Community: In Honor of Thomas Julian Talley*, edited by J. Neil Alexander, 153–170. Washington: Pastoral Press, 1990.

Hennig, John. "The Feasts of the Blessed Virgin in the Ancient Irish Church." *Irish Ecclesiastical Record*, 5th series, 71 (March 1954).

——. "The Historical Work of Louis Gougaud." *Irish Historical Studies* 3, no. 10 (September 1942): 180–186. jstor.org/stable/30006631.

——. "Old Ireland and Her Liturgy." In *Old Ireland*, edited by Robert McNally. Dublin: M. H. Gill and Son, 1965.

Henry, Françoise. *The Book of Kells: Reproductions from the Manuscript in Trinity College Dublin with a Study of the Manuscript by Françoise Henry*. New York: Knopf, 1974.

——. *Irish Art in the Early Christian Period to 800 A.D.* Ithaca, NY: Cornell University Press, 1965.

Herbert, Máire, and Rev. Martin J. McNamara, eds. *Irish Biblical Apocrypha. Selected Texts in Translation*. Edinburgh: T. and T. Clark/Bloomsbury Academic, 1989/2004.

Herren, Michael W., and Shirley Ann Brown. *Christ in Celtic Christianity: Britain and Ireland from the Fifth to the Tenth Century*. Cambridge, UK: Cambridge University Press, 2004.

Hillgarth, J. N. "Visigothic Spain and Early Christian Ireland." *Proceedings of the Royal Irish Academy: Archaeology, Culture, History, Literature* 62 (1961–1963): 167–194. www.jstor.org/stable/25505106.

Hole, Charles. *Early Missions to and within the British Islands*. London: Society for Promoting Christian Knowledge, 1888.

Hopkins, Stephen C. E. "John Carey (trad.), *The Ever-New Tongue: The Text in the Book of Linsmore*." Memini Travaux et Documents. OpenEdition Journals. https://journals.openedition.org/memini/1478.

Hughes, Kathleen. *The Church in Early Irish Society*. Ithaca, NY: Cornell University Press, 1966.

Hull, Eleanor. "Observations of Classical Writers on the Habits of the Celtic Nations, as Illustrated from Irish Records." *Celtic Review* 3, no. 9 (July 1906): 62–76.

Hunwicke, J. W. "Kerry and Stowe Revisited." *Proceedings of the Royal Irish Academy: Archaeology, Culture, History, Literature* 102C, no. 1 (2002): 1 19. www.jstor.org/stable/25506158.

Irmscher, Johannes, and Anthony Cutler. "Gospel of Nicodemus." In *The Oxford Dictionary of Byzantium*, edited by Alexander Kazhdan. Oxford and New York: Oxford University Press, 1991.

Jeffery, Peter. "Eastern and Western Elements in the Irish Monastic Prayer of the Hours." In *The Divine Office in the Latin Middle Ages: Methodology and Source Studies, Regional Developments,*

Hagiography, edited by Margot E. Fassler and Rebecca A. Baltzer, 99–143. New York and Oxford: Oxford University Press, 2000.

Jenner, H. "The Gallican Rite." In *The Catholic Encyclopedia*, vol. 6. New York: Appleton, 1909. Online ed. New Advent. https://www.newadvent.org/cathen/06357a.htm.

John Paul II, Encyclical Letter on Commitment to Ecumenism *Ut Unum Sint*. May 25, 1995.

Johnston, Elva. "Religious Change and Frontier Management." *Eolas* 11 (2018): 104–119. jstor.org/stable/10.2307/26605110.

J. R. Review of *L'ancienne liturgie gallicane: Son origins et sa Formation en Provence au V et VI siècles*, by P. J.-B. Thibaut; review of *Der Entail des Volkes an der Messliturgie im Frankeneiche von Chlodwig bis auf Karl den Grossen*, by Georg Nickl. *Studies: An Irish Quarterly Review* 20, no. 78 (June 1931): 346–347. jstor.org/stable/30094779.

Jungmann, Josef A. *The Early Liturgy, to the Time of Gregory the Great*. Liturgical Studies. Notre Dame: University of Notre Dame Press, 1959.

Kelly, Amanda. "The Discovery of Phocaean Red Slip Ware (PRSW) Form 3 and Bii Ware (LR1 Amphorae) on Sites in Ireland—an Analysis within a Broader Framework." *Proceedings of the Royal Irish Academy: Archaeology, Culture, History, Literature* 110C (2010): 35–88. www.jstor.org/stable/41473662.

Kenney, James F. *The Sources for the Early History of Ireland*. New York: Columbia University Press, 1929. Dublin: Pádraic Ó Táilliúir, 1979.

King, Archdale. *Liturgies of the Past*. Milwaukee: Bruce. 1959.

——. *Liturgy of the Roman Church*. Milwaukee: Bruce, 1957.

——. *The Rites of Eastern Christendom*, vol. 1. Rome: Tipografia Poliglotta Vaticana, 1947.

Laing, Lloyd. "The Romanization of Ireland in the Fifth Century." *Peritia* 4 (1985): 261–278.

Lapidge, Michael. "Columbanus and the Antiphonary of Bangor." *Peritia* 4 (1985): 104–116. https://codecs.vanhamel.nl/Lapidge_1985a.

Lasareff, Victor. "Studies in the Iconography of the Virgin." *Art Bulletin* 20, no. 1 (March 1938): 26–65. https://doi.org/10.2307/3046561.

Leask, Harold G. *Irish Churches and Monastic Buildings*. Vol. 1, *The First Phases and the Romanesque*. Dundalk, Ireland: Dundalgan Press, 1955.

Lerner, Elizabeth A. "Virgins and Mothers: Feminine Ideals and Female Roles in the Early Irish Church." *Proceedings of the Harvard Celtic Colloquium* 14 (1994): 162–174. jstor.org/stable/20557281.

MacCarthy, Bartholomew. "Hibernia Christiana." *Irish Ecclesiastical Record* 16 (May 1895): 442–452.

Mac Niocaill, Gearóid. *Ireland before the Vikings.* The Gill History of Ireland, vol. 1. Dublin: Gill and Macmillan, 1972.

McDonnell, Kilian, and George T. Montague. *Christian Initiation and Baptism in the Holy Spirit: Evidence from the First Eight Centuries*. Collegeville, MN: Liturgical Press, 1991.

McKinnon, James W. "The Origins of the Western Office." In *The Divine Office in the Latin Middle Ages: Methodology and Source Studies, Regional Developments, Hagiography*, edited by Margot E. Fassler and Rebecca A. Baltzer, 63–73. New York and Oxford: Oxford University Press, 2000.

McNally, Robert E. "St. Patrick: 461-1961." *Catholic Historical Review*, no. 3 (October 1961): 305–324. jstor.org/stable/25016896.

McNamara, Martin. "De Initiis: Irish Monastic Learning 600–800 AD." *Eolas* 6 (2013): 4–40. jstor.org/stable/10.2307/26193960.

Meehan, Bernard. *The Book of Kells: An Illustrated Introduction to the Manuscript in Trinity College Dublin*. London: Thames and Hudson, 1994.

Mews, Constant J. "Apostolic Authority and Celtic Liturgies: From the Vita Samsonis to the Ratio de Cursus." In *St. Samson of Dol and the Earliest History of Brittany, Cornwall and Wales*, edited by Lynette Olson, 115–136. Woodbridge, UK: Boydell Press, 2017. doi.org/10.1017/9781787440319.008.

Meyer, Kuno. "Learning in Ancient Ireland." *Irish Review* 2, no. 21 (November 1912): 449–459.

Moran, Patrick Francis. *The Catholic Prayer Book and Manual of Meditations*, Dublin: Browne and Nolan, 1883. Available at https://archive.org/details/TheCatholicPrayerBook/mode/2up.

Mytum, Harold. *The Origins of Early Christian Ireland*. London and New York: Routledge, 1992.

Nî Chatháin, Próinséas. "The Liturgical Background of the Derrynavlan Altar Service." *Journal of the Royal Society of Antiquaries of Ireland* 110 (1980): 127–148. www.jstor.org/stable/25508780.

Nordenfalk, Carl. *Celtic and Anglo-Saxon Painting: Book Illumination in the British Isles* 600–800. New York: Braziller, 1977.

——. "The Diatessaron Miniatures Once More." *Art Bulletin* 55, no. 4 (December 1973): 532–546. jstor.org/stable/3049162.

——. "An Illustrated Diatessaron," *Art Bulletin* 50, no. 2 (June 1968): 119–140. www.jstor.org/stable/3048527.

O'Donoghue, Neil Xavier. *The Eucharist in Pre-Norman Ireland*. Notre Dame, IN: University of Notre Dame Press, 2011.

——. "Insular Chrismals and House-Shaped Shrines in the Early Middle Ages." In *Insular & Anglo-Saxon Art and Thought in the Early Medieval Period*, edited by Colum Hourihane, 79–90. University Park, PA: Princeton University Index of Christian Art, 2011.

O'Dwyer, Peter, O. Carm. *Towards a History of Irish Spirituality.* Dublin: Columba Press, 1995.

O'Loughlin, Thomas. "The Many Feasts of Mary in the Contemporary Catholic Liturgy: A Study of the Persistence of the Protoevangelium of James within Liturgical Memory." *Maria: A Journal of Marian Studies* 1, no. 1 (July 2021): 1–20.

Olver, Matthew S. C. "Connections between the Roman Canon Missae and the East Syrian Anaphora of Mar Theodore." *Questions Liturgique* 101, no. 3–4 (January 2021): 276–304. doi.org/10.2143/QL.101.3.3290090.

Pelikan, Jaroslav. *Mary through the Centuries: Her Place in the History of Culture.* New Haven, CT: Yale University Press, 1996.

Plummer, Rev. Charles. *Irish Litanies: Text and Translation.* London: Harrison and Sons, 1925.

Raftery, Joseph. "Ex Oriente ..." *Journal of the Royal Society of Antiquaries of Ireland* 95, no. 1/2 (1965): 193–204. jstor.org/stable/25509589.

Raya, Most Rev. Joseph, ed. *Byzantine Daily Worship.* Allendale, NJ: Alleluia Press, 1969.

Richardson, Hilary. "Lozenge and Logos." *Archaeology Ireland* 10, no. 2 (Summer 1996): 24–25. www.jstor.org/stable/20562263.

——. "Observations on Christian Art in Early Ireland, Georgia and Armenia." *Proceedings of the Royal Irish Academy* 87 (1987): 129–137.

Roe, Helen M. "The Irish High Cross: Morphology and Iconography." *Journal of the Royal Society of Antiquaries of Ireland* 95, no. 1/2 (1965): 213–226. https://www.jstor.org/stable/25509591.

——. "The Orans in Irish Christian Art." *Journal of the Royal Society of Antiquaries of Ireland* 100, no. 2 (1970): 212–221. jstor.org/stable/25509749.

Ryan, John, S.J. *Irish Monasticism: Origins and Early Development.* Dublin: Four Courts Press, 1931/1992.

——. "The Mass in the Early Irish Church." *Studies: An Irish Quarterly Review* 50, no. 200 (Winter 1961): 371–384.

——. "The Sacraments in the Early Irish Church." *Studies: An Irish Quarterly Review* 51, no. 204 (Winter 1962): 508–520.

Shoemaker, Stephen J. "The Virgin Mary in the Ministry of Jesus and the Early Church according to the Earliest *Life of the Virgin.*" *Harvard Theological Review* 98, no. 4 (October 2005): 441–467. jstor.org/stable/4125276.

Smith, Allyne L., Jr. Review of *St. Andrew Service Book: The Administration of the Sacraments and Other Rites and Ceremonies according to the Western Rite Usage of the Antiochian Orthodox Christian Archdiocese of North America*, 2nd ed., edited by Michael E. Trigg, John Dowling, and Karl Steinhoff. *St. Vladimir's Theological Quarterly* 41, no. 23 (1997): 249–268.

Smyth, Marina. "Monastic Culture in Seventh-Century Ireland." *Eolas* 12 (2019): 64–101. jstor.org/stable/10.2307/26763328.

Stalley, Roger. *Early Irish Sculpture and the Art of the High Crosses.* London: Yale University Press, 2020.

Stancliffe, Clare. "Columbanus's Monasticism and the Sources of His Inspiration: From Basil to the Master?" In *Tome: Studies in Medieval Celtic History and Law in Honour of Thomas Charles-Edwards*, edited by Fiona Edmonds and Paul Russell. Woodbridge, UK: Boydell Press, 2011. jstor.org/stable/10.7722/j.ctt81mmk.8.

Stevenson, Jane. Review of *The Antiphonary of Bangor*, by Michael Curran. *Peritia* 5 (2009): 430–437. www.brepolsonline-net.ucc.idm.oclc.org.

Stewart, Columba. *Cassian the Monk.* Oxford Studies in Historical Theology. New York and Oxford: Oxford University Press, 1998.

Stokes, George T., D.D. *Ireland and the Celtic Church.* 6th ed. Revised by Hugh Jackson Lawlor, D.D. London: Society for Promoting Christian Knowledge, 1907.

Stokes, Whitley, ed. and trans. *Lives of Saints from the Book of Lismore.* Anecdota Oxoniensia. Oxford: Clarendon Press, 1890.

Sullivan, Sir Edward. *The Book of Kells.* 2nd ed. New York: Crescent Books, 1986.

Taft, Robert, S.J. *Between East and West.* Washington, D.C.: Pastoral Press, 1984.

——. *The Liturgy of the Hours in East and West.* Collegeville, MN: Liturgical Press, 1986.

——. "Mount Athos: A Late Chapter in the History of the Byzantine Rite." *Dumbarton Oaks Papers* 42 (1988): 179–194. jstor.org/stable/1291596.

Telepneff, Gregory. *The Egyptian Desert in the Irish Bogs.* Etna, CA: Center for Traditionalist Orthodox Studies, 1998.

Tertullian, *Corpus Christianorum* 1:265.

Thompson, Bard. *Liturgies of the Western Church.* Cleveland and New York: Collins World, 1961/1974.

Walsh, Fintan. *The Road to Kells: Prehistoric Archaeology of the M3 Navan to Kells and N52 Kells Bypass Road Project.* Dublin: Wordwell Books, 2022.

Warren, F. E. *Antiphonary of Bangor.* Part 2. London: Harrison, 1895.

——. *Liturgy and Ritual of the Celtic Church.* Oxford: Clarendon Press, 1881. (This includes the Stowe Missal.)

——. *The Liturgy and Ritual of the Celtic Church.* 3rd ed. Edited by Neil Xavier O'Donoghue. Piscataway, NJ: Gorgias Press, 2010.

Weeda, Peter. "The Irish, the Virgin Mary and Proclus of Constantinople." *Peritia* 22–23 (2011–2012): 83–106. doi.org/10.1484/J.PERIT.1.103281.

Werckmeister, O. K. "Three Problems of Traditions in Pre-Carolingian Figure-Style from Visigothic to Insular Illumination." *Proceedings of Royal Irish Academy: Archaeology, Culture, History, Literature* 63 (1962–1964): 167–189. https://www.jstor.org/stable/i25505109.

Werner, Martin. "The Madonna and Child Miniature in the Book of Kells: Part I." *Art Bulletin* 54, no. 1 (March 1972): 1–23.

——. "The Madonna and Child Miniature in the Book of Kells: Part II." *Art Bulletin* 54, no. 2 (June 1972): 129–139.

Whitfield, Niamh. "Brooch or Cross? The Lozenge on the Shoulder of the Virgin in the Book of Kells." *Archaeology Ireland* 10, no. 1 (Spring 1996): 20–23. jstor.org/stable/20562237.

Windschuttle, Keith. "Edward Gibbon and the Enlightenment." *New Criterion* 15, no. 10 (June 1997). https://newcriterion.com/issues/1997/6/edward-gibbon-the-enlightenment.

About the Author

Connie Marshner fell in love with Ireland when she was in middle school and with the Eastern Church when she found Holy Transfiguration Melkite Greek Catholic Church in McLean, Virginia, a few years later. She heard echoes of Eastern hymnody in some late antique Irish prayers and poetry, and the pursuit of a master's degree in Gaelic literature at University College Cork gave her the opportunity to do in-depth research on the topic. *Monastery and High Cross* is drawn from her 2022 dissertation. A teacher of Gaeilge, she is the chair of the Saints and Scholars Foundation, which supports a new model of faithful Catholic education for modern secular Ireland, www.saintsandscholars.us. She lives in Front Royal, Virginia.

Sophia Institute

Sophia Institute is a nonprofit institution that seeks to nurture the spiritual, moral, and cultural life of souls and to spread the gospel of Christ in conformity with the authentic teachings of the Roman Catholic Church.

Sophia Institute Press fulfills this mission by offering translations, reprints, and new publications that afford readers a rich source of the enduring wisdom of mankind.

Sophia Institute also operates the popular online resource CatholicExchange.com. *Catholic Exchange* provides world news from a Catholic perspective as well as daily devotionals and articles that will help readers to grow in holiness and live a life consistent with the teachings of the Church.

In 2013, Sophia Institute launched Sophia Institute for Teachers to renew and rebuild Catholic culture through service to Catholic education. With the goal of nurturing the spiritual, moral, and cultural life of souls, and an abiding respect for the role and work of teachers, we strive to provide materials and programs that are at once enlightening to the mind and ennobling to the heart; faithful and complete, as well as useful and practical.

Sophia Institute gratefully recognizes the Solidarity Association for preserving and encouraging the growth of our apostolate over the course of many years. Without their generous and timely support, this book would not be in your hands.

www.SophiaInstitute.com
www.CatholicExchange.com
www.SophiaInstituteforTeachers.org